BILLIONS

BILLIONS

SELLING TO THE NEW CHINESE CONSUMER

TOM DOCTOROFF

First published 2005 by
PALGRAVE MACMILLAN™
175 Fifth Avenue, New York, N.Y. 10010 and
Houndmills, Basingstoke, Hampshire, England RG21 6XS.
Companies and representatives throughout the world.

PALGRAVE MACMILLAN is the global academic imprint of the Palgrave Macmillan division of St. Martin's Press, LLC and of Palgrave Macmillan Ltd. Macmillan® is a registered trademark in the United States, United Kingdom and other countries. Palgrave is a registered trademark in the European Union and other countries.

ISBN 1-4039-7169-2

Library of Congress Cataloging-in-Publication Data
Doctoroff, Tom.
    Billions : selling to the new Chinese consumer / Tom Doctoroff.
      p. cm.
    Includes bibliographical references and index.
    ISBN 1-4039-7169-2
    1. Consumers—China—Attitudes. 2. Consumers' preferences—China.
3. Intercultural communication—China.   4. Communication and culture—China. 5. Marketing—China. I. Title.

HF5415.33.C6D63   2006
658.8'343.0951—dc22

                                                                              2005049303

A catalogue record for this book is available from the British Library.

Design by Letra Libre, Inc.

First edition: December 2005
10 9 8 7 6 5 4 3 2 1

Printed in the United States of America.

Dedicated to the memory of our mother and father,
Judge Martin and Dr. Allene Doctoroff

ACKNOWLEDGMENTS

This book could not have been written without the creative and strategic brilliance of my partners since 1998, Lo Sheung Yan and Ratan Malli.

CONTENTS

LIST OF ILLUSTRATIONS

FOREWORD

BY SIR MARTIN SORRELL

In 1989, I traveled up to Guangzhou from Hong Kong. It was our first WPP board meeting in China. Even then, the sheer power, scale, and bustling vitality of the country were overwhelming. At that time, the second railway line from Hong Kong to Guangzhou was being built. It was as if an entire industrial and economic world was being built by hand.

I've since been to China about a dozen times. Every time I am impressed by its people's hard work and commitment. Indeed, the most impressive characteristic of the Chinese people is that they never fail to listen and learn. They are extremely adaptable. This ability is crucial and we in the West ignore it at our peril. China has already made its presence felt in electronics and textiles. Its insatiable thirst for oil and steel is causing tremors around the world. Even if China is not a powerful rival in your sector now, it will be soon. And not only to us in the West, but to the South Korean chaebols and Japanese multinationals.

Many in the West still don't really get China. At 1.3 billion people, it is the equivalent of four or five USAs. It's an extraordinary number, but some scoff that few of these people can actually afford goods and services. But even if, say, only 150 million to 200 million Chinese consumers have significant disposable income now, that is three-quarters of America—hardly a market that can be ignored. And goodness knows how many Chinese consumers will have significant disposable income in a few years' time.

China is essential to WPP's growth and development. By the time the Beijing Olympics arrive in 2008, China's advertising market will be the second biggest in the world. We already operate in 9 locations and will bring the total to 12 by the end of this year. We believe it is important to look at China as a whole, and not just focus on Beijing or Shanghai.

As Chinese industry becomes more sophisticated, so will its advertising, marketing, and branding. Inexorably, it is moving from being a maker of cheap generic goods to producing distinct brands at premium prices, taking the journey Japan started four decades ago and South Korea more recently. Chinese marketing has already come a long way in a short time. Once, they simply shouted their product name at customers. Now the messages and images are more subtle, with food manufacturers extolling their brand's health benefits and other manufacturers proclaiming their green credentials.

There has never been a market like China. It's the fastest-growing, most interesting, least bureaucratic place around. At the same time it is a paradox. This frenetic commerce is still directed by the Communist Party. China sees things differently: understanding the world through Chinese eyes is the same as trying to understand the world through Muslim eyes. We in the West tend to believe that our value systems and beliefs are the same as theirs, that what we consider good or bad is the same for them. It is not necessarily so, and gaining a deeper understanding of the Chinese mind is exceedingly important.

China's influence will not confine itself to trade. It would be arrogant to say that a country with 1.3 billion people should have less of a say about the world's political and economic agenda than a country with 280 million. China will be the major counterbalancing force to the United States and the world. Since the fall of the Soviet Union, the United States has enjoyed political, cultural, social, and military hegemony. That will not last. Inevitably, there must be something to fill the vacuum and that something is China.

So a bipolar world between China and the United States is inevitable. That's already happening. China is now a huge investor in the United States; the world's banks are jockeying to get a foothold in mainland China. The military side of that bipolar equation is worrying. We're seeing ever closer links between China and Cuba. We've seen Beijing's direct investment in Europe's Galileo satellite, which could be used for security purposes, and the Pentagon's jumpy reaction. Taiwan remains an issue. And energy will continue to be a big concern, because China has few resources of its own. It needs Russia and Middle East oil and gas and will not be willing to rely on the United States to protect those sources. Again, big changes in the world order are coming.

Most of those who've bought this book will need little further persuasion of China's immense potential. China is one of the few certainties in an uncertain world. In 25 years its importance will have multiplied beyond recognition. Far less certain, however, is how non-Chinese businesses, relatively unfamiliar with the country and its culture, can be sure of taking part in that explosive growth; of not being sidelined forever by this once-in-a-generation phenomenon. And herein lies the real value of Tom Doctoroff's book.

He knows his subject with an almost native sensitivity, but this is no empty academic study. He unveils precious insights and identifies motivations—then translates them directly into thoroughly practical and manageable marketing strategies. Tom Doctoroff is a consummate writer, with a compelling turn of phrase, grounded in real knowledge of his subject—the Chinese consumer. He confirms all that I believe myself about the future of this country; and is then profligate in the advice he gives as to how we can share in it. Business is already competitive in China and is destined to become more so. Tom Doctoroff's masterly book will at least ensure that we enter this competition brilliantly briefed and comfortingly well-armed.

INTRODUCTION

THE EXTRAORDINARY CHINESE

We're ambitious. Our goal is nothing less than to crack the reputedly indecipherable code of marketing to the New Chinese Consumer. This book articulates what I've learned over the past eleven years in Greater China (four based in Hong Kong and seven in Shanghai) with JWT, one of the region's largest and most respected advertising agencies. I am the company's Northeast Asia Area Director and Greater China Chief Executive Officer. I make no claims to being a historian or economist but will confess to being a bit of an amateur cultural anthropologist. More practically, I've had the privilege of partnering with over fifty clients, both multinational (e.g., Unilever, Ford, Kraft, Unicharm, De-Beers/DTC, Siemens, Pepsi, PepsiCo Foods, Nestle, Kimberly-Clark, Avon, Shell, Reckitt Benckiser, HSBC, B&Q, Vodaphone, Samsung) and domestic (e.g., TCL and Konka televisions, China Mobile, China Unicom, Lenovo computers, Yili dairy, Sedrin beer, 999 pharmaceuticals), and it is this experience that I believe permits me to make a few observations regarding the contours of the Chinese mind and the topography of the People's Republic of China (PRC)'s commercial terrain. Yes, I confess my generalizations are sweeping and, therefore, I offer a preemptive apology to those who put a high price on nuance or shades of gray. You have to break shells to make omelets, so in the spirit of healthy debate, I'm willing to have a bit of egg on my face.

IT'S THE CONSUMER, STUPID!

China's growing importance to the world economy is indisputable. The country isn't a flavor of the month. Within the consumer sector, the acquisitive appetite of today's mainland shopper has played a large role in thrusting the PRC to the world's third-largest trading force. Many, many companies, both foreign and domestic, are angling furiously to grab a piece of the action. Multinational corporations (MNCs) are, slowly but surely, becoming more sure-footed in many areas. Fewer and fewer are entering the market oblivious to what they'll find. Despite MNCs' growing sophistication about the Chinese commercial terrain, companies with dreams of selling to such a huge emerging market seem to have forgotten that the mainland consumer is different, too. Westerners are more comfortable with the objective, discrete, and quantifiable. But the mindset of 1.3 billion people is notoriously hard to read, so most of us choose not to bother. Denial and avoidance set in. Even marketers of some of the world's leading brands tend to land in China with an erroneous belief in the applicability of Occidental cultural norms. But the topic can't be ignored, because the Chinese *are* different. Culturally, if not individually, we are moral absolutists, and they are relativists. We value social dynamism. They value order. We view history's march as linear. They view it as cyclical, driven by fate. We believe society is "good." They believe it "corrupts." We are monotheists, empowered as individuals by our personal relationship with God Almighty. They are, for the most part, atheistic, unified on a "spiritual" plane by a belief in Chinese "culture."

THIS BOOK'S CONTENT

Billions covers three broad areas. First is the critical importance of culture in shaping buying decisions. We delve into the psyches of contemporary Chinese consumers. We uncover the core "drivers" of behavior and preference across key market segments: the emerging middle class (only now achieving critical mass), the urban mass market, men, women, and youth (the "new generation"). We explore both the dynamism of contemporary China and the enduring legacies of thousands of years of history. On a more concrete level, we will translate these cultural tendencies into marketing guidelines that can be applied to the vast majority of consumer goods.

Second, we provide tools to increase the odds of entering the Middle Kingdom with a bang rather than a thud. Many of these principles are relevant even outside of China. However, given the scale, newness, high investment cost, and complexity of the PRC battlefield, learning one's ABCs is particularly critical. We review how to:

- Harness the power of "insights" (i.e., consumers' fundamental motivations for behavior and preference);
- Forge a relevant brand vision (i.e., a long-term identity that seamlessly combines emotional aspiration and functional differentiation);

- Create a product portfolio that maximizes brand extendability (i.e., the range of categories that can coexist under the same trademark);
- Anticipate the peculiarities of the Chinese media scene;
- Uncover the real power of the Beijing Olympics and identify ways to optimize sponsorship opportunities.

In the final section, we analyze the pitfalls into which multinational brands and their local competitors often fall, many of them a function of either cultural ignorance or rigidity. We applaud the few getting it right, chastise those getting it wrong, and review the tactics of both camps. More specifically, we'll survey:

- ten basic tips of effective China advertising;
- five mistakes most often made by multinational companies;
- five structural barriers within Chinese corporations that preclude the development of strong local brands;
- three areas of domestic brand stagnation, three areas of domestic brand progress, and six MNC-counterattack strategies;
- ten ways to shape international brands into global icons with Chinese characteristics.

PRIDE AND PREJUDICE: WHAT'S AT STAKE

Some commentators suggest we are living at the start of the Chinese century. This is perhaps a bit much. As Morton Abramowitz concluded years ago in a critique of Asian triumphalism, economic strength is not enough. "In an interdependent world," he wrote, "those that aspire to lend their name to centuries must also have political strengths and value systems that enable them to project influence persuasively." On a diplomatic plane, the PRC is increasingly proud but still insubstantial. It will remain so until the Communist Party cedes its monopoly on power. Furthermore, enduring leadership—both economic and political—is lubricated by "responsive innovation," a quality nurtured only in democracies and societies rooted in individualism.

There is no question, however, that the rise of China—and industrially, it will rise, bumpily yet steadily—heralds a fundamental financial, diplomatic, and psychological realignment of historic proportions. Not since the debut of industrial America after World War I has the world seen such a drastic reshuffling of the economic deck. The Middle Kingdom's commercial potential is huge. Moreover, the country boasts both a seemingly endless supply of cheap migrant labor and increasing success in high-end sectors such as microprocessing and component design. I'll leave it to the scholars and consultants to quantify this two-headed dragon's impact on global prices, labor markets, and output. Suffice it to say the upheaval is vast. By 2020, the Chinese juggernaut will both threaten and enhance the livelihood of everyone, even the most inward-looking, Wal-Mart-loving evangelist in George W. Bush's red America.

How will we respond to the (re)emergence of a great nation, a new twenty-first-century superpower destined to rival the West in terms of trade and financial clout? As Tevye the milkman often quipped when asked questions of the ages, "I don't know." But the risk of Sinophobia metastasizing into something insidious cannot be discounted. And if the United States gets its clock cleaned by Beijing in the 2008 Olympics, as many expect, we may need to undergo national psychotherapy. Our last great rivalry, the epic battle between the darkness of Soviet totalitarianism and light of liberal democracy, was perceived as a struggle between "good" and "evil." Chinese civilization, on the other hand, is rooted in proud, time-tested tradition. Although our perceptions of China are twisted by cliché, the country has always been part and parcel of our collective awareness. Chinese people are already woven into the fabric of Western society. They are at our universities. They write our software and cure our illnesses. Despite shrill alarmism, we know China is not "bad." That said, unless inspired leadership infuses us with the boldness to embrace and understand different value systems, xenophobic fears of a new dark force threatening our Shining City on a Hill, the glorious destination of Mankind, will mushroom. A *New York Times* editorial in response to CNOOC's aborted 2005 Unocal takeover bid put it nicely: "Instead of bashing China, Congress and the administration should be putting money into bolstering retraining programs to help American workers whose jobs migrate overseas. American school systems, American parents and American students are going to have to focus on the fact that young people with mediocre educations are not going to be able to compete with energetic, educated (Chinese) young people. . . ." The root of all dysfunctional behavior is insecurity.

China frightens us because, as suggested above, it is "unfamiliar." The next hundred years will hinge on whether we, as nations and people, can achieve a "harmony of opposites," an appreciation of our own strengths and limitations.

In the short- and medium-term, can Western companies jettison ethnocentric pride, prejudice, and a narrow worldview quickly enough to earn a profit in the PRC? For the sake of robust Return on Investment (ROI), they had better. American and European multinationals usually come to China with preconceived, stubborn notions of how their products should fit into consumers' lives. Such biases can be suicidal. Without awareness of fundamental motivations for behavior and preference, all is lost. Regardless of whether you're selling detergent, diamonds, motor oil, or M&Ms, there is an iron link between culture and commerce. Insight is the key to advancement, both geopolitical and commercial.

THE EXTRAORDINARY CHINESE

Are we really sure the sweat and toil required to chop down the Bamboo Curtain is worth the effort? China experts generally fall into two polarized camps: starry-eyed optimists and self-righteous pessimists. The former are convinced that China will become a peaceful superpower and a pillar of the global economy. The latter survey the PRC's unproductive industry and morally ambiguous commercial terrain with premonition of disaster. Oligarchic dictatorships and capitalism don't mix. The country's economic institutions are primitive and, worse yet, schizophrenic. It's a Communistic bazaar, a clanging oxymoron destined for either implosion or explosion. China both enrages and inspires. So, where are we?

The Doubting Thomas's aren't crazy. Anyone with a yen for bursting bubbles need only spend an hour at Pudong International Airport, Shanghai's municipal disgrace. From afar, the French structure is magnificent, broad-shouldered, thrusting skyward. Inside, everything is designed and produced locally, on the cheap, a disastrous embarrassment to a city with cosmopolitan pretension. It's inhuman and ultrafunctional, albeit inefficiently so. The moving sidewalks are absurdly narrow; a poky, passive-aggressive traveler can slow everyone behind him to a crawl. (Now that's power!) Putrid bathrooms are underground and, in the entire building, there's only one elevator. Escalators only go down but never up. Second-rate signage marring third-rate stores scar the entire shopping arcade. Prada sits adjacent to the "International Shop," a bin of stuffed pandas and faux cloisonné. Departures are unreliable and, worse, delays are unannounced and unexplained. Gum wrappers set off alarms, prompting agents to tug, pat, and grope every body part. Customs feels like a refugee camp. Lines are interminable. All planes are scheduled to arrive and depart at the same time. Immigration officials are beyond surly; they're robotic, preprogrammed to remain dead-faced or scowling. "Customer service" is an alien concept to the automatons who oversee baggage scanning. Tumbling suitcases pile out of x-ray machines and there's no one to help organize anything; it's not part of anyone's job description. The attendant "only handles baskets." The compartmentalized, sclerotic bureaucracy isn't flexible enough to deal with unforeseen complications (e.g., rain). It simply can't respond; instead, it freezes, foreshadowing collapse.

On a broader scale, China's economy is fraught with danger and head-scratching contrasts. Ostentatious wealth coexists with crushing poverty—on the same city block. The country's private enterprises are dynamic while the majority of state-owned enterprises are dinosaurs—bloated, profitless corpses straight out of nightmares. Capital allocation is inefficient. The banks lend to curry political favor, usually on behalf of coddled state-owned enterprises (SOEs), rather than to optimize wealth. Most private companies can't get a loan from the Big Four banks. Despite overcapacity in key sectors (autos, steel, cement, real estate), interest rates are frozen and so is the renminbi, China's currency that, until mid-2005, was pegged to the dollar and now trades within an extremely narrow range against a basket of foreign currencies. Hot money is still flooding the market, potentially destabilizing the entire financial infrastructure. Rampant corruption impedes efficient investment or horizontal integration. Managers are more focused on currying political favor than maximizing long-term return. At most local companies, the two-hour lunch *cum* nap is an institution. Books with scary titles—*The Coming Collapse of China*—have hit the bookshelves. Is the wave crashing?

No one knows. Truth be told, confidence in China's future is an article of faith. But even religious conviction can be underpinned by reason. In the PRC, straight-line projections are hazardous. The Chinese believe that destiny is cyclical, constantly changing, shifting from *yin* to *yang* and good times to bad. As a result, both the central government and the Chinese people anticipate and prepare for crisis. More often than not, they skirt it. SARS was nipped in the bud with draconian tactics. The country's "soft landing" may yet be realized. (Knock wood.) Chinese believe fortune can't be fundamentally altered but it can be *managed*. It is no coincidence that China is the only country on earth run entirely by engineers, masters of micro-analysis. The PRC is a technocrat's ultimate fantasy. The West regards China's enigmatic contradictions as fixed variables, insurmountable obstacles on a treacherous road to modernity. But the Chinese are brilliant at weaving around barriers; across millennia of history, they have adopted a splendidly detailed, realistic worldview. The power structure's embrace of Wal-Mart is but one example of pragmatism. Equipped with radar that anticipates threats, the Chinese have disarmed skeptics over and over again. They will continue to do so. While a rosy outcome is never assured, we can push fear and occasional anger aside to embrace hopeful admiration. The Chinese dragon will, ultimately, evolve into a productive and affluent member of the world community.

China's economy,* while not fully hatched, is amazingly diverse given its low per-capita income and emerging market status. As mentioned earlier, the PRC has an endless supply of cheap labor. (Or does it? A few rural disturbances and pock-

---

Warning: the following opinions will be expressed without the consent of McKinsey & Co.

ets of migrant-worker shortages in Guangdong are said to signal the end of the low-cost gravy train, but few buy this. Sixty percent of citizens still live down on the farm. Although the pace of urbanization is amazingly rapid, China will have underemployed workers available thirty years from now.) And the Middle Kingdom is more than a cut-rate flea market. From silicon chips to industrial molds, its prowess in value-added sectors makes managers from Germany to Thailand break out the Pepto Bismol. *Business Week* hyperventilated that "The China Price" were perhaps the spookiest words since "prosperity is around the corner." To boot, different regions now specialize in different sectors (e.g., auto components in the South, telecommunications and information technology in the North), facilitating the formation of supplier-and-producer clusters that slash transaction costs. What's more, the emergence of China's new middle class completes a virtuous investment-production-consumption circle, the same one that allowed America to become an industrial powerhouse in the twentieth century. Currently, there are approximately 100 million middle income individuals with enough disposable income to purchase nonessential goods; by 2010, there will be 200 million.

Second, the hope that China can evolve into a rule-based society is more than a hazy pipe dream. True, China's courts are partial to local interests, and civil rights essentially don't exist. The business world is still dominated by a web of impenetrable *guanxi*-obsessed wheeler-dealers (in Chinese business, guanxi is a network of cozy relationships based on a "you scratch my back and I'll scratch yours" mentality), not risk-sensitive banks. And the Communist Party, while not opposed to carrots and sticks, ruthlessly protects its hold on power. But we shouldn't underestimate the impact of the WTO. For the first time in China's history, the PRC is poised to benefit from *structured* relationships with other countries and international *institutions*. China's most impressive characteristic has always been, and continues to be, a holistic worldview. It has always had wisdom to recognize the strengths of other cultures and leverage them in a Chinese context. (When a Starbucks opened in the Forbidden City, it was considered an integration of East and West rather than a betrayal of tradition.) And, unlike in dynastic times, today's give-and-take will be optimized by the rule of law. During the Han, Tang, and Ming dynasties, the Middle Kingdom had extensive dealings with other governments and embraced many foreign ideas (e.g., Buddhism). But the relationships were never institutionalized; they existed at the discretion of an emperor. This isn't the case today. Multilateralism is conventional wisdom, in both "hegemonic" America and "totalitarian" China. Another factor that shouldn't be ignored is former President George H. W. Bush's much-maligned New World Order. Despite his problem with the vision thing, he had a point. Terrorism and neo-McCarthyism notwithstanding,

China's outside links are being established during *relatively* stable domestic and international circumstances.

China, post-accession to the World Trade Organization, is slowly but surely integrating itself into the fabric of the global trading system and, this time, no side has a clear upper hand. Import duties are falling. Services, including banking and investment, will open to foreign competition, an utterly unthinkable proposition just a few years ago. Even the advertising industry, now burdened with exorbitant taxes and restrictive joint ventures, will open up. (That said, as long as the Communists remain in power, media ownership/content will always be strictly controlled. Any liberalization will be cosmetic, designed for propaganda purposes.) Intellectual property rights, while still largely ignored (92 percent of all software is licensed illegally), are at least a hot topic. In short, China will be forced to play by the rules—laws designed to promote efficiency and spur growth—or it will be bounced from the party. China simply can't afford for that to happen, lest the grand Job Creation and Urbanization Paradigm crumble to pieces, an outcome that would be nothing short of disastrous, not just for China but for the world.

Third, and most fundamental, the Chinese are, in the end, an amazing, even inspiring people. Each of the above arguments is coldly rational; they can be debated, dissected, picked to pieces. However, anyone who has spent any length of time in China will be impressed by the dynamism and intelligence of its citizens, at least the ones not crushed by industry or bureaucratic implosion. Westerners think the outside world is, more or less, safe. Chinese believe it's dangerous; life is precarious and can't be taken for granted. To survive, let alone advance, adaptive traits are required and the Chinese have them in spades. They are cleverly resourceful. They boast a broad (albeit ethnocentric) worldview and are fascinated with anything new. Anti-individualism fuels a patriotic fervor that unifies the nation behind a common goal of national advancement. A profound respect for intelligence, the ultimate weapon in a dog-eat-dog world, has created a country that reveres the scholar. Their mindset emphasizes knowledge over might, defense over offense, skill over brute force, concentration over impulse. Smart kids are actually cool. Parents would sell their souls to get their children into Harvard. As a result, Chinese are analytically and tactically brilliant. While creativity is not China's forte, dazzling application is. The Chinese are, simply put, the most striving, ambitious people on the planet and that counts for a lot. They are pragmatic yet human, wary yet hopeful, patient yet quick to respond. They are the hope of their future. I'm betting on them. (See figure I.1.)

The China market is real. The China opportunity is real. The promise of Chinese consumerism is real . . . but easy to squander.

Fig. I.1. Nokia knows that, for 3,000 years, Chinese culture has stressed the importance of understanding the world around you as the fundamental adaptive trait. In today's ever-changing business environment, such an orientation remains a powerful competitive weapon.

PART I

CHINESE CULTURE AND BUYER MOTIVATIONS

CHAPTER 1

BIG DREAMS, SMALL POTATOES

THE MOTIVATIONS OF CHINA'S NEW MIDDLE CLASS

OVERVIEW

The psychology of the new middle class is marked by contradictions. China's history, its unity of spirit, and a missionary zeal to elevate the nation's role in the world are all net positives that will create a great modern nation. However, China's millennia-old dynastic and Confucian culture creates apparent "conflicts" that need to be carefully managed by marketers. The mindset of the newly affluent paradoxically blends an aggressive hunger for social and financial advancement with a rigid, hierarchical social structure that rewards conservatism. As a result, the Chinese psyche has always been torn between the polarities of ambition and caution. (Japanese, on the hand, are unadulterated safety seekers. Western countries, fueled by individualism, pretty much "go for it.") Denizens of the Middle Kingdom are pulled by a desire to both *project* individual status and *protect* family welfare. They are motivated by both a dynamic and impulsive "*now*" orientation versus a stable and balanced *future* focus.

The ambivalence between conspicuous consumption and conformist conservation has historically divided the hearts of Chinese. An explosion of lifestyle and economic opportunities, combined with the other reality of low incomes, rusted iron rice bowls, and expensive housing, exacerbates this tension. And smart marketers must help consumers resolve it. This chapter concludes with six ways to do this.

DEFINITIONS FIRST

When we speak of the "Chinese middle class," to whom and to what do we refer? The economic answer is fairly straightforward, though difficult to quantify. Middle class means having enough disposable income to buy "stuff," not necessities. Middle class means *cai* (food to please), not *fan* (food to fill). Middle class means home ownership, a long-term savings plan, and car purchases (if not now, then one day). Middle class, in the parlance of the Sixteenth People's Congress, winks at a robust, yet pliable, *xiao kang,* which loosely translates as "petite bourgeoisie," beneficiaries of Jiang Zemin's self-aggrandizing (but still important) "Three Represents." (See page 23.)

Psychographically, however, the answer is rich, full of nuance, and challenging. The middle class defines the soul of a nation. It is the heart of a culture. It projects values intrinsic to a society not struggling for material survival. Around 90 percent of the United States' populace considers itself to be middle class. In China, a nation only recently liberated from the shackles of inefficient state planning and force-fed egalitarianism, that figure is probably no more than 10 percent. But China's middle class is still the essence of a culture boasting 5,000 years of often glorious history. Therefore, in defining the identity and motives of China's middle class, we are articulating the crux of Chinese civilization. As marketers, we are pinpointing its fundamental motivations of behavior and preference.

THEY'RE HERE

The business world has woken up to the power and size of China's fast-growing middle class. And, this time, it is sober-minded, finally abandoning fantasies of 1.3 billion souls releasing decades of pent-up consumerism. Distribution death traps, kamikaze sales teams, infectious corruption, and seemingly indecipherable regional preferences—not to mention 800 million rural dwellers living on less than three dollars a day—have shattered the illusion of gold in the topsoil.

However, the Chinese, particularly in the primary "cluster cities" of Beijing, Shanghai, and Guangzhou—as well as important secondary cities (e.g., Chengdu, Hangzhou, Dalian, Qingdao, Xiamen, even Chongqing)—*are* getting richer. There are at least 100 million individuals with "middle class" purchasing power (enough disposable income to indulge in nonessential goods ranging from a can of youth-cool Pepsi to a meticulously appointed living room). And this "middle class" is unlike any other in history in terms of scale, growth rates, and ambition. A couple of headline statistics:

- Starting from scratch five years ago, China is the largest mobile phone market in the world with over 300 million handsets in use. Nokia, Motorola, and Samsung have major research and development centers in the PRC.
- According to the Diamond Trading Company (DTC, formerly DeBeers), engagement ring penetration is approximately 80 percent in some key markets, up from less than 10 percent in 1994. Shanghainese are more susceptible to the sparkle factor than the much-wealthier Japanese, for whom acquisition rates hover at just above 50 percent.

Things are looking sunnier than one might have thought possible only a couple of years ago. However, the middle class is not an easy nut to crack. Its purchasing power is limited and, at the same time, the "newly affluent" are experiencing a great deal of angst as they sort thorough competing life-choice demands. The dilemmas faced by a market with a population of twice the size of France are invitations to harness the ambitions buried in them and extract the energy to fuel in-market success.

One of the keys to unleashing these forces is first identifying the underlying drivers of middle-income Chinese citizens who are only now achieving critical mass. As a result, we must explore both the dynamism of contemporary China and the enduring legacies of thousands of years of history. We then translate a "master" or "unifying insight" into six marketing guidelines that can be applied to the vast majority of consumer goods.

SOME CAVEATS, NATURALLY

Yes, this is an ambitious goal and one rife with subjectivity. So it makes sense that, even before beginning, we will start off with a few caveats. First, the conclusions drawn about Chinese are just that—about *Chinese*. However, one might glean an impression that they articulate the drama of the entire human condition . . . but this is not the case. Emotions are universal but the degree to which each is expressed is not. Second, one might question whether these findings are ephemeral, bound to change during what *Time* magazine called "The Next Cultural Revolution." Rest assured that they are not a passing fad. In fact, it is likely that these conclusions trend toward timeless. Such an assertion is not intellectual megalomania. Instead, it recognizes the role of cultural roots, however they may be defined, in a society's make-up. Across time, across socioeconomic strata, across geography, the essence of "Chineseness" has applications. That said, the *expression* of Chinese values does assume different forms. They reinforce—perpetuate, rather—the presentness of the past. They are the keys to deciphering the code of China's cultural blueprint; and deci-pher it we must to make a profit selling a bar of soap, a mobile phone, or a car. (According to Kristin Stapleton, a professor of Asian history at the University of Kentucky, claims of cultural "permanence" have been intellectually discred-ited to the point of scorn. Of course, culture is not genetic and, therefore, not as unchangeable as skin color or eye shape. However, mores are not ephemeral. "Internationalized" Hong Kong is still "Chinese." Oil-rich Saudi Arabia is still tribal. Culture—and, in particular, Chinese culture—withstands the test of time.)

MIDDLE CLASS CULTURAL ROOTS

Confucianism

To explore the country's soul, let's take a journey back a few thousand years. Any theorizing regarding "What makes China Chinese?" must start with a basic understanding of *ru jia,* the Confucian school of thought. We must also absorb the influence of a Daoist worldview ("Cyclical Dynasticism") that contrasts with the West's monotheistic humanism. Together they form the contours of the contemporary Chinese heart and economic engine.

So, what is the essence of Confucianism? Confucius articulated a model of an ideal social structure based on "conformist reward." He lived in the later Zhou dynasty, around 500 BC, a time of civil war and diminished cen-tral government power. *Kongzi,* as the Chinese call him, set his gaze to the past, an idealized golden era when society was perfectly ordered and harmo-nious. Confucius and disciples of his, such as Mencius, laid out an intricate code of conduct, centered on five key "relationship dyads" or *wu lun* in which everyone had strictly defined roles and responsibilities: (a) father to son, (b) husband to wife, (c) ruler to minister, (d) friend to friend, and (e) older brother to younger brother. Over centuries, with neo-Confucian rigidity peaking during the Qing dynasty in the nineteenth century, society's struc-ture became a fixed variable. Things were regimented, hierarchical. In large part, the burst of early-twentieth-century reform was a reaction against an os-sified Confucian order that militated against modern reform. But it came too late.

And yet, for a couple thousand years, Confucian thought was a hugely pos-itive force in the evolution of Chinese artistic, political, philosophical, and eco-nomic sophistication. In its time, Confucianism ignited a revolution of inestimable magnitude. To a certain extent, it shifted emphasis away from heaven to the here and now. It also spawned the first socially mobile society. In theory, even a field hand could study the *Si Shu Wu Jing,* take the Civil Service exam, and enter the ranks of the noble gentry or the dynastic court. By unconditionally accepting—internalizing—the social order, one could move up within it. And what rose eventually fell. As early as the Han dynasty (220 BC), equal inheritance was mandated. Wealth was divided between the sons to ensure that economic entitlement did not sustain a complacent clan.

Confucius therefore created a somewhat schizophrenic society. On one hand, the human world was regimented. On the other, it was incredibly *alive.* It was dynamic, rising and falling, collectively morphing into something different time and time again. It fueled a system of rewards designed to encourage drive and initiative. Of course, individualism—a challenge to the supremacy of the emperor's order or a "me before us" worldview—was immoral. So, dynastic China was regimented, but it was ambitious. It was mechanical but fluid. It was okay to push, but not too hard. Progress was good. Challenge was bad. This is one layer of conflict among contemporary denizens of the Middle Kingdom— aspiration versus rigidity. This leads to the next layer described below, the tension between the hopefulness of upward mobility and the helplessness of an unavoidable destiny.

Western Individualism and Empowerment

Moving 4,000 miles to the west, to Israel, the cradle of Judeo-Christian civilization, when the Biblical patriarchs (Adam, Abraham, Isaac, et al.) spoke with God, He offered a quid pro quo: "Accept my 'word' (i.e., law), and I will reward you with a heaven on earth." The deal triggered a series of contracts between man and God culminating in the Ten Commandments and Jesus' Sermon on the Mount, both articulations of the rules governing ideal society.

Confucius and Moses were, on some levels, similar. They both disseminated a perfect order, an idealized social structure. But Confucius was a man with no links to a supreme being. Moses and his forefathers had direct, one-on-one relationships with God. The moral code conceived by a single deity was a gift articulated by the infinite Unknowable and then given to individuals.

It was more than divine generosity. The Torah is a covenant, an empowering pact that offers a clear reward for accepting God into the heart. Heaven also served as a readily identifiable return on investment. But both Judaism and Christianity are rooted in individualism: a man or woman, through a one-on-one relationship with God and acceptance of His Word, has the ability to change a nation's or individual's fate. Not just circumstances, but *destiny.* True,

God's ways are unknowable. He always puts obstacles on the path, but the ultimate reward is clear and within reach of the individual.

The freedom to touch the face of God is the ultimate empowerment. It is also the soul of monotheistic—Western—society. Our history is a bumpy yet steady progression to a Promised Land. It is also "linear" in the sense that, over time, man and God work together to achieve an increasingly evolved moral consciousness. Furthermore, Europeans and Americans view their moral "destination" as absolute, a place at which cultural relativism becomes irrelevant.

Asian Randomness and Insecurity

Most Asian societies, on the other hand, regard history as a combination of randomness and cyclicity, despite the centeredness of Confucianism. More specifically, fears of random chaos are alleviated through the imposition of a structured, cyclical code of conduct and worldview.

In China, Japan, Southeast Asia, and ancient Greece and Rome, God doesn't exist. But gods do. They are all too knowable. They have human flaws, including caprice, the one most likely to cause mortals grief. A man can pray from sunrise to sunset, even sitting atop a mountain close to heaven's ear, with no guarantee of reward. Polytheistic cultures are built around a "pain but no gain" credo. They do not expect progress. They crave appeasement, predictability, and shelter from the next crop-flooding storm or life-snuffing earthquake.

Such randomness is unsettling and leads to collective helplessness. It also nurtures legal and social codes that maximize predictability. Dynastic China imposed structure in a multitude of ways. Confucianism ordered the world of Small Things. The Mandate of Heaven explained—and predicted—history's sweep.

Structure as Safety

Man's inherent state is precarious. As a result, religious, political, and philosophical institutions are naturally geared toward propagating order. Chinese were, and continue to be, obsessive about balance and predictability. Daoism's *yin* and *yang* (i.e., feminine versus masculine forces) are an integration of the *ba gua,* or eight natural elements evenly divided between feminine and masculine forces that can be combined in only sixty-four pre-set ways (see figure 1.1). The lunar calendar is cyclical, with each "animal" corresponding to one of twelve "earthly branches." Lucky dates for marriage, auspicious office openings, and astrological license plates are all structure-obsessed manifestations of a preordained temporal rotation. Then there are the ten *heavenly* stems that correspond to times of the

Fig. 1.1. The Ba Gua, *from* I Ching, *represents the cyclical nature and immutable structure of the entire universe. More concretely, it represents the flow of the eight elements that make up everything.*

day, but let's not obsess about the mathematics. Suffice it to say, when you combine an earthly branch and a heavenly stem, fate is the result. Every man, woman, and child is marching toward a fundamentally unalterable destiny. And destiny is a function of immutable cycles against which no one had better put up a fight. The best he can hope for is to understand—and, possibly, *manage*—his fate. (If it's meant to rain, it will rain. But he can bring an umbrella.) He can never avoid what must be. In the words of Henri-Charles Puech, author of *Man and Time:* "No event is unique, nothing is enacted but once . . . every event has been enacted, is enacted, and will be enacted perpetually; the same individuals have appeared, appear, and will appear at every turn of the circle."

The Clan, the Emperor, and a Lack of Civil Institutions

In the grand scheme of things, a god can't be counted on and the individual doesn't count for much. So society is structured around two polarized centers of gravity: the clan and the emperor. Under the watchful eye of Confucius, each has a responsibility to the other. The extended family must submit to the ruler and the ruler must wield power correctly, working for the collective good.

When an emperor abuses or squanders his might, he forfeits the Mandate of Heaven (so says Mencius). Preceded by a brief period of spectacular disaster, history inevitably returns to its natural and tranquil state. The relentless order is reestablished. Another cycle of time has run its course.

When governing power gravitates *away* from the mainstream, the institutional hallmarks of a "civil society" fail to take root. As a result, China has never seriously flirted with any form of representative government. (The 1911 Republican revolution doesn't count. Even before Yuan Shikai made his restorative power play, suffrage never exceeded 5 percent of the population.) The country's judiciary—today and in the past—is designed only to reinforce the legitimacy of central authority. Despite several emperors' benevolence (*ren*), China has never enjoyed a more progressive form of government than benign dictatorship. There was no Roman forum, no Bill of Rights, no Renaissance. Never liberated by humanism, there was no Magna Carta or Declaration of Independence. The focus on the *responsibility* of the individual, rather than his rights, manifested itself in countless ways, from a thousand years of highly stylized art that downplayed the human form to the unquestioned submission of son to father and wife to husband.

And what has been the result? Stoic powerlessness. Confronted with misfortune, Chinese sigh, "*mei you ban fa*" (literally, "no way to handle"). The laid-off cabbie will curse his fortune but rarely revolt. Destiny is the driver. "Fairness" rarely enters the discussion except in particularly egregious circumstances (e.g., massive government corruption, famine), and, even then, it is a question of the emperor's failure to lead, not of respect for individual rights. China is a socially mobile culture but advancement is linked to the acceptance of a prescribed order. It is a nation where intellectual adventurism dies a sad death. It is a nation that, despite powerful ambition, is haunted by insecurity.

Perpetual Insecurity

It has always been this way. Power or security have always been precarious, always a function of currying favor in high places. "*Ban jun ru ban hu*," a Mandarin maxim, means, "Sitting next to a lord is like sitting next to a tiger." In other words, he who lives by the sword dies by the sword. In dynastic China, power was given and taken by dictators who were often capricious and cruel. The first Emperor Qin's ruthlessness was epic, but even today he is respected for centralizing China. The last de facto imperial sovereign, the Dowager Empress Cixi, was an equally bitter pill to swallow. She is not detested for brutality but, instead, colossal mismanagement. (Historians claim her last words were,

"Never again entrust the power of the State to a woman.") Results-driven vindictiveness is respected. Emperors have always consolidated, established, or reestablished power through purges, snuffing out bright stars along the way:

- Shang Yang, a Warring States legal reformer, was executed in 338 BC.
- Qu Yuan, a Warring States patriot, poet, and statesman, was outcast in 277 BC.
- Si Ma Qian, the most respected historian of the Western Han period, was emasculated in 99 BC.
- Yue Fei, a brilliant Yuan dynasty military strategist, was tortured to death in 1142 AD.
- Lin Zexu, the Qing dynasty negotiator before the Opium War, was exiled in 1842 (admittedly, at the urging of the British).
- Peng Dehuai, a general who accompanied Mao on the Long March but had the temerity to call the Great Leap Forward "flawed," was savagely persecuted during the Cultural Revolution, starting in 1966.
- Liu Shao Qi, Mao's right-hand man and partner in crime, was banished from the Party during the Cultural Revolution and died in prison.

Paranoia Pops: The Cultural Revolution

The ten-year period from 1966 to 1976 was both tragic and ironic, not to mention a direct result of the role of insecurity in Chinese culture. From McCarthy to Hitler, demagogues establish legitimacy via fabricated enemies "within." The United States government was infested with Reds. Jews were polluting Aryan purity. Mao's genius, however, was to declare war on Chinese civilization itself and, in doing so, wield insecurity as a weapon of control. Scholarship was bad; illiteracy was righteous. Nobility was evil; poverty noble. Genuine artistic expression was profane; dime-a-dozen, cookie-cutter operatic pulp was glorious. Filial piety corrupted; the blind worship of the Chairman beatified.

No Chinese was safe because the fiber of China itself was under siege. The Cult of Mao became the only sanctuary. Values that had seeped into each pore of every Chinese were toxic, in need of purging. Tradition was vilified. Ink drawings, sloping roofs, calligraphy, silk dresses, Buddhism, Daoism, monks, Ming furniture, Tang poems, Beijing University, porcelain, and the Great Wall were tainted. And yet, paradoxically, "New China" was built on the back of the Old. Confucian values such as respect for strong central authority, the supremacy of the emperor (i.e., Mao), and an instinctive anti-individualism were instrumental in the 1949 revolution's mass seduction. They were useful once again during the tumult of "Ten Difficult Years." The Cultural Revolution's betrayal of the past underscored future precariousness. The insecurity of Imperial times was magnified exponentially.

Deng's Insecure Wealth

It was Deng Xiao Ping who snatched the nation from the jaws of this hysterical self-destruction. Sanity was restored first in the countryside during the decollectivization of the 1980s. But things really got rolling in 1992 when Special Economic Zones (SEZs) began offering aggresive tax breaks to foreign enterprises. During a tour of the Southern provinces, Deng declared, "To get rich is glorious!" He also tipped his hat to the inevitability of capitalistic income disparity when he said, "Let some prosper first." (Importantly, this acknowledgement had nothing to do with economic "rights." Indeed, capital generation was imperially proclaimed the individual's most sacred *obligation* to the motherland, a nation destined to assume her rightful position on the world stage.) Since then, China's economic transformation has been nothing short of dazzling. In the past ten years, real per capita income has more than doubled. The eastern seaboard, despite environmental pillage and a huge migrant population of rural workers (*wai lai min gong*), is incontestably dynamic. Consumerism has crept into the consciousness of even society's more modest strata. Shanghai, Beijing, Guangzhou, Shenzhen, Hangzhou, and Wenzhou all boast average yearly incomes of at least $4,000, a level economists peg as the threshold to "middle-class society."

But, still, the people worry. China's Stalinist banking system and decrepit state-owned enterprises allocate capital with mind-numbing inefficiency. Yawning gaps in spending power may (or may not) threaten social stability. But the vulnerability is more than structural; it is felt on a deeply personal level. China's new wealth is viewed as hard won and easily lost, particularly by those who have it, 74 percent of whom consider themselves to be "self-made." How come?

First, the Iron Rice Bowl is rusted. Until the mid-90s, any urban employee of a state-run *danwei* (work unit) could, in exchange for sheepish obeisance, count on cradle-to-grave subsidization of every basic need. Food, clothing, education, housing, medical insurance were all taken for granted. Now, however, there are no more free lunches. It is a dog-eat-dog world with most expenses borne by the individual. Self-reliance translates into a long-term "savings anxiety" that encourages an extremely high savings rate (higher than 30 percent in practically every Chinese city).

Second, aggregate wealth is dependent on the Party's continuing endorsement of economic reform. Shanghai, in particular, has benefited from the central government's blessing. The Whore of the Orient's charm is no longer faded; it sparkles. But Shanghai is no entrepreneur's Mecca. Its success is a bureaucratic and political triumph, realized by fiat. Pudong's impressively soulless skyline was built on the back of arbitrary edicts. For example, Deng himself dictated the SEZ tax rates and Jiang and his Shanghai Clique further tinkered with them. China's most vibrant showcase of economic reform is a case study of administrative efficiency, not creative vision or entrepreneurialism. Continued success is by no means taken for granted, particularly given Beijing's recent "Go West!" campaign. As a result, Shanghai's print and television media are some of the tamest in the nation. Its work force is subservient, eminently adaptable to the regimentation of corporate hierarchy. The city glances over its shoulder in anticipation of the next incoming threat.

Third, newly affluent individuals sense their wealth is unprotected. The past—an era of meal coupons, famine in the hinterland, unschooled "patriotic" doctors, and backyard furnaces—is still a fresh memory. More fundamentally, an individual's recent gains are not protected by the political system. Even socialism with Chinese characteristics is still frosty to private enterprise, despite a nod to "advanced forces of production and culture" within the "Three Represents." (They are now enshrined in the CCP constitution: The Communist Party must always represent the development trend of: (a) China's advance productive forces, (b) the orientation of China's advanced culture, and (c) the fundamental interests of the overwhelming majority of the people.) Property rights are only nominally protected by the constitution. The judiciary is still light years away from impartiality, with its judges either poorly trained or beholden to local power brokers. The banking system is rigged against the interests of the entrepreneur; raising capital for non-state-owned entities is an exercise in extreme frustration. (Only one non-SOE businessman, the CEO of Haier, has been appointed to the policy-setting Central Committee.)

Wealth is insecure, so people are, too.

MIDDLE-CLASS BEHAVIORAL CHARACTERISTICS

Defense Mechanisms against Insecurity

The populace of the People's Republic is squeamish. The concoction of Confucian ambition and regimentation, Daoist passivity, dynastic helplessness, plus the insecurity of wealth in the Communist era, is not the easiest to stomach. People stride toward greatness but every step is measured. There is a lack of true individualism and few paths of success, so everyone climbs the same creaky, narrow ladder. It's crowded and competitive. One's position must be both loudly declared and jealously guarded. The Chinese are pulled between defensive self-protection and assertive projection of status.

"Protection" for a Safe Future

Although blighted by racism, high crime rates, guns, and gum on the sidewalk, Western life is pretty stable. The corner coffee shop is a Starbucks. Most elections elicit yawns. Business isn't a battlefield; it's a minuet. The newspapers alert us to dark forces but, in normal times, we're a pretty happy-go-lucky bunch, shaken from fat and friendly torpor only when a tragedy (e.g., the Cuban missile crisis, 9/11, Hurricane Katrina) breaks through our complacence.

Chinese, on the other hand, are always suspicious. In the past one hundred years, they have lived through the Republican revolution (1911), twelve years of regional warlords (1916–1927), Japanese occupation (1937–1948), civil war (1945–1948), the Communist "liberation" (1949), a counter-rightist movement (1953), a hundred flowers blooming (1957), the Great Leap Forward (1958–1962), the Cultural Revolution (1966–1976), agrarian reform (1980s), the single-child policy (1978-), socialism with Chinese characteristics (1992-), the return of foreign barbarians (1995-), and the shredding of the state safety net (1998-). And, as we have seen, recent times are the rule, not the exception. Chinese, particularly Mainlanders, instinctively shield themselves from abrupt change. Stability is a blessing; society, structured around the clan and a mercurial, all-powerful ruling class, is fragile. People live between crystal walls in danger of shattering.

For thousands of years, adaptive individuals have protectively cocooned themselves in safety. The first emperor, Qin Shi Huangdi, surrounded himself with thousands of life-sized terra cotta warriors (each with unique facial expressions) on the bumpy road to the afterworld. A protective instinct is also evident in moats surrounding the Forbidden City, walls as thick as ramparts enclosing private residences with steel-gated front doors and barred windows on upper floors, a half-continent-long Great Wall built to seal civilization in and barbarians out, school uniforms to ensure no "sticking out," a germ-killing soap with a 25 percent market share (Safeguard), joss sticks warding off evil, fortune tellers, amulets, lucky numbers, auspicious wedding dates, and, last but not least, feng shui to suck in the "dragon winds." All these practices are manifestations of a collective insecurity about the future. Each is designed to protect from what cannot be controlled.

The protection instinct often assumes passive forms. The greatest challenge many Western managers have in cultivating leadership centers on locals' unwilling to express a point of view, particularly when a topic is shaded in gray. The subjective is uncomfortable even for the brazen. Saying what you think is like walking a tightrope with no safety net. Without six-sigma confidence, silence reigns.

Projection of Today's Status

Most protective elements are Daoist or Buddhist in origin, both of which are said to propagate "passivity," but China is also boldly Confucian—and thus status-driven, ambitious, assertive, and socially mobile. Japanese appear to take genuine comfort in "fitting in"—that is, regressing to the mean. (When advertising sanitary napkins to young Japanese women, the message is, "Pssst! Don't worry. No one's going to notice anything." In China, it's, "Fear not! Nothing will come between you and success!") Chinese want to advance, even if there are sharks swimming in the sea. Compelled to mark their territory within a regimented social structure, Chinese are proudly conspicuous consumers. Status is a weapon to be wielded, not locked in a box for posterity's pleasure. Victory is projected, loudly and in Technicolor. Why? Competition is fierce. So, to encourage others to "keep away," one has to let others know who he is and what he has achieved.

Chinese project greatness. (So does Motorola in its "Moto" branding campaign. Trendy types are literally screaming its name from rooftops. And Unilever's Lux shampoo and soap is all about assertive projection of star-like glamor. See figure 1.2.) Neon lights flood the street. Their colors are bold, blazing reds, yellows, and golds. Signage is not flush against buildings; it stretches into the middle of the street to proclaim, "Something important is going on here!" Modern Chinese architecture (e.g., Shanghai's new Jin Mao building, the Beijing opera house, any airport) is grand and imposing, often shoddy inside but impressive from afar. (In fact, substandard materials—junky door handles, stained carpets, rusted toilets—and lack of environmental harmony don't matter if the effect is big and bold.) Facades of apartment complexes are colorfully painted, but, around the corner, out of sight, stained gray and white motifs reassert their monotonous dominance. There are clear demarcations between public spaces and private quarters, the latter often tranquil and unassuming.

On an individual level, status must radiate. For example, parents carefully select given names designed to project a heroic character—Morning Sun, Strength, Wisdom, Victory, Shake, Cosmos, Forward, Success, Climb, Bright, Great, Thunder, Dragon, Surpass, Radiate, Peak. Where you live is also a reflection of who you are, so the nomenclature of homes must inspire—Peacock Dynasty, Heavenly Horse, Tycoon Court, Gathering of All Heroes under Heaven, Genesis Villa, Prestige, and Riverside Mansion. Common areas are dripping with marble, jade, and gold, all of questionable quality.

Fig. 1.2. Lux personifies "projective," star-like beauty. The brand is much more successful in China than in Western European markets.

Projection of status occurs with every breath. (A famous Chinese maxim: "It's better to be the head of a rooster than the tail of an ox.") The business card exchange is ritualized. Presented with the reverence of a college diploma, every character is meticulously analyzed. The receiver usually vocalizes the job title, as if to recognize the bearer's achievements. Professional forms of address are also elaborate: "boss," "manager," "owner," "leader," "chairman," "vice mayor," "big brother," or "father's uncle" taking the place of "Mr." or "Sir." Only intimate relations use first names.

During an initial encounter, one expects a rapid-fire interrogation worthy of the Spanish Inquisition: income, title, marital status (and satisfaction), home address, spousal pulchritude, number of children and their gender, etc. Given the Chinese protective instinct, this assault might seem incongruous, but it is an expedient manner of sizing someone up and placing him some-where—high or low—on the social hierarchy. Social intercourse is lubricated only after life station has been ascertained. And he who projects more of it has the upper hand.

Project, Protect, and Internal Conflict

The PRC's newly affluent are pulled between two poles. The projective instinct encourages a crass materialism worthy of America's Gilded Age. (In second-tier cities, it is still common to see a professional wearing a new suit with its label sewn on the outside of the sleeve.) Expensive brands are bought for status, not functionality. Price is used as a surrogate indicator of quality, particularly when the consumption is public (e.g., alcohol at a business dinner). Buying decisions can be irrational, even for big-ticket items; consumption is designed for material gratification. Shopping centers buzz with guilty titillation. Over the past five years, a swaggering, avaricious consumer culture has penetrated China. In 1995, Beijing, Shanghai, and Guangzhou each had one upscale mall. Today, primary "clusters" boast more than a dozen apiece. Local Chinese, not just expatriates, frequent *Xin Tian Di,* or New Heaven and Earth, an upscale entertainment complex serving $10 beers and imported Cuban cigars. In a world of projected wealth, the "nouveau riche" class has cachet. Just outside Shanghai, one of China's newly minted multimillionaires recently built a replica of the White House as his private residence. Such chutzpah is greeted with a straight face.

But China is still not a wealthy country, even in glittering coastal cities. Beijing, for example, has a Purchase Power Parity (PPP) per capita income of under $5,000, almost eight times less than most American cities. Granted, this figure (1) includes the municipality's rural area, (2) excludes income from tax-free moonlighting gigs, and (3) doesn't adjust for a low cost of living. (Taxis are very cheap and a lovely apartment—except in the center of town where prices have skyrocketed—costs around $100,000.) But Shenzhen is not Monaco. Pennies are pinched. Belts are pulled tight. Even proudly displayed "VIP" cards— issued for everything from ice cream parlors, corner cafés, and launderettes to massage halls and underground DVD stalls—are ultimately snapped up because of the 10 percent discount they provide.

Projection is further dulled by insecure self-protection. As discussed, today's wealth can evaporate. China's Leninist political system has no legal system capable of addressing middle-class interests. Stock speculation is riskier than a gambling binge. Ten years ago, homes and education were free. Today, both require a carefully hatched savings plan. Unemployment, consistently underreported by officials, has risen to 11–13 percent of the urban work force. And, most critically, the jittery ethos of a nation whose people do not believe they can alter destiny cannot be expunged. For thousands of years, cautiousness has honed Han instincts. The combination of new China's cutthroat capitalism and old China's ruler-dominated dynasticism also fuels fiercely protective consumption. The focus is on the child or other members of the extended family, not the self. It is conservative, stability-minded, and future-focused. It plays right into the hands of an insurance industry ready to take off like a rocket.

INSIGHT APPLICATION

When selling products to a middle class with such a mindset, how can we reconcile bold projection with anxious protection? The recognition of this dilemma is a uniquely Chinese insight. Addressing it will establish an empathetic bond with consumers, sowing the seeds of long-term loyalty. The next section outlines six specific strategies to achieve this goal.

#1: Charge More for Public Consumption

Chinese need to project status. However, keeping up with the neighbors costs money, and the vast majority of the "newly affluent" don't have a lot of cash on hand. As a result, they are highly selective regarding the *categories* for which they will pay a premium. Products that are publicly displayed—brands that can double as badges—will justify a higher price relative to the competition. The leading home appliances, for example, are domestic (e.g., TCL, Haier, Konka, Changhong, Little Swan); while they do not provide a status fix, they are reliable. Sony, Panasonic, and other Japanese trademarks drip prestige but few consumers (except for upscale yuppies) buy them. They are not displayed; only the family uses them. (See figure 1.3.)

Mobile phones are a different story. In Beijing, Shanghai, and Guangzhou, not a single local brand penetrates the top five, despite price points 50 percent (or more) below Nokia, Motorola, and Samsung. Cell phones represent a revolution in personal communications. They are also the most powerfully public means of projecting individual identity. A young person's "cool" is more than tangentially correlated with his mobile phone "badge." It is a personalized calling card, both literally and figuratively.

Diamonds, glaringly obvious status projectors, have experienced phenomenal growth in primary and secondary cities. In 1994, urban coastal penetration was in the single digits. Today, in Shanghai, acquisition exceeds Japanese rates. The diamond, a stone that reveals feminine sparkle for the whole world to see, is a luxury good. But, as a public display tool, it's an essential. Gold, no less expensive than diamonds, is suffering stagnant sales, largely because of its musty associations (i.e., "my father's Oldsmobile").

Personal car shipments are mushrooming. Consider this: when an individual's salary approaches $1,250 per month, he's a juicy target for the burgeoning auto industry. The average "low end" imported vehicle costs approximately $15,000, 100 percent of yearly income and twice as much as a perfectly functional local model. Despite this astronomical price/income ratio, the auto market is burgeoning with annual unit sales topping one million vehicles for the first time in 2002. Why the momentum? A shiny new Buick (yes, *Buick*) is the ultimate public "success demonstrator." Its horn honks, "I've made it to the top. I'm worthy. Respect me. Now."

2: Use Status as a Tool

Unlike Europe or, to a lesser extent, the United States, the "socio" component of socioeconomic status is not heavily weighted in the new China. Of course, the concept of "coming from a good family" exists, but the hierarchy of prestige is still under construction. Furthermore, despite limited income and insecure wealth, middle-class folk are optimistic about their future. But, as with their ancestors, the newly affluent are skittish about advancement's fragility. So they need "weapons of success." Status is not an end in itself. It is a means to an end, a vehicle of progress. Status should never be inert; it must be productively alive. For example, Audi's television advertising has depicted a sartorially splendid man striding down an endless red carpet surrounded by applause. It print work leverages the taste required to appreciate fine art as a reflection of the Audi driver, a man who relies on "connoisseurship" to "lead the road." (See figure 1.4.) Clearly, automobile advertising doesn't target the man who *has* but, instead, the man who *will* have.

In a recent DTC print ad for men's diamonds, the headline reads, "One sparkle is enough to make a powerful man." Dynamic status is active. With a ring on his finger, his qualities shine through, dazzling both superiors and competitors. A Motorola spot shows competitive brands' users (literally) aflame, stumbling through an urban war zone. The "Moto man," armed with GPRS connectivity, calmly sips coffee, savoring his recent promotion. Passat, an upscale Volkswagen, aired an increasingly common "manifesto TVC" with copy celebrating the importance of "internal tools" or, in American parlance, "the right stuff." It states: "He who controls, wins. He who creates the road, writes the

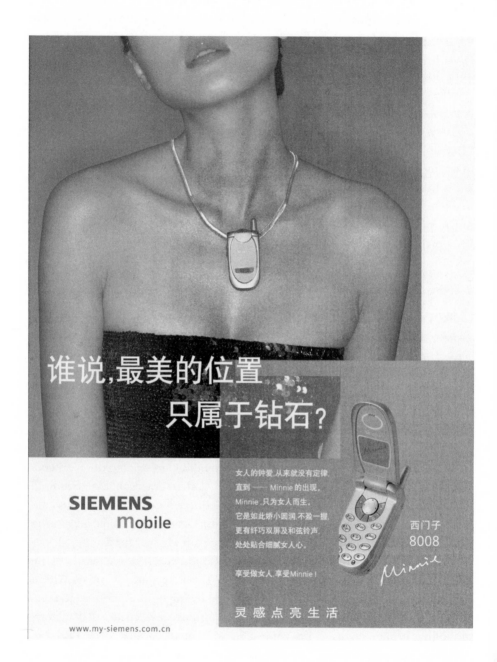

Fig. 1.3 (previous page and above). These ads for the "Minnie," Siemens phone for women, highlights the product's dual role as an eye-catching accessory.

Fig. 1.4. This print campaign suggests that a man's success is ultimately advanced by higher-order connoisseurship, one demonstrated by a preference for the top-of-the-line Audi 8.

rules. He who moves forward fastest, achieves greatness." The ad closes with a Passat driving through an elegant museum and past a larger-than-life portrait of Napoleon taming a bucking stallion.

Status must be used as a weapon. It must protect whatever success an everyday warrior has managed to achieve. Business is a battlefield; life is an endurance test.

#3: Make Aspiration Accessible

Chinese are Confucians and Confucians are goal-driven, so all advertising should be scrubbed clean down to the shine. Its must emit the comforting glow of a 1950s Disney short. It must project the idealized economic aspirations of a wide-eyed, yet hungry, Generation Next. Every woman is a *xing fu nu ren* (blessed with material, professional, and romantic satisfaction). Even marriage should be *mei man* ("complete" with love, cash, and kids). Men should be on the way up. Families should beam Father-Knows-Best serenity. However, given limited disposable income, ambitions should not be light years from today's reality. A middle-class dad should drive home in a Buick, not a Ferrari. Props, sets, and situations must navigate the gray area between dreams and delusion. An out-of-touch promise will be forgotten or disliked, but future goals, achievable or not, should be glorified on film. (See figure 1.5.)

True, it's a fine line. How far is too far? It depends on the consumer market and the product category. Low-involvement, cheap goods have mass appeal so they're broadly targeted. For example, Zuo An coffee uses a "taste of Paris" platform. The advertising's palette is romantic, rainy, and poetic. The visuals are drenched with sophistication and the gleam of cobblestone streets at sunset. This is appealing because it's *meant* to be a moment of *fantasy*, not a portrait of ambition. On the other hand, a recent Lux ad starring Karen Mok presented soft hair as almost a passport to the lifestyle of the rich and famous. Its delusional premise alienated a broad swathe of middle-income hair washers.

Fig. 1.5. All advertising in China should be aspirational, reflecting the tomorrow that might be. But they have to be realistic enough to avoid snapping believability. The "perfect family"—with one child, preferably a boy—is often employed to achieve this balance.

The purchaser of luxury products is wealthier. As a result, aspirational cues can be more glamorous. Diamond advertising may show a couple summering on the Italian Riviera. The man who drinks cognac can fly first-class on Singapore Air to enjoy the pampering of a pretty stewardess.

Know your market. Have insight into dreams; the glimmer of your campaigns will hypnotize, not blind.

#4: Keep a Low Profile

Now things get a bit tricky. We have established the role of braggadocio in the new middle class, but how can we subtlety fit it into the equation? Chinese are status conscious and, indeed, will go to great lengths to demonstrate clout. But *modest* grand-standing is the best way to make an impression. Let's not forget that Confucianism is two-sided, with opposites in balance. The alter ego of ambition is conformity; the partner of aggression is understatement. Greatness should be *discreetly* on display.

Luxury cars are a case in point. A Mercedes has a practically Pavlovian power to trigger envy, but the price is ostentatiously over the top. True, the "little people" will express admiration, but what they will think is: "He must be corrupt." The Audi A6 is more prudent. Styling products that exist in Western markets because they "let your hair make a statement" must achieve a difficult balance in China. On one hand, they must promise to transform a woman's "look"; on the other hand, application must not result in aggressively nonconformist coif creation. In fact, the largest styling players succeed on a demure "keep your hair in place" platform.

Mont Blanc pens are prestigious because their design is unobtrusive. Consumers applaud an elegant style that doesn't scream for attention. However, the white star that tastefully sticks out from the front pocket is an eye magnet. Even diamonds must tread the tightrope between recognition and ostentation. In a recent DTC spot, a woman stands in front of a reflective glass, sexily admiring her pendant. The heroine doesn't realize that the mirror is two-way; she doesn't know the stone has caught the attention of a couple on the other side, its distaff member piqued with delicious jealousy. The commercial, "Blame it on the Diamond," teasingly asks, "Can I help it if they can't help noticing?"

Chinese consumers often need an excuse to show off. In this context, it's important not to confuse a "reason to believe" with "permission to believe." Ultimately, teenagers want a cool pair of Nikes to make an impression. But, the product's underlying promise of "standing out" must be wrapped in the legitimacy of the sporting world. The dazzle of the latest Gucci handbag should be underpinned with "Italy's finest soft leather."

Finally, for the first time in the modern era, "the masses" are buying private homes. As Chinese grow into their wealth, a fresh interior aesthetic is taking root. "Shanghai Chic" is a far cry from the gaudy neo-rococo (Grecian fountains, gilded bed frames, ornate ceilings) that, until recently, was the stamp of sophistication. This new style boasts streamlined elegance. Chrome is out; glass is in. Overstuffed cushions are déclassé; earth-toned sofas are power seats. (Some have postulated that the "new minimalism" is a reaction to the loud opulence of the initial get-rich-quick characters, many of them princelings' sons or corrupt fathers, all with dubious reputations.)

Yes, get noticed, but standing out isn't the same as sticking out. China cool is "monochromatic with a burst of color" or "a gaze punctuated by a wink." There should be no muscle flexing, no I'm-in-charge-here bravado.

#5: Position the Home as a Fortress

The world of Project and Protect is stressful. A person bent on success must simultaneously project forward while shielding behind. The public stage is never safe from predatory competitors. Project/Protect also obviates a sense of self. Adherence to conventional standards comes naturally. Yet, unlike most Japanese, Chinese ache to be perceived as a cut above. Realization of "what I want, what I like, and who I am" (regardless of an absolutist template imposed by society) is a repressed yet emerging need.

In achieving a sense of safety as well as self-worth, the home plays a critical role. "Burgeoning" doesn't do justice to describing the growth of private residences. Ownership now exceeds 70 percent in major cities, up from practically nothing just a few years ago. Granted, a portion of these transactions is facilitated by government buy-back schemes. However, a stroll around any middle-income neighborhood will quickly highlight the ubiquity of new housing targeted to local Chinese. These estates look good and feel solid. The urban landscape is being transformed for the better. It has been liberated from the homely monotony imposed by central planning.

Owners have the freedom to treat the home as a canvass, and self-expression is blossoming. Nippon paint produces some of the most beloved advertising on the Mainland. Their strategy, "Explosive colors that brighten your world and the world around you," gently hits the bull's eye of domestic dreams.

One of their most memorable commercials, gorgeously shot with saturated hues, captures modest families transforming not only their homes but also the drab horizon with brilliant red, yellow, and purple.

Self-expression is more than doing what you want *with* your home; it's doing what you wish *in* your *own* home. TCL, the Mainland's most innovative television manufacturer, dramatized its plasma display screen with an empowering proposition: "When your set is only seven centimeters wide, no one can tell you where to watch TV." (In one ad, a handsome man places it in the bathroom so, while shaving, he can ogle an attractive woman on the screen.)

The home is also a haven, a bunker, the fortress of a field hand. In the outside world, the winds are bitter, but, in Sanctuary, they caress and soothe. Thinkers Garden, an upscale housing complex, alluded to its apartments being as safe as a mother's womb.

#6: Project, Protect, and the Child

A woman's ultimate responsibility in China, despite fifty years of holding up half the sky, remains having a son or daughter (and a son still is preferable, even in advanced markets). Cultural values are relentlessly pounded into the minds of the next generation. Project *and* Protect instincts are directed to the offspring, little darlings who represent the family's hope for tomorrow. Youngsters must be "optimized." (The single-child law reinforces an already sharp "investment instinct," since all eggs are now in one basket.)

"Protecting" the child assumes two forms: (1) shielding from danger and (2) cultivating talent, real or imagined.

Mothers assume it's never safe for their children to leave the house. Every time he or she ventures out into the world, warning bells ring. So she cocoons the child to shield him from danger. In food advertising, women reject growth-enhancement messages. Milk should not "unnaturally transform"; instead, it should build up resistance to illness. (Bright Dairy, a large state-owned enterprise, produced an award-winning campaign that adopted a Western transformation approach: "Faster, higher, stronger. With just a sip, your kid can perform like superman." But, it bombed in focus groups and never aired.) Even taste-driven categories flirt with protective messages. Lao Cai, a soy sauce purchased by Unilever in the late '90s, *appears to* focus on "bringing out the 'xian' of cooking" (*xian* is "straight from the farm" freshness desired in meats and vegetables). However, on closer inspection, the ad appeals to this protection mentality: (1) great taste leads to the family "wanting more," (2) "wanting more" leads to eating more, (3) eating more leads to ample nutritional intake, (4) ample nutritional intake leads to illness avoidance, and (5) illness avoidance leads to a happy, balanced family. All this from a soy sauce! Germ-killing claims appear in a huge range of product advertising including mini-washing machines, air conditioners, bathroom cleansers, detergents, and, of course, personal grooming. Safeguard soap, a power brand with a 25 percent share, directly links elimination of germs to motherly love. ("How can you love them if they're not protected from bacteria?") (See figure 1.6)

To some extent, all agrarian societies treat offspring as economic entities—Confucian societies to an even stronger degree. (China is only today making the transition from a pre-industrial economy to one with a service sector.) Education, naturally, is a passion for many parents everywhere. In China, however, there isn't a whiff of rebellion against Saturday cram schools, three hours of nightly homework, ballet lessons for the flat-footed, and piano courses for the tone deaf. Children internalize wildly unrealistic expectations because their sense of self is stunted. Modest families will mortgage a home to send a five-year-old to a magnet kindergarten (price tag: $2,000, or half an average family's yearly income). In Beijing, Shanghai, and Guangzhou, personal computer penetration is approaching 50 percent, despite costing two months' wages. Epson color printers are sold as an educational tool; parents' needs barely get a mention.

Even low-involvement products can be pitched as aiding a kid's development. Omo washing powder, in a manner consistent with its global "dirt is good" proposition, encourages mom to allow her kid to "explore his environment" even if it means getting clothes dirty. "With such effective stain removal, there's no need to pay a price for your baby's development." The message, while still not sufficiently simple, has the potential to redefine the category, one largely driven by low-end functional or value benefits.

Once a child is on the right track, parents project his success into the sky like klieg lights. The classroom, violin recital, and science fair are platforms on which a child's gifts can be displayed. Feng Cao, a rural market detergent, dramatizes its whitening power by making a little dancer's tutu look like new. When the child is performing on stage, a neighbor notes that she "is as lovely as a little swan." The mother is then bathed by warm applause, just as her little girl takes a bow.

IN CONCLUSION

The Confucian and dynastic heritage of China has resulted in an insecure middle class pulled in opposite directions—protection of self and projection

Fig. 1.6. P&G Safeguard's "heart hands surrounding the family" is one of the most powerful mnemonic devices in Chinese ad history. It represents the quintessence of maternal protection.

of status. Confronted with polarized drivers, the emerging affluent needs help in managing the conflict of "modest aggression." We have identified six ways marketers can pull off this strategic sleight of hand:

1. Charge more for publicly consumed products;
2. Use status as a tool, an investment that pays dividends, not an end in itself;
3. Ensure that a brand's image is both aspirational and accessible;
4. Keep a low profile even when demonstrating success;
5. Position the home as a fortress of self-expression and escape;
6. Recognize a parent's drive to both protect and project (the achievements of) the next generation.

As suggested earlier, these six imperatives will remain constant over time. Of course, their expression will morph as material and cultural triggers evolve. However, in uncovering the fundamental motivators of China's new middle class, we have also revealed its dominant cultural orientation. Despite the huge impact of international integration, global media, and relentless economic progress, it is impossible to sweep away "identity." If you wade into the world's largest and oldest market, leave assumptions on the shore. Let insight be a weapon on unfamiliar terrain; let profit spring from respect for the Middle Kingdom's unique civilization and magnificent heritage.

CHAPTER 2

DREAMS AND DISASTERS

CHINA'S MASS MARKET MINDSET

The last chapter dealt with the emergence of the PRC's new middle class. It consists of upwardly mobile professionals, numbering around 100 million, clustered in Eastern coastal cities. They are fueling the rise of twenty-first-century China with their slick cars, sparkling diamonds, youth-cool Pepsi, gadget-loaded mobile phones, vertigo-inducing stock investments, and the latest designer garb. Conspicuous consumption is in. Indeed, the rise of an optimistic (though cautious), empowered (though hierarchy-conscious) middle class in China promises to be the story of our lifetime. It is the story of the rise of an alternative mode of consumption that does not threaten the existing Western model. Instead, it is likely to strengthen it by challenging its inherent convictions on everything from commercial savvy to ethical integrity.

Yes, the impact of the Chinese middle class will be colossal. But the *zhong chan* represents just a small fraction of the total opportunity available to companies in today's Middle Kingdom. Of China's population of 1.3 billion, 1.2 billion lead modest lives, spending little compared to their wealthier middle-class cousins. Because of this, they have been ignored by most Western marketers. By focusing exclusively on the "tip of the pyramid," these marketers may, indeed, have gained a first-mover advantage in the "market of the future." However, for the time being, they have also relegated themselves to niche positions, straddling the fringes of mainstream urban existence. Medium-term revenue potential is capped.

The importance of a broad consumer franchise is an increasingly vital element of success on the PRC business battlefield. China is still burdened with a layered distribution system and Byzantine, fickle sales networks. Bigness counts. "Mass" creates the gravitational pull needed to shape order from chaos. "Mass," ultimately, means a "mass market." This chapter outlines the fundamental motivations of the 400 million people who comprise the "urban" mass market—the second wave of Chinese consumers who will benefit from China's continuing economic boom. To fully tap into the awesome opportunities unleashed by China's rise, any manufacturer—foreign or local—must come to grips with their behavioral and attitudinal triggers. Only then can effective marketing strategies emerge.

(Note: A further 700–800 million consumers comprise the third segment of the Chinese population—the rural mass. Despite their large number, they are not likely to contribute significantly to the Chinese consumption landscape because of their extremely limited means. Because of this, they are not the focus of this book.)

TRANSFORMATION VS. PROTECTION

As discussed in the last chapter, during his 1992 Southern Tour, Deng Xiao Ping predicated China's rise on "letting some get rich first." Permitting economic stratification resulted in one of the world's widest chasms between "haves" and "have nots."

As a result, there are two Chinas, one extraordinarily optimistic and the other much less so. The lucky 8 percent whose lives have been transformed by the economic boom of the '90s are progress-driven and aspirational. This Chinese middle class plan their futures meticulously—they are fully cognizant that it's a jungle out there. They seek a competitive advantage in the game of life. Dazed yet titillated, they are driven by conflicting needs to *protect*—through sweat and toil—their achievements, and to *project* new status in an ultra-regimented and badge-conscious society. The middle class is not naïve. However, they believe—they have *faith*—that the future is bright.

The urban mass, on the other hand, has not directly benefited from the economic restructuring of the past two decades. In fact, many of them have borne its brunt. Incomes at the top have skyrocketed. But the rest of the population has moved forward marginally, if at all. Layoffs triggered by the collapse of walking-dead state-owned enterprises are feared by every blue-collar worker. Prices have risen as subsidies on daily essentials evaporate. Things are not (yet) desperate; the masses are not incapacitated by learned helplessness. However, they are much more pessimistic about the future than their wealthier comrades. The middle class strives to transform its circumstances and achieve a brighter, more exciting tomorrow. The less fortunate are busy trying to not fall off a cliff.

A fear-based approach to daily life isn't a recent phenomenon fueled by the jumble of socialism and Chinese characteristics. It has been reinforced over thousands of years of history, an endless struggle between order and chaos, between stability and despair.

MASS MARKET CULTURAL ROOTS

Western Institutions vs. Chinese Mandate

Culturally and socially, China and the West are fundamentally different. Shaped by religious doctrine (Moses' Ten Commandments, Jesus' Sermon on the Mount) and classical philosophical works such as Plato's *The Republic* and Immanuel Kant's *Critique of Pure Reason,* many in the West believe morality is absolute. Chinese, however, reject this. According to Shen Dingli, an expert in international relations at Fudan University in Shanghai, "China's (world)view is not a moral view, but a view based on realism; it's one that hasn't got much to do with human rights." Yes, cultural values are relative. True, they are etched over generations and are fixed neither temporally or geographically, but they are deep-seated and can't be blown away by the first gust of "change."

China, spread across the huge Asian landmass, is polytheistic and collective. Western civilization, born under the Middle East's arid sun, is monotheistic and humanistic. Individuals, created in the image of an omniscient, omnipresent, and omnipotent God, are the building blocks of society. Every person had the ability and right to change the world around him. Dennis Praeger, in his review of Thomas Cahill's book *The Gift of the Jews: How a Tribe of Desert Nomads Changed the Way Everyone Thinks and Feels,* describes the revolution of thought inherent in the movement beyond what Cahill terms the pre-monotheistic "Great Wheel." "If all is a circle, nothing we do matters, none of us matter, life does not matter. It will all happen again. What we do doesn't matter. For our actions to matter, they must be able to influence the future. But the future cannot be influenced if everything happens over and over. If, on the other hand, the Jewish view is adopted, everything matters. Every act I engage in matters, and therefore I matter so much so that each one of us changes history by everything we do."

Many argue it was this recognition of the individual's worth that allowed Western civilization to reach a new height during the Renaissance. Realizing that the individual's ability to generate capital was the key to greater wealth, the

Italian and Dutch city-states of the sixteenth century established a number of institutions to ensure that economic resources were distributed as quickly as possible to those individuals who could make the most of them. These institutions—including the wide extension of credit, impersonal management of businesses, and the pooling of service facilities into banks and similar entities—have become the basis for modern capitalism.

Unlike Europe, China never created civic institutions capable of either protecting individual rights or managing capital flows. An "institution"—from marriage to the International Advertising Association—can be defined as an "impartial" mechanism intended to both regulate and *optimize* the "utility" of human interaction. In dynastic China, from the glorious early Zhou to the dysfunctional late Qing, there were no *economic* institutions. Interaction between clans, while not forbidden, was frowned upon, furtive, and haphazard. Entities such as commercial courts or risk-based lenders never existed. (They still don't today.)

There was no way for "commoners" to productively pool resources across families or provinces. Money was regarded as something unclean. Taxes were collected by the long arms of central government. Peasants could only hope that one day, they might benefit from imperial largesse. Capital flowed up and back down again. There were no bodies established to smooth "lateral transfers," sparks that ignite a dynamic private sector. The Mandate of Heaven encompassed fiscal administration.

The Mandate of Heaven was withdrawn when dynasties could not control the hinterland. More specifically, every dynasty—from the Qin to the Qing—fell due to inefficient resource allocation. Collapse was caused by powerless emperors with no control over the nation's purse strings. Peasant rebellions boiled. Palace intrigue brewed. Demands for "stability" challenged the throne's authority. Ineffective fiscal management—corruption, unproductive investment, and a lopsided balance between urban and rural growth—remains a principal threat to the CCP's reign. Imperial incompetence shatters "natural order."

Chaos was, and continues to be, the only absolute evil under Heaven.

The Chinese State: Survival Is Job One

The Middle Kingdom's symbol is a dragon that projects the essence of manly, powerful *yang* (see figure 2.1). It's not friendly looking, but certainly not fierce in an Arthurian sense. Long and spindly, it breathes fire in an oddly static way. And, unlike the female Phoenix, a representation of *yin,* the creature can leap

Fig. 2.1. With the teeth of a horse, claws of a chicken, skin of a snake, and antlers of a deer, China's unofficial "logo" is the hardy, powerful dragon. The symbol is all about survival.

but can't fly. The Chinese dragon is not transcendent. It doesn't inspire. It's an utterly earth-bound creature and, not coincidentally, encapsulates the crux of Chinese culture, the root of national purpose. Actually, the dragon isn't really a dragon at all but more a concoction of different animal parts. It's Franken-stein-like, somehow more than the sum of its parts, with the teeth of a horse, antlers of a deer, claws of a chicken, and body of a snake. True, the thing is ugly, but it's *ALIVE*. The China dragon is a life force, symbols of which exist in practically all animistic, nonmonotheistic religious (and perhaps in the roots of some monotheistic ones as well, as fans of *The Da Vinci Code* might argue). But the China dragon has more on its mind than reproduction. A sturdy beast, living in a brutal environment, it regenerates and *survives*. Resourcefully eternal, it makes it through another year, by hook or by crook. As Deng might say, it "crosses the river by feeling the stones." Eventually, the Chinese dragon makes it to the other side.

Order: China's Imperative

And what does survival, China's raison d'etre, hinge upon? To Chinese, the answer is instinctive: stability and order. Order is, and continues to be, the only absolute *good* under Heaven. The emperor was responsible for maintaining order. His ultimate duty was to ensure nothing less and nothing more than survival. Why? Because the external world was both naturally and militarily dangerous.

When explaining Chinese culture, agrarian roots are a red herring. All preindustrial cultures were agrarian. Topography and geography, however, are extremely important. Stretching from Mongolia to Vietnam and from Shanghai to Chongqing, China was vulnerable to myriad forms of disaster and death. The loess carpeting the bulk of its land is shallow and sparsely vegetated, a perfect recipe for crop instability and famine. The Yellow and Yangtze rivers, overflowing with silt, have burst their banks like clockwork for thousands of years. As recently as 1976, an earthquake decimated a small city in Northeast China. Due to high population density and low construction standards, a few strong jolts wiped out hundreds of thousands of people.

Mother Nature has not been the only enemy. The invaders from the north were even fiercer. The nomadic *Xiong Nu* (and other Altaic-speaking) tribes were a constant menace along thousands of miles of unshielded, naturally exposed territory. In an eternal battle against cruel weather and warriors, China has always, bravely and nervously, protected life. The masses didn't look up or out; instead, they glanced over their shoulders for the next danger.

Mobilize! When survival is at stake, people are called to arms. The concept of "me" is dangerous, a threat to collective survival, so China has always denied the self. Human beings have been "commoditized" to serve the greater good.

The entire population has rallied time and again to defend the motherland. In the fifteenth century, immediately after emperor Zhu Di suspended his ambitious maritime expeditions, 250,000 soldiers from all corners of the country were plucked from villages to cross the Kerulen River and defeat the Mongols. The fourteen-year construction of Beijing engaged 100,000 artisans and a million workers. The city wall, forty feet high, had a circumference of fourteen miles. Five million people were harnessed to construct one of the greatest engineering feats of the pre-industrial age, the 1,500 kilometer Grand Canal. More than three million were dispatched to (re)build the Great Wall during the fifteenth and sixteenth centuries. More recently, thirty million were sacrificed during history's most destructive utopian experiment, the Great Leap Forward, Mao's misguided attempt to industrialize the countryside. During the Cultural Revolution, sixteen million youth and intellectuals were "sent down" to the countryside to "learn from the peasants." In 2003, a million "volunteers" scoured the inner provinces to "educate" people about AIDS.

Culture: China's Adhesive

Again, there were no institutions or mechanisms expressly designed to manage human interaction. So how was mobilization possible? It was Chinese culture—its artistic, spiritual, and behavioral code of conduct—that glued the nobility, civil service, and peasantry together. Culture was the gravitational pull from which nothing in China's orbit could escape. Every law, every prayer, every bedroom, textbook, and pagoda, every morsel of food, grammatical structure, and porcelain cup, *everything* was consistent with cultural imperatives. Every dimension of China's world view—legal, societal, or spiritual—demanded and reinforced the belief in order as the key to survival. (Chinese believe they and Jews are kindred spirits. Both share a passion for education, family, and wealth. More fundamentally, both regard cultural cohesion as a bulwark against uncertainty. The Jews are deeply admired for a culture that has endured—indeed, thrived—despite endless oppression and struggle. The politically correct slogan *tuan jie jiu shi li liang* says it all: From unity comes strength.)

Legalism: Presumed Guilty. Zhang Yimou's hugely popular 2002 movie *Hero* depicts the story of a highly skilled assassin (played by Jet Li) who has trained for years with the single goal of killing Emperor Shi Huang Di, one of the most ruthless, inhuman dictators mankind has ever known. From 213 to 191 BC, he and his followers burned books, executed millions, buried scholars alive, and adopted black as the imperial color. Jet Li's character initially hopes to end this cruel reign. However, just when the assassin's plans have come to fruition and his opportunity to kill the emperor is there, he chooses to forego it. The assassin comes to realize that despite the emperor's cruelty, he is the one great hope for a glorious China. In the end, he trades his life for the emperor's, and by extension, China, as should all "heroic" Chinese. China's first emperor is still considered a great man because he unified the country. He forged order after the chaos of the Warring States period. He standardized weights, measures, currency, and characters. He abolished hereditary nobility and implemented "rational," merit-based selection for the civil service. Through sheer force of will, he built an infrastructure far more expansive than its equivalent in the Roman Empire.

Like Mao 2,000 years later, he brutally imposed a new order. He justified his barbarous tactics with a new moral code, legalism. Its core tenets are still felt today. Legalism essentially holds that: (1) man's nature is evil, (2) a strong state is required to squeeze good out of him, and (3) to maintain order, laws should punish offenders rather than safeguard rights. The Chinese state propagates a belief in its own infallibility. Courts serve the interest of the state, which serves the interest of the masses by, again, preserving unity. Amnesty International estimates that China executes at least 5,000 people every year, none of whom have been tried by a jury of peers. The vast majority of Chinese accept indiscriminate application of the death penalty since "China has too many people." Still today, chaos is evil, so most people will submit to a state with absolute power, so long as it maintains order while elevating the living standards of the country. Clamor for political—i.e., democratic—reform must be suppressed, lest China descend into Russian-style dissolution.

Confucianism: Hierarchical Regimentation. As discussed in the previous chapter, to preserve *societal* order, Confucius articulated a model of social structure based on "conformist reward." The hierarchical nature of Confucian society is obvious. Yet, again, dynastic China was not completely rigid; indeed, it was the world's first socially mobile culture. Emperors feared "institutionalized" local special interests (i.e., nobility based on birth) so, during the Qin era, the aristocracy was purged. From the rise of the Han to the fall of the Qing, advancement was tied to the meritocratic civil service examination system. Mastery of Confucian canon, a fixed code of conduct articulated in the distant past, was the passport to glory. Progress hinged on conformity. Conventional wisdom was absolute. Challenge to the order was social and professional suicide. The marriage of acceptance and advancement created a national character at once restrictive and ambitious. From the sovereign's perspective, the yin and yang of restraint and aspiration created a virtuous cycle of incentive and acceptance of imperial order.

Most young Chinese can more easily discuss Arnold Schwarzenegger's legislative battles in California than Confucian thought in contemporary China. Nevertheless, Confucianism remains China's cultural blueprint and dominant moral force. Felt everywhere, it explains why thirty-year-old unmarried children live with their parents. It explains why material security, not romance, remains the basis of marital endurance. It explains refusal to contradict anyone up the chain of command, even within Western companies where challenging conventional wisdom is often rewarded, not punished.

It also explains the obsession with titles and business cards, the steep sales curves of diamond rings and automobiles, the Little Emperor Syndrome, and a rural male-to-female birth ratio of 100:118. The fabric of China's cultural tapestry, from acceptance of totalitarianism to rejection of American hegemony, reflects a Confucian worldview.

Daoism: Balancing Heaven and Earth. Regardless of whether you consider Daoism a philosophy or a religion, it is also about order. The *ba gua,* the centerpiece of the Zhou dynasty's seminal *Book of Changes,* reduces the universe to an immutable sequence of eight elements. To ensure harmony, the *yin* and *yang,* or female and male "energy," must be "balanced" in everything from food (*qi bu*) and office space (*feng shui*) to exercise (*qi gong*). Balance restores natural order. And natural order is good. The Zhou era *Book of Changes* (I Ching), a "how-to manual" on achieving harmony with the universe, rejects a pioneering spirit and stresses the mathematical impossibility of changing nature. Daoism reinforces a cosmological view that humans are insignificant; forward momentum is contingent on "going with the flow." Like water, we advance only when we achieve and accept harmony with our environment. Daoism is a paradoxical fusion of progress and passivity.

Legalism, Daoism, and Confucianism: all three militate against freedom of thought. All three propagate anti-individualism. Compliance is tantamount to survival.

Culture's Manifestation: Walls Everywhere. Order was (and still is) required to harness resources, both natural and monetary, to protect the nation's very existence. Defense was (and still is) a primal urge. Discipline was required for the state to shield itself from attack. *People Daily's* propaganda is true; the PRC has never been an aggressive power. The Yuan and Qing were the only eras during which China vigorously expanded its borders; both dynasties were ruled by foreign powers—i.e., the Mongols and Manchus, respectively. Gavin Menses' recent tome, *1421: The Year China Discovered the World,* describes the Ming dynasty's uncharacteristic flirtation with colonial exploitation. Despite the promise of territorial and financial gain, massive investment in ships, a navy, and technology, was abruptly cut off. Funds were redirected to ward off Mongol attack. (The Chinese obsession with face is also defensive. In a country where hierarchy regulates human interaction, loss of the precious commodity occurs when the safety of "social structure" has been compromised.)

The PRC, led by a technocratic legion of engineers, loves mammoth projects (e.g., the Three Gorges Dam, "Special Economic Zones"). But they are defensive, not offensive. The government only recently began modernizing its decrepit military. The People's Liberation Army's mission is to safeguard territorial integrity. (The vast majority of Chinese believe reclaiming Taiwan—i.e., "reunifying" China—is not offensive.) China's most famous landmarks are also protective. As mentioned in the previous chapter, the first emperor Qin Shi Huangdi, not the most loved dictator, was buried with an army of terra cotta warriors. The Forbidden City, constructed during the early Ming dynasty as a bulwark against the Mongols, is a fortress, replete with moats, turrets, and a labyrinthine inner structure. Cities had walls. Residential areas did, too. In Guangdong province, Hakka clans lived in *wei wu,* massive citadel-like circular structures with tiny windows at the top (see figure 2.2). They were large enough to accommodate an entire village, making it easy to know who was where and doing what to whom.

The Peasant: To Be Seen and Not Heard

China was, and still is, an agrarian culture. Society was crudely stratified into two levels, an ultra-elite bureaucracy and farmers. Under Confucianism, the former had an obligation to keep the latter from starving to death. The latter had an obligation to obey and pay taxes to the former.

Resignation. The "little people" accept their lot. Chinese not only bow to but also believe in fate. Western culture for the most part does not. Sure, there are exceptions—Calvinist predestination and the like—but it is rare to find people in the West who own up to believing that their lives are controlled by the stars. And those who do are often ridiculed. (Remember the furor in the 1980s when it was revealed that Nancy Reagan consulted an astrologer regularly? That is not a reaction that would be understood in China.) Encouraged by a monotheistic faith that provides a personal relationship between the individual and an all-powerful deity (although in some cases this relationship is mediated by clergy, like in Roman Catholicism), Westerners are much more open to the idea that each individual can change the world. They believe that history is shaped not by "us," but by "me." The future is a steady but bumpy progression to a Promised Land. Individuals are the pistons of progress. In stark contrast to this, the Middle Kingdom's worldview is cyclical, not linear, so independent thought serves no adaptive role. The tide comes in and recedes, lapping the same shore again and again. The elements of the world—the *ba gua*—are cyclical. The pas-

Fig. 2.2. Wei Wus such as this one were found in Southern China. They are round fortresses that could accommodate everyone from the same village. They are also a perfect manifestation of China's historical obsession with "protection ensuring survival." Photoccme picture.

sage of time—i.e., the ten heavenly branches and twelve earthly stems—is cyclical. The movement of sun, stars, and moons is cyclical. Humankind, an insignificant speck in Heaven's rotation, must bear the hand dealt to it. Fate is ineluctable; fortune is preprogrammed.

Chinese society is and remains fatalistic, obedient to the whims of Lady Luck. The inhospitable landscape was an inescapable reality. Collective submission, an adaptive trait, was manipulated by the ruling class to keep the masses in their place. An authoritarian culture rewarded subservience. Despite crushing poverty and no civil or economic rights, rebellion has broken out only intermittently. True, peasant resistance was, with few exceptions, the catalyst for imperial change, but dynasties lasted hundreds and hundreds of years, and challenge to the power structure was only intermittent. Mass passivity sustained corrupt or inept dictators for extended stretches of time and preempted agricultural productivity gains. The Chinese countryside stagnated.

In *The Search for Modern China*, historian Jonathan Spence, one of the foremost experts on dynastic peasant life, limns daily Han existence: "The common people wore pajama-like garments while working. . . . Millet, wheat and rice were the major food crops. Women attending to silkworms were almost universal. . . . We know that conditions of poverty were commonplace. Han emperors frequently issued edicts mentioning natural disasters and crop failure. Some of the destitute eventually ended up as slaves, as cases of selling wives and children are mentioned often in the sources. Most of the slaves became household servants, and thus did not contribute significantly to the national economy. . . ." Conditions did not really improve through the Tang, Song, Yuan, Ming, and Qing dynasties. For two thousand years, days were long and brutal. Tedium was interrupted by calamity. Monotony was punctuated by catastrophe. It was not a bright and happy reality. And nothing could be done to alter that reality.

Interlude: Order and the Chinese Language

Pardon the digression, but "culture" is not the only factor that hammers home the importance of stability and discipline. The Chinese language, itself a window to the Red Heart, does too. The Chinese tongue is a lot like an algebra equation. Elegantly complex, it's ultimately structured and quantifiable. To foreign speakers, Chinese has five "traps"—characteristics that, in effect, limit access to full understanding of the written language: (1) the use of characters, (2) the gray area between characters and "words," (3) the prevalence of "condensed meaning" phrases, (4) extremely rigid sentence structure, and (5) the ubiquity of "measure words." (The more you study, the more ignorant you feel.) Together, they not only keep foreigners at a distance but also buttress the importance of conformity. The inflexibility of Chinese also militates against linguistic dynamism and semantic evolution. Even considering the early-twentieth-century death of classical Chinese, contemporary Mandarin is beautiful but a bit ossified, surprisingly similar to what was written 2,000 years ago.

First, Chinese characters are very complex. (The number of characters is a matter of some debate. The *Kangxi Dictionary* lists about 40,000 characters, while the modern *Zhonghua Zihai* lists in excess of 80,000. To be considered literate, one must know at least 2,000. Educated people know between 6,000 and 10,000. Good nonnative speakers recognize more than 3,000.) Without willful memorization, there is no way to master them and no two are contextually identical. Every character contains a "radical" or *bu shou,* one of over 200 meaning "hints" that categorizes—and fixes—a word's essence. All characters, therefore, are "slotted" into one of 200 conceptual straight jackets. There's no way to look up a word in the dictionary without knowing its classifier(s). For hundreds and hundreds of years, no *bu shou* has been invented. The stroke sequence of each written character is also nonnegotiable. (School children get their knuckles rapped for incorrect order.) To communicate, conformity is mandatory.

Second, individual characters are not "words." They are concepts, more than a morpheme but less than a dictionary entry. (Single-character words are, yes, unbalanced.) "Real" words are character combinations, usually two together so the meaning, context, and flavor of each and every word are more or less fixed. "Manifestation" will always have a "material" or "physical" and "shining" feel. "Rape" cannot be associated with men, only women. "Heaven," vivid and concrete, is a glorious palace on clouds, not Western religion's utopian abstraction. In stark contrast to English's dynamism, every Chinese word has a concrete "core," a nondebatable, inflexible, immutable, static constant.

Third, abstruse *cheng yu*—i.e., ancient four-character maxims that are used in modern Chinese—show up everywhere. So do four- and eight-character political slogans (and other sayings). *Yi ju liang de* more or less means "killing two birds with one stone." *Lai re fang chang* fuses "Rome wasn't built in a day," "All roads lead to Rome," and "Good things come to those who wait" into a demand for patience and perseverance. But wait. Let's not forget endless two-character "abbreviations." The Tiananmen Square "incident" is referred to simply as *liu si,* or "six four" (which itself is short for the date on which the tragedy occurred). Beijing University (*Bei jing da xue*) is always shortened to *"Bei Da."* Newspaper headlines are loaded with these two-character traps. In order to be truly well-versed in pithy proverbs, condensations, and abbreviations, a foreigner must spend years on Chinese soil buried in books. Chinese vocabulary is inaccessible to all but the faithful and true. Only one who has been educated in politically and culturally correct boot camps, can speak with true grace.

Fourth, sentence structure is etched in stone. Grammatical simplicity—i.e., lack of conjugations, tenses, inflections, and articles—renders strict word order the only way to avoid ambiguity. In English, we can say, "I'm taking my pretty girlfriend to the airport at seven o'clock" *or* "My pretty girlfriend is being taken by me at seven o'clock to the airport" *or* "At seven o'clock, I *will* take my pretty girlfriend to the airport." Mandarin leaves no choice; one *must* say "seven-hour-I-take-my-pretty-girlfriend-arrive-airport." The concrete—in this case, time—always precedes the abstract. The "solid" always takes precedence over the ambiguous. In addition, sentences should be "balanced" and symmetrical. Our metronomic, restrained "not only . . . but also" construction has at least twenty Chinese equivalents. Speech, therefore, is "harmonious" (not lopsided) and obeys the rules.

Finally, "measure" or "counting" words ensure that nouns—each and every one of them—are clumped into no more than forty or so concrete categories. In English, we can say, "a chicken, two chickens." In Chinese, the chicken must be "classified" as a *zhi;* it is slotted into the same category as other small mammals and birds (dogs, cats, pigeons). A table is a *zhang,* as are other flat, thin, slab-like objects (tickets, slabs, dominoes). An ordinary person is a *ge.* A high-status individual, on the other hand, is a *wei.* In order to count with dignity, respect for preordained labeling is strongly advised.

What's the point? Well, there are two. First, adherence to convention occurs with every utterance. In the PRC, you can't open your mouth without signaling embrace of the Chinese worldview. Such an air doesn't exactly fuel challenge to conventional wisdom. Once again, the supremacy of order manifests itself in the crannies of social consciousness. More practically, Chinese copywriting is both an art and a science. Mastery of style requires years and years of formal training. "Back translation" is suicidal. Taglines must dance. Copy must sing. But singing and dancing requires rhythm and a Chinese beat is difficult to acquire. Hire a good advertising agency, lest your first utterance shatter eardrums.

MASS MARKET BEHAVIORAL CHARACTERISTICS

Contemporary Urban Acquiescence

The masses' mindset has not changed, even in cities. The masses are conditioned to accept "abuse of power by the powerful," hence, the prevalence of their striking passivity in the face of corruption and yawning income disparities. There is no sign of public dissatisfaction coalescing into the kind of nationwide movement inspired by the Tiananmen Square demonstrations. When confronted with a hopeless situation, urbanites instinctively lapse into passivity. *Mei you ban fa* (literally, "no way to handle") is one of the first phrases any foreigner learns, usually from disgruntled taxi drivers complaining about wages or from sales clerks explaining stock shortages. Despite the widespread awareness of the party's iron-fisted control of media, the masses don't bother to challenge blatant propaganda. It is white noise, instantly tuned out. Demonstrations against the arbitrary and illegal "fees" imposed by crooked local leaders are only sporadic (but spreading). Tormented passengers on China's delay-ravaged, non-communicative, cancellation-prone, noncompetitive airlines are docile lambs led to slaughter. Corruption is as inevitable as sunset. While often grumbled about (and occasionally rebelled against), its pervasiveness is largely met with a collective and resigned shrug.

Chinese admire the efficiency of our *system* of checks and balances but not necessarily our values. Many local governmental organs *are* detested due to inefficiency and corruption. However, the central government is admired for its intelligence, far-sightedness, and "management" skills, even more so since "fourth-generation" President Hu Jintao and Prime Minister Wen Jiabao rose to power. Political reform is broached (anonymously) only by defanged party elders who are more interested in the relationship between bureaucratic structure and economic efficiency than civil rights. The people are blasé about the central government's refusal to apologize for, or even reconsider the wisdom of, the 1989 Tiananmen crackdown. Many Chinese believe the government "did the right thing" in 1989 because, "order must be preserved at all cost." On the economic front, layoffs, an inevitable side effect of state enterprise restructuring, are accepted as a fact of life, despite the absence of a dependable safety net. Wildcat protests, some violent, are increasingly common in impoverished towns but they are instigated by the coexistence of fat-cat gluttony and unpaid back wages rather than a thirst for representative government. To make way for shiny skyscrapers and trendy boutiques, millions of citizens have been relocated from the city center to far-off, sterile suburbs. Barely a peep of protest has been heard. For the masses, genuine property rights are still a fantasy despite their recent incorporation into the Chinese constitution. There are no functioning institutions to protect the little guy.

Disasters and Coping

Due to the reality of both history and contemporary life, today's urban masses are driven by two polarized instincts. The first, risk avoidance, is much more pessimistic than the anxiety of disorientation that characterizes the middle class. It is based in fear. The masses still do not take "survival" for granted.

Here's an example. Even though China has fewer than 8 vehicles per 1,000 citizens—compared with 940 vehicles per 1,000 Americans—the country ranks #1 in the world in auto fatalities with 104,000 traffic accident deaths in 2003. Craig Simmons, in a *Newsweek* "Letter from China" column, highlights that "Chinese explain the carnage in several ways; there are too many inexperienced drivers; the police don't enforce traffic laws; nobody wears seat belts. But there is a more important reason: Chinese are bad drivers because everyone wants to be first. China was held back for so long that its people are now rushing forward en masse, like water from a broken pipe. This is the national psychology." Off the highway and in the city, taxi drivers weave, honk, dodge, and push through traffic. There is no pedestrian right of way. Hailing a taxi during rush hour is a blood sport. Crossing the street, even at a crosswalk, is death-defying.

Social Darwinism—"survival of the fittest" in a societal rather than evolutionary or biological context—had its genesis during America's Industrial Revolution, when talk of mechanical dehumanization was all the rage. Now it fits twenty-first-century China like a glove. From subtropical Guangzhou to subarctic Harbin, it is a jungle out there. Queues don't exist. Elevator etiquette is an oxymoron. Space-age skyscrapers tower over slums. Families (including grandparents) are crammed into tiny, forty-eight-square meter flats, many of which have no bathroom. The factory worker isn't "fired"; he euphemistically "retires," leaving a son or daughter to support the entire family. The average monthly wage for high school graduates is $25 per week; spending on food eats up more than $12. The quest for competitive advantage is ruthless. Four-year-olds attend cram school. Every day, students go through school evading humiliation by both teachers and peers. The college entrance exam is an edge-of-the-seat cliffhanger for parents who pace outside schools on the day of the test.

Every day, the Mainland consumer takes precautions against ruin. Disaster avoidance, therefore, figures prominently in Chinese advertising. John Hancock, for example, suggests that, without insurance, life would be a series of illnesses (cut to snapping alligators), accidents (fade to fiery meteorites), and financial calamity. Inspired by the film *The Perfect Storm*, China Mobile positions GPRS internet connectivity as the difference between death and rescue. The commercial ends with a warning: "At critical moments, don't be caught without China Mobile."

Dreams and Escaping

This is not to say that the average person in China is on the verge of a nervous breakdown. It's not all doom and gloom.

If the first instinct of the Chinese masses is constantly worrying about and thinking of ways to avoid disaster, the second is a defense mechanism against this by concentrating on escape, albeit via dreams and fantasies. It's a world of vivid imagination, freedom from all trouble, and spiritual transcendence.

This escapist instinct has its roots in two important aspects of China's history and culture: the Buddhist notion of Nirvana and the secular tradition of the civil service examination system.

Before the arrival of Buddhism in China in the first century AD, the Chinese never had a well-defined idea of "freedom from suffering." While they yearned for it, like they do today, none of their philosophies and beliefs gave this state of being a name or form. In Buddhism, they not only found their most heart-felt aspiration named and promised, they also found a clearly defined route to achieving it.

If Buddhism gave the Chinese something to aspire for in the afterlife, the civil service examination system gave them something more immediate and concrete to dream about in this life. Established to make China's bureaucracy a meritocratic, rather than aristocratic, institution, the exams theoretically gave every Chinese man an equal chance to enter the privileged ranks of the country's bureaucracy. Within these ranks, reward generated further reward, and power, wealth, and influence were guaranteed. Never mind that just being able to sit for the exams took an investment of time and money that was beyond the reach of the vast majority of the population. The dream of what was on the other side of a successful exam (actually, a series of exams) was a potent one— a dream of social mobility that has survived to this day.

This faraway promise inspires the Chinese to transcend their lot by finding joy in the most modest corners. The urban landscape is blessed with scattered flowers on a concrete field. Massage parlors, offering comfort for the head, foot, and anything in between, are found on every block. At sunset, unassuming neighborhood parks become ballrooms. Luxurious bathhouses, ubiquitous and cheap, boast rococo ceilings and herbal ponds. A haircut isn't complete without a shoulder rub down (and in some places a wink, a nudge, and a trip up a flight of stairs will buy "special service").

Pastimes and entertainment are not anchored in reality; instead, they liberate the spirit from the mundane. Film and TV dramas are escapist. Popular music is cotton-candy pap. Li Ning, the local athletic gear company, positions sports as release, not a platform for showing off. In their advertising, text floats across the screen: "Goodbye fatigue; goodbye toil, fear and fat. . . . Yesterday's worries are over." Lenovo computers' branding campaign revolves around dreams, not bits and bytes. A child throws a paper airplane that turns into a rocket. The copy doesn't mention productivity enhancement. It's all about "hope," "fantasy," "glory," and "a future beyond imagination."

Karaoke halls are palaces in which every room is fit for a star. The most popular video games (e.g., Charming Baby, Legend) involve role-play. Carrefour, Wal-Mart, and Ikea are worlds of choice, amusement parks where shoppers often gawk but don't buy. Nostalgia for the sepia-toned 1930s and the primary-colored Revolutionary era is in. The lottery is a passion. Spiritualism—*tai qi*, Buddhism, Catholicism, and *falun gong*—soothes the soul.

INSIGHT APPLICATION

Survival and transcendence are basic instincts. The former is about fighting despair, while the latter is about escaping it. Survival is firmly grounded in ugly reality; transcendence has very little to do with reality. Survival and transcendence: two instincts that are worlds apart and manifested in very different ways. When targeting the Chinese masses, marketers should address one or the other.

Sometimes, but not always, it's even possible to unify these divergent worlds of need, transforming a sow's ear into a silk purse. The following are five ways of capturing the urban mainstream's heart.

I. Position Brands as Safety

In an environment perceived as dangerous, the promise of protection is a powerful motivator. Under Chinese custom, people born under the sign of the current "animal year" wear red underwear to keep themselves extra safe. At the gates of small cities, an elderly man, bell in hand, greets sunset with a warning to "lock your doors and watch your belongings." The immense success of Haier, the local appliance behemoth, is founded on its reputation for after-sales service, rather than product quality.

Due to the protection imperative, products are popular in China and the West for different reasons. In the West, nutrition benefits are "transformative," the key to a taller, smarter, and more handsome kid. In the PRC, immunity is king, especially in infant food. In the West, the leading paint is advertised as an "explosion of color." In China, a toxin-free seal of assurance commands a price premium. In the West, soap should soften skin with "1/4 moisturizing cream." As mentioned earlier, P&G's Safeguard commands a 25 percent share in China because of its germ-killing claims. Invasion is a threat even in the shower!

Societal Endorsement is another form of safety. "The individual" has never been relevant in China. His or her needs, hopes, and rights have always been sublimated to those of the clan, work unit, or society. While Confucian culture is not "collective" in the Japanese sense—i.e., taking genuine comfort from "fitting in"—individualism has always been dangerous. Chinese culture was born not of a *desire* but rather a *need* for security. Physical survival could never be taken for granted, so "teamwork of the masses" was crucial. The individual existed, first and foremost, as part of society. Public approval, therefore, is still a cherished guarantee against isolation and rejection. China's new middle class, motivated and rewarded by entrepreneurialism, at least *aspires* to a self-definition independent of the group. The masses do not. The "model residential unit" remains a stirring bureaucratic designation. Groupthink is pervasive within even the most Westernized companies. Only the bold dare to express a point of view not predigested by conventional wisdom.

Products will be warmly embraced if they deliver third-party approval. Unilever's Fang Cao, a market detergent targeted to lower-income consumers, leverages the public domain as a torture test for cleansing efficacy. Its tagline, "New clothes? No, Fang Cao!" is a hit because it turns mother into a Supermom capable of making old clothes new. By demonstrating her skills as a home-maker, she moves up in the eyes of her peers. Hazeline shampoo's recent TV commercial depicts a beautiful girl whose dry, tangled hair is accidentally projected onto a screen in a crowded lecture hall. "Boos" turn into "oohs" when, days later, she appears with a soft and flowing mane, armed with enough confidence to sit in the front row.

Famous Brand, Big Relief. At their most basic level, brands are indicators of reliability. In the past, Chinese companies were notoriously undependable and, in many ways, some companies are still burdened by state ownership and "bean-curd manufacturing." Put bluntly, many local corporations are not yet trusted to deliver basic quality standards. On the other hand, if a product is from a big multinational corporation, it's probably okay.

The embrace of JV brands debunks the claim that rising Chinese national-ism leads to preference for local brands. For Mainland consumers, joint ven-ture or wholly owned foreign status is a signal of quality. Even in categories where "local flavor" is paramount (e.g., food), the appeal of indigenous brands is an open question. In the absence of standards authorities such as the Food and Drug Administration, JV pedigree means clout. When Unilever launched soy sauce, a quintessentially Chinese product, its research found "culinary ex-pertise" outweighed by "multinational resources" in determining brand appeal. Foreign preference in high-involvement categories such as cars, computers, and telecommunications is even more notable. Therefore, anything a manu-facturer can do to highlight "international heritage" will be a plus.

"Stretchability" is also a distinct feature on China's marketing landscape because a *big* brand comforts. In developed countries, basic product quality is more or less assumed. On the Mainland, an environment of fake goods and no con-sumer protection, new brands are eyed suspiciously; furthermore, establishing their credibility is an expensive proposition. (Media rates in Beijing and Shang-hai and Guangzhou are no less expensive than in Chicago or Sydney.) Brands, therefore, tend to extend across relatively unrelated categories. P&G's Olay, for example, covers everything from its premium "anti-aging system" to mass-mar-ket shower gel. Unilever's Hazeline is a soap, shampoo, conditioner, and skin cream. Haier, the local white goods giant, produces mobile phones, refrigera-tors, dishwashers, and televisions. Chunlan churns out everything from air con-ditioners to motorcycles and consumers don't bat an eyelash. Size counts. Swagger impresses—hence, the portentous *basso profundo* voiceover found in third-rate, cut-and-paste advertising ("China's largest, most prestigious bath-room tile maker . . .").

Third party endorsements are another useful sign of trustworthiness. In advertising, public relations, and on packaging, Crest toothpaste highlights its standing with the China Research Institute. For fifteen years, Safeguard has successfully built its credibility on the back of microscope-wielding "lab coats" from the China Medical Association. Seals of approval are effective for health and nutrition products. They are practically mandatory for anything consumed by a child.

II. Reinforce the Family Rampart

Anti-individualism, an authoritarian government, and a physically inhospitable external world mean each day is precarious.

The sanctity of family—and the inviolability of familial obligation—can be felt everywhere in contemporary China. Adult children automatically give a portion of income to elders as a gesture of respect, no matter how much money mom and dad make. Failure to return home for Chinese New Year, irrespective of the number of planes and trains required to get there, is a cardinal sin. Intergenerational relationships are formal and noncommunicative. Problems of the heart are rarely discussed and, until marriage, sons and daughters live at home, obeying the wisdom of their father. If a financially independent couple wishes to move out into their own apartment, they must negotiate terms with the mother-in-law, for it is she who micromanages the rearing of the grandchild.

Keeping Safe. There are several ways in which marketers have tapped into the importance of family. The most basic, of course, is to highlight a brand's role in keeping family members safe from physical harm. Safeguard, the champion in capitalizing on "protection as a demonstration of love," portrays germs as enemies; mom's hands are joined in a powerful visual icon, a heart-shaped shield. Many financial services (e.g., *Ping An,* or "peaceful safety," insurance) link investment products with a *xing fu* ("fortunate and secure") family enjoying a *ta shi* ("solid and stable") future. ICI was the first multinational company to launch paint targeted at the mass market. Its brand, Guardian, emphasizes "low toxicity," far and away the category's most persuasive benefit. Aesthetic appeal is not relevant for many new homebuyers, ones still unable to take health and safety for granted.

Ties that Bind. Beyond safety, marketers have tapped into the resonance of preserving family cohesion. A close-knit family unit, unified by ritual, responsibility, and reliance, is a bulwark against destruction. A Chinese maxim asserts, "Brothers may fight within the house but will join hands to battle the insults from outside." (Family unity is also required to assuage spirits hovering around the ancestral village. An angry ghost is even more formidable than flesh and blood enemies.) *Gui Bie Wan,* a health supplement, latches on to Confucian values and, specifically, a son's obligation to his father. The brand has been positioned as a gift for elderly parents during traditional Chinese festivals. The copy in one of its heart-warming commercials: "When I was a child, it seemed like every day was my special day. All dads remember their son's birthday. Now that we've grown up, how many sons remember their father's birthday? Express your respect with *Gui Bie Wan.*"

As mentioned earlier, even Lao Cai, a basic soy sauce, deftly links a taste benefit (*xian* or, crudely translated, "just-slaughtered freshness") with family health and harmony. The closing shot of the commercial shows a mom beaming as her husband and son, clean plates in hand, ask for a second serving. In China, (a) eating more means more nutrition, (b) more nutrition means a healthy family, and (c) a healthy family means a "durably balanced" family. In a country adept in logical analysis, if A = B and B = C, then A = C. In a country where students possess an uncommon ability to ace the GMAT, taste satisfaction miraculously yields harmony. In China, "enjoyment" or "delight" is beside the point.

A Beautiful Backdrop. Even if domestic unity is not explicitly part of a product's benefit structure, the family can be leveraged as a milieu to dramatize brand performance. The clan, not the individual, sits at the universe's center; therefore, intrafamily dynamics are often used as an attention-grabbing "executional context." Rejoice shampoo, for example, recently launched an "affordable" variant targeted to the mass market. While the main brand's equity focuses on "confidence from soft and shiny hair," this variant's anti-oil benefit is demonstrated by a little girl, delighted as she touches her mother's clean hair. *Diao Pai,* the leading laundry detergent, tugs at heartstrings. It communicates value by elegantly weaving more-washes-for-less-money into a melodramatic story about a laid-off factory worker. Family bonds aren't strengthened per se. However, they have been used to breathe emotionality into a fundamentally functional message. *Diao Pai,* not surprisingly, dominates the category despite a price point slightly higher than market average.

III. Turn Bargain Hunting into Smart Shopping

Before exploring the nuances of this theme, let us proclaim the first commandment of marketing in China: Thou Shall Not Overcharge. You won't get away with it.

Although savvier than in the late 90s, MNCs still make lots of mistakes: (1) ignoring cultural imperatives, (2) overestimating the reliability of local joint venture partners, (3) underestimating media investment costs, (4) failing to localize products, and (5) optimistically overestimating market size. However, the biggest blind spot is pricing. Driven by willful ignorance, inefficient distribution, high costs or old-fashioned greed, we underrate the critical importance of "accessible pricing." Kellogg entered the PRC with a box of corn flakes costing 40 percent more than its U.S. equivalent. JV shampoos are still no cheaper than in Western markets, even after P&G slashed prices.

Unreasonable premiums are suicide. First, the masses are not rich. Even in glittering Shanghai, per capita income, *after* adjustment for purchase power parity, is around a third of Taiwan's and an eighth of the United States'. Without a very compelling reason, locals won't pay more, particularly for products used out of the public eye. Second, in many categories, Chinese are first-time buyers. High price points preclude trial, the required behavioral response in a low-penetration market. If a brand is not "launched cheap" by charging a low price, introducing a second-tier brand (e.g., Unilever's Zhonghua toothpaste) or extending the mother brand downwards (e.g., Colgate), it will die.

That said, a cheap price is a double-edged sword.

"I am the World's Best Bargainer!" In China, when struggling to favorably impress, I establish that I am: (a) Jewish and (b) not a Republican. Once these two classifiers are known, camaraderie deepens. When probed regarding affinity toward Jews, even nationalistic citizens will express that Jewish people have "Chinese strengths" but not "their shortcomings." Like the Han, Jews are regarded as believers in the importance of education and family. However, unlike the Chinese, Jews have suffered degradation yet remain both culturally cohesive *and* a powerful economic/political force. Vulnerability has been transformed into strength. The humiliation of poverty has evolved into financial clout. (A phrase that elicits howls of laughter when spoken in Mandarin with an American accent: "There's nothing to fear under Heaven and Earth except a Jew who can negotiate in Chinese.")

Stinginess is a quotidian necessity. Within a regimented social hierarchy, it also threatens to expose a buyer's low status and questionable character. Marketers should make efforts to turn a low price into something more splendid— a signal of clever resourcefulness, even a hint of future greatness. "Aspirational bargaining," a contradiction in terms to many in the West, is admired in the PRC. VIP cards, usually printed in cheesy embossed gold, are distributed in every corner restaurant, massage parlor, hair salon, and fourth-rate hotel. Consumers hoard them like toiletries from five-star spas. The thicker the stack, the more a guy gets around town. Adept at stitching together a business network and navigating social barriers, the little big person wields VIP cards for status or economic benefit. With pride he or she shows they are someone, and, at the same time, gets 10 percent off.

Smart, Not Cheap. To reconcile the reality of daily struggle with dreams of grandeur, "bargain hunting" can become "smart shopping." Negotiation should be ritualized so both buyer and seller can claim victory. At street stalls and corner shops, there are no price tags. The rule of thumb: any discount less than 50 percent means lost face for the buyer, but a markdown of more than 60 percent humiliates the merchant. B&Q, the do-it-yourself retailer, allocates a prominent chunk of its floor space to the "special deal site," not "final clearance bins." Price points shouldn't look "desperate"; they should signal savoir faire. China Telecom's prepaid calling card sells for 40 RMB but the face value states 100, giving the buyer a feeling of having gotten a bargain. (See figure 2.3.)

Value, Not Price. However, marketers who rely solely on discounts to entice customers, no matter how seductively framed, are playing a loser's game. The competitive battlefield is fierce and the forces of commoditization haunt the landscape. Sustaining a premium remains a strategic imperative. "Price point," therefore, should be reconstructed into a *"value* equation" and margin erosion insulated by incorporating value-added, elasticity-reducing benefits. Dulux, for example, sells "five-in-one" emulsion paint at prices 13 percent *above* market average; the package prominently draws attention to its anti-toxic, anti-stain, anti-fume, anti-odor, and anti-fungal attributes. Once again, we must tip a hat to P&G's Rejoice. Ten years ago, it revolutionized the shampoo market by creating "two-in-ones," the cleaning-plus-anti-dandruff segment that now occupies 50 percent of the category. Nescafé addressed the taste preferences of a tea culture while strengthening its value proposition with "three-in-one," a blend containing coffee, milk powder, and sugar. Today, Nescafé owns the coffee high ground, leaving Kraft's Maxwell House in the dust.

Satisfaction, Not Price. Perceived value can also be enhanced by dramatizing sensorial satisfaction. Nestlé's 1 RMB wafer is tailored for the China market, where chocolate suffers from being perceived as too "heaty" (causes too much internal heat, which results in anything from pimples to poor metabolism). By increasing the wafer-to-cocoa ratio (and lowering cost of goods), a Kit Kat–like candy bar is sold as an everyday snack, not an occasional indulgence.

Fig. 2.3. In these B&Q ads, discounts are not given to consumers. Instead, smart consumers "squeeze" money out of B&Q. Shoppers are skillful bargainers, not needy beggars.

Furthermore, thanks to a new advertising "critter," Mr. Big Bite Shark, it owns a new chocolate benefit, "chompability." The combination of low price and superior service enables Shanghai Mobile's "Jia Jia Ka" to offer "double satisfaction." Its advertising features a brightly drawn "double thumbs up" and "double smile." (See figures 2.4 and 2.5.)

IV. Glorify the Mundane

The world is dangerous. The future is unsure. Many question whether gray skies are going to clear up. Still, the Chinese put on a happy face. The points of light that dot an otherwise drab cityscape are evidence of an inspiring transcendence. To forge an emotional bond with consumers, marketers should respect that impulse and present products as joyful releases.

Political Predisposition. The Mainland's greatest "brand" is the Chinese Communist Party. It is a master of elevating the ordinary to a spiritual plane. True, the

Fig. 2.4. This Nestlé wafer ad, hugely successful, refers to chocolate "chompability" at only 1RMB ($.12). It savvily dramatizes taste satisfaction, not low price.

全新的神州行加加卡倾力上市,更多实惠,更全面功能任您选择, 一切的一切,只为让您满意加倍!

 客户服务热线:1860　话费查询专线:1861
www.sh.chinamobile.com　上海移动通信有限责任公司

全新的神州行加加卡欣喜上市,更多实惠,更全面功能任您选择,一切的一切,只为让您满意加倍!  客户服务热线:1860 话费查询专线:1861
www.sh.chinamobile.com 上海移动通信有限责任公司

Fig. 2.5 (left and above). Two very simple prints ads for Shanghai Mobile that present a discounted phone card as not cheap but doubly satisfying.

CCP's relationship with the masses has shifted over time. When Mao was alive, the Party, not the parent, was the spiritual center of everyone's existence. Despite anti-rightist movements, the Great Leap Forward, and the Cultural Revolution, Mao was a savior, a demigod who chased away the "foreign barbarians" that had carved up the Middle Kingdom. (Deng Xiao Ping released the nation from its cultish straight jacket with a pragmatic covenant: if the masses accepted the Party's leadership, it would provide material wealth. Yes, the CCP's message has evolved; however, its tactics—e.g., control of capital allocation, clampdowns on the media, behind-the-black-curtain decision making—have remained the same.)

The government also knows how to turn the prosaic into the sublime. In the '70s, a dead peasant named Lei Feng was elevated to martyrdom. The Party's famous exhortation, "Learn from Lei Feng!" is perhaps the most vivid example of the masses whipped into orgiastic bliss over, well, nothing. Lei's heroism sprang from small "acts of kindness" such as helping the elderly cross the street. His deification tantalized every taxi driver, every construction worker, with frustrated dreams of grandeur. In Ma Jian's cynical novel *The Noodle Maker*, a little man who earns money by selling blood argues his life is the stuff of history books. He contends, "I'm an 'advanced blood donor,' a selfless Lei Feng devoted to the cause of the people. I'm more Lei Feng than Lei Feng! . . . I gave blood twice a day to help out a man who had been ordered to give blood by the Party. Not even Lei Feng would have done that!" Today, factory hands dream of becoming "model workers." The central leadership descends from its lofty perch to bless an ordinary state-owned enterprise, praise a student, or celebrate a mechanic who has achieved "model worker" status. Western Mainstream media supposes the public has grown tired of these dog and pony shows. But it has not. For those craving emancipation from daily ennui, they are a glimmer of hope. (The Party's recent selection of Yao Ming as a model worker was not appreciated. In the words of one loquacious taxi driver, "Even though he comes from a nice family, he's not one of us any more. He makes the Chinese people proud but he's not a role model. He's a hero. A very rich hero. This award shouldn't be allowed for people like him.")

Beyond Politics: Sparkling Modesty. Due to its Confucian roots, China is a culture that projects status with bold signage, mammoth airports, soaring skylines, and high-speed trains. (Unlike Japan, a meticulous country, the PRC looks much better from afar than close up. The cliché of "good hardware, bad software" is also true.) But the Chinese are most masterful at "micro-dazzle," little touches meant to satisfy, not impress. A capacity to rise above everyday tedium yields *small-scale* twinkles. Tiny street-level apartments are graced with decorative blinking lights. Palm trees are wrapped in neon. Shanghai's elevated highways are streaked with miles and miles of (scraggly) potted plants and (garish) blue lighting. The most unassuming alley is dotted with lanterns.

The masses know how to ornament their lives. Nonbranded, dime-a-dozen clothing is brightly hued. National holidays are excuses to spruce up a humble home. Inexpensive reversible sofa slips are one of B&Q's best sellers; they enable consumers to instantly change an ordinary coach from pale blue to orange or yellow. Cheerful cushions and throw rugs—upbeat accents against a sea of white walls—are also popular. Wedding ceremonies, once bureaucratic affairs supervised by the state, have evolved into grand parties where anything goes, from talent shows to bridal fashion parades and acrobatic performances. Bridal photos are beyond romantic; they are dreamscapes displayed in cookie-cutter living rooms. Grooms are knights, rescuing brides. Couples are in heaven, adorned with angel wings.

More and more marketers are catching on to all this. *Kongfu* fruit juice, in one of 2004's most popular commercials, dramatizes the need to shake before drinking with adorable children bouncing up and down in the middle of a dilapidated lane. Smart brands know small victories are big moments. Cooking the dish well, getting the package out in time, or winning the ping pong game can be triumphs. Nike produced a "Sports Anytime" series of ten-second TV spots in which sitting in class, catching a bus, and receiving flowers become unexpected bursts of athletic excitement. (See figure 2.6.)

V. Fuel the Fantasy of Control

The Chinese mainstream believes in preprogrammed destiny, and has been conditioned to obey edicts from above. They live in circumstances that are, at best, unpredictable and, at worst, doomed. No one believes he or she controls the future. As a result, even the most modest person craves empowerment, the "Chinese tip" of Maslow's oft-quoted "hierarchy of needs." When it's dangled in front of them, they grab at it with a vengeance. China's roads are scary, but the seventy-eight-year-old amateur traffic guard who will punish you for stepping off the curb before the light turns green is even more terrifying. During the SARS scare, smiling little neighborhood ladies morphed into dragon queens, endowed with the authority to investigate, report, and punish anyone for "suspicious travel."

The Little Person's attitude toward authority is a mixture of compliance and repressed resentment. As a result, everyone is eager for opportunities to give overblown bigwigs their just dessert. Film producers churn out an endless

Fig. 2.6 (left). In this :10 Nike ad—one of a series of eight—an everyday moment is transformed into a burst of sporting excitement. Life for the masses should be filled with small joys. The campaign won the China Advertising Association's 2004 Grand Prix.

stream of cookie-cutter kung fu (*gong fu*) flicks, each one almost guaranteed to be a timeless blockbuster. Why? Kung fu's unique combination of a silent build-up of energy and an effortless release of spectacular, larger-than-life force mirrors the tension between the common man's everyday life of quiet frustration and his dream of glorification. Through discipline and forbearance, an insignificant man can become a superhero. Chinese fables are also filled with Davids triumphing over Goliaths. Sun Wu Kong (i.e., the Monkey King) fights monsters with magical power to protect his master on a quest to locate the Buddhist Sutra. Na Zhe is a small child guarding his hometown from evil dragons.

Marketers, too, should create a sense of empowerment brimming with bravado. Nike has signed basketball sensation Yi Jian Li as spokesman. Yi, a shy, unassuming, baby-faced sixteen-year-old who, against all odds, qualified for the national team, represents a new, fluid style of Chinese play. The advertising of Nestle Ice Cream's X Crunch portrays a typical teenager who shakes and rattles the world around him with every bite of his crunchy cone. (See figure 2.7.)

IN CONCLUSION

Having coped with far greater risk and uncertainty than their middle-class cousins, the Chinese urban mass market is fearful and cautious. Challenging circumstances, throughout history and in the present, have created a pair of polarized impulses: safety seeking and transcendent escape. We have considered five ways of speaking to, or better yet, *linking* these divergent states. Specifically:

- Strengthening "reassurance credentials" among risk-averse consumers;
- Leveraging the protective role of the family to maximize brand relevance;
- Transforming price-consciousness from a necessary evil to a source of pride;
- Glorifying the mundane; and
- Offering a fantasy of control to counter an everyday sense of helplessness.

CODA: RECONCILING THE MASS MARKET AND THE MIDDLE CLASS

Is there one big market in China or are there two? Is the middle class fundamentally different from the mass market? Do the people who have gained from the past twenty years of economic reform view the world in a radically new way? Are they still "Chinese in the traditional sense" or have they evolved into Western wannabes?

Despite all the tumult, the two groups are not poles apart. And they never will be. Chinese are united by an unbreakable cultural bond. No matter what a

Fig. 2.7 (left). One bite into Nestlé X Crunch's crunchy coating results in the explosion of the mythic Five Finger Mountain. It's a large-than-life release of aggression.

family's income, it exists in a rule-bound society where acceptance of conventional order is second nature. The "Confucian code" mandates stasis is good and (abrupt) change is bad. Order is sublime and chaos is evil. Evolution is tolerable but revolution is not. The hierarchically minded favor no tax bracket. Fathers and sons interact in the same way no matter how "modern" the New Generation professes to be. "Your son is smart and he will be successful" is the greatest compliment a parent can receive regardless of family status. Furthermore, "rights"—both economic and human—are not safeguarded for either class. No slice of China has evolved into a society where the individual is respected (and institutionally protected) as a legitimate agent of change. As a result, all Chinese live in fear of "losing it all," assuming a defensive—and, at times, ruthlessly offensive—posture throughout life. Self-made men, even some state-sponsored apparatchiks, still want a green card "just in case." And a low-income mother will do everything humanly possible to make sure her child is safe and sound, shielded from germs and bullies. (Intel is one brand that can hit the bull's eye, existing at the intersection of aggression and self-preservation. On one hand, it's a reassurance of quality, a "stamp of approval" that a computer's insides are state-of-the-art. On the other, the chip itself is dynamic, a "wand" that can make New Generation wishes come true. It powers dreams. It transforms silicon into the soul of machines. If the American company manages to link Western hi-tech with Confucian ambition, it will become a Chinese icon, cementing the loyalty of both consumers and channel managers. If not, the brand will represent no more than a commoditized gizmo in a box.)

Still, the two groups *are* distinct. The masses are, first and foremost, fear-based protection seekers. And they can only dream of transcending daily burdens. (Even non-Buddhists find refuge in their Own Private Nirvana.) The middle class is different. Yes, they are always on the alert for possible dangers. And, as defense mechanisms, they simultaneously protect and project status. But, ultimately, they're optimistic about moving forward in life. Lingering anxiety is productively channeled. Alan Brown, the former Chairman of Unilever China, pithily summarizes the difference: the middle class advances with weight on the front foot. The masses steady themselves—practically digging a hole in the ground—with the back one. And, given an environmental trigger, both groups instinctively rebalance at a moment's notice.

The differences between a middle-class and mass worldview, real as they may be, are not black and white. They are all shades of gray, reflecting that China's cultural blueprint has been consistent for millennia. Twenty years of economic reform will not erase the unifying "Chineseness" of the Chinese. Regimentation will not yield individualism when dollars are sprinkled about.

Therefore, the class-based discrepancies are tendencies, not mutually exclusive preferences. Hazeline shampoo, for example, is rooted in a mass market, conservative benefit: "No artificial ingredients so it's safe for your hair." And more than a few well-to-do also seek the "reassurance of nature." But, overall, the latter are more drawn to the glamorous (projective) beauty of Lux or L'Oreal. Similarly, given the opportunity to indulge in a bit of conspicuous consumption, an ordinary worker would get great joy from driving down Chang'an Avenue in a Buick. His life, however, is spent under the harsh light of reality—i.e., the need to feed his family. He is not motivated by bourgeois positioning statements, except in fantasy.

One final point: marketers should remember the middle class exists in not only Tier I but also Tier II and III cities. And coastal jewels such as Beijing, Dalian, Shanghai, and Hangzhou obviously boast large mass markets. Omo, an upscale detergent, has a loyal, albeit small, consumer base in Wuhan. But Diaopai, a value-for-money brand (and market leader), also has a franchise in Shanghai.

So the new middle class and the great mass market are unified by cultural imperatives but separated by economic circumstances and the latter's inevitable impact on a relatively homogenous Han worldview.

CHAPTER 3

BALANCING HALF THE SKY

WHAT CHINESE WOMEN WANT

She is elegant. She is tough, soft, ambitious. The Chinese woman is a jumble of intriguing contradictions. Her desires and drives are as confusing to herself as they are to men. One cannot understate the impact of economic reform (*gaige kaifang*) on her aspirations, lifestyle choices, and sense of self. Today, she can travel to far-off romantic spots, plan an extravagant wedding, climb a corporate ladder, bear a child (or two, assuming both she and her partner come from single-child households), and obsess over her "look." Before Deng Xiao Ping opened a Pandora's Box of Western temptation, the Chinese woman's life was decidedly monochromatic, comfortingly stable, and uncomfortably repressed. Today, fashion explodes with color and shops seduce with discounts. Professional horizons are boundless and her role within the family (she controls the purse strings) has never been stronger or, from a man's perspective, more intimidating. History offers no parallels; the impact of the pill, *Roe vs. Wade,* and the failed Equal Rights Amendment pale in comparison. While American and European females still are "further ahead," their Chinese counterparts have sprinted from behind at nearly warp speed. Life is a dizzying whirl. Things have never been better.

And yet today's Chinese woman isn't satisfied. China is still a regimented society where conformity to convention is paramount. And that's a tall order. She is conflicted, torn between polarized societal expectations and tensions exacerbated by a new aspiration: individualism. In short, she suffers from "triangulation," caught between three incompatible paradigms, two of them imposed by a regimented social structure and the third by the individual herself. Whereas

China's anxiety-prone men require confidence-building (see next section), she craves a balance between tasting the fruit of today's bold new era and the imperatives of Confucian stricture. Savvy marketers can position their brands as a means of resolving conflicts that linger in the heart and, in doing so, enhance consumer loyalty, the lynchpin of profit and price premiums.

(Before proceeding further, let me anticipate some rebuttals to these conclusions. Again, the Chinese woman's struggle is, again, just that—Chinese. Although women around the world, particularly in developed economies, strive to achieve a balance of family obligations and personal goals, the "extremes" between which the PRC females are pulled—i.e., societal archetypes—are unique. Second, Western women seek self-actualization—that is, personal enrichment. Ambivalence afflicting contemporary Middle Kingdom women is, as we shall see, fueled more by clashing social mandates than true individualism.)

CHINESE WOMEN'S CULTURAL ROOTS

Fathers and Sons (Only)

Confucianism, China's cultural blueprint and dominant social force for the past 2,500 years, is patriarchal. Confucius' *wu lun*, or five key relationships that define social intercourse and order, both explicitly and implicitly reinforce the notion that men are superior to women. Unlike the Biblical commandment to "honor thy mother and father," the Master defines a son's respect for (only) his father as civilization's most important pillar. Mom doesn't merit a courtesy mention. Furthermore, Confucius' third *lun* unambiguously asserted that a wife, in essence, should "report" to her husband. She had no right to own property, inherit fortune, or initiate divorce, even under abusive conditions. (Although the treatment of Western women was not much better before the twentieth century, cultural beliefs inherent in Western philosophy—personal freedom and a broadened sense of equality—provided them with the keys to their own liberation. Confucianism has not provided similar tools to Chinese women.) Needless to say, her role in determining whom she married was nil. (Traditional wedding ceremonies, from the bride's anonymous trek to his home village to her red bridal attire—symbolizing fertility—reflected a woman's sacred duty to procreate.) He, in no uncertain terms, wore the pants of the family. From a very early age, females were taught to stand silently (and, perhaps, in pain) by her man. In the Qing-era "Book for Girls," the specifics of coquettish subservience are inculcated with rhythmic cadence: "Make tea and meals to respect your parents; wash and comb often to keep clean; learn to sew and don't be lazy; don't talk back when parents scold; listen before brothers and their wives; keep quiet while laughing; when married respect your in-laws; don't complain if your husband isn't rich; don't be stubborn when your husband scolds; raise your children to honor the ancestral line." (Despite this call for obsequy, women in dynastic China weren't domestic slaves. While her fealty was absolute, he had an obligation to ensure the family's material security and social standing.)

So what was the point of womanhood? Posterity. Wives' most sacred duty was to bear children (sons) and fiercely protect them until they reached maturity and could contribute to the clan's well-being. A famous Chinese maxim, *bu xiao you san wu hou wei da,* warns that if a daughter fails to bear a child, she has no value in the grand scheme of intergenerational harmony. Polygamy, legal until 1949, was not morally abhorrent. Indeed, it was perfectly acceptable "insurance" that increased the odds of fathering sons and passing down one's genes. (As discussed below, even today, marriage is not a "romantic institution." For the most part, it represents social and material obligation. It is a mutual defense pact against the vicissitudes of fate.) Women, therefore, were expected to satisfy a man's needs, clearing any obstacles that could prevent him from fulfilling his duties to society. In the process, she was obliged to suppress any impulse for achievement or ego expression. She was gentle, tender, mild, and caring. She was "sensually passive," alluring before marriage, and maternally constricted afterwards. (The barbaric, fetishistic practice of feet binding, outlawed only after the Communists rose to power, speaks for itself.) Her weapons were "big breasts and wide hips," indispensable child-bearing anatomy. A woman consoled, calmed, and caressed. Most of all, she quietly shielded the family from harm. She was the very model of Confucian comfort and woe unto her should she stray from this noble path.

(In the Middle Kingdom, the urge to protect is still instinctive. True, maternal instincts are universal, hard-wired into women's DNA. However, the Chinese are conditioned to: a) perceive the unfamiliar as insidious, primed to "invade" if given the opportunity and b) fear illness as an immediate threat to life.)

Revolution

The Communist takeover was, for all the utopian blather, a bureaucratic and an economic paradigm shift. (In the early '50s, things were reasonably well managed. Living, health, and education standards improved dramatically.) For the first time in history, an "emperor" (i.e., Mao) attempted to consolidate imperial power by *structurally* binding the peasant and governing and merchant (i.e., urban) classes. This required an economically self-sufficient countryside, a rosy vision that, when corrupted by Mao's megalomaniacal ambition, resulted in the 1958–1962 Great Leap Forward, a manmade disaster in which up to 30,000,000 people perished. Mao's goal to empower his rural base hinged on naïve dreams of massive wealth creation. Exploiting all means of production became an urgent imperative. He rallied the entire nation to industrialize and exhorted women to join the labor pool. When he proclaimed *"fu nu cheng ban bian tian"* ("women hold up half the sky"), China's ruler wasn't flirting with Jeffersonian Enlightenment. It was not a right but their *responsibility* to contribute to the construction of a secular, Communist paradise.

Regardless of whether Mao's objectives were idealistic or utilitarian, women's fortunes changed dramatically after "Liberation." Graham Hutchings, author of *Modern China,* describes the breakthroughs: "The marriage law of 1950 abolished concubinage, bridal 'gifts' or dowries, and arranged marriages. It also provided for the dissolution of forced unions, sparking a wave of divorces across the country instigated by unhappy women. Marriages had to be registered, one of several moves that brought the state into direct contact with ordinary people. Land Reform, a second measure, empowered women economically. Not only could they own property, they were *granted* it in a massive exercise in redistribution." (It can be argued that both landmark acts smacked of hypocrisy. First, Mao himself had many wives and concubines; in his prime, his sexual appetite was insatiable. Second, beyond tokenism, women never entered the political or military power structure. Third, in most cases, their household roles stagnated as throwbacks to subservient, dynastic times.)

Gains were not without cost. Chinese women sacrificed their femininity. Fashion was illegal. Hair, traditionally long and sensual, was bobbed. Make-up was dangerously provocative. Romantic yearnings were downright immoral. Love was an irrelevant, unproductive emotion. Wedding ceremonies were downgraded to drab, administrative affairs. Premarital sex was practically unheard of. Men and women addressed each other as "Comrade." Females entered the military and drove tanks. They climbed telephone poles, sweated in foundries, manned assembly lines, and harvested fields. Personal ("given") names became gender-neutral. Erotic, high-pitched, baby-doll voices were lowered to a vocal range appropriate for disciplined task mistresses. *All* husbands and wives were urged to call each other *ai ren,* or "loved person," a community-endorsed, politically correct appellation that now sounds prudishly quaint.

Despite the trade-offs, however, the overall state of Chinese womanhood improved dramatically after the Revolution. For the first time, both sexes could express (and sometimes fulfill) personal ambition. Both men and women were granted the right to pursue political and professional objectives as long as they were consistent with those of the state.

CHINESE WOMEN'S BEHAVIORAL CHARACTERISTICS

Two Contemporary Standards

The contemporary Chinese woman is, not surprisingly, confused. She is pulled between coexisting mandates of soft (albeit protective) subservience and aggressive productivity.

The Confucian. The "caring wife and mother" is alive and well in twenty-first-century China. A modern woman handles practically all of the domestic chores (except in Shanghai, where men man the kitchen). Her child, not her job, is the center of existence; femininity is still a cherished ideal. During courtship's early stages, she lowers eyes to signal discretion. After marriage, she unsheathes an "iron fist" to protect the child. She worries about air conditioners spewing germs, televisions emitting radiation, classroom bullies, kindergarten academic performance, and character stroke order. But she rejects overtly mannish public behavior. In a crowd, she rarely raises her voice. During crises (e.g., funerals), she neither wails or moans nor remains dry-eyed. She masters the art of the "public dainty sob," muted whines interrupted with gentle gulps. (In the excellent 1994 documentary *Tiananmen*, Chai Ling, the ruthlessly narcissistic student leader whose demagogic misjudgments contributed to the demonstrators' tragic fate, appears in front of the camera, the night before the 1989 massacre. Pretty and vulnerable, her crocodile tears were worthy of an Oscar.) Round, open faces trump high cheekbones. Even makeup is subdued, "inclusive" rather than "transformative." Skin whitening cream is bought to eliminate blemishes, not enhance radiance. Women rarely buy cars, the ultimate stimulant of aggressive (male) status seekers. But she'll pay a huge price premium for digestion-enhancing infant formula. Risqué, husband-pleasing underwear sells, as long as the price is right. (Dr. Ruth would be pleased. Sex shops are ubiquitous. They are managed—and frequented—by women.) The contemporary Chinese woman has rediscovered the natural joys, burdens, and allure of traditional femininity.

The Socialist Striver. But Maoist ambition still thrives. The PRC's fairer sex is, relative to other countries like Japan, very aggressive. In a 2000 study conducted by JWT, 74 percent of Mainland women stated that "my own success is an area to put effort into." The figures for "wealth" and "friendship" were 53 percent

Fig. 3.1. In today's world, Confucian values are alive and kicking. A woman needs a child to complete her identity and her ultimate role, that of mother.

and 19 percent, respectively. The contrast between Chinese and Japanese women is striking. Only 28 percent and 33 percent of the latter described "success" and "wealth" as "important." "Friendship," on the other hand, came in at 44 percent. Despite a lingering preference for boys (particularly in second- and third-tier cities), more than 50 percent of university students are girls. Over 80 percent of married women hold a job. In the office, women are no less expressive than the guys. Furthermore, strong women are admired by both sexes. (Men's respect, however, remains ambivalent.). Wu Yi (whose nickname is the "Iron Lady"), the only female member of the CCP Steering Committee, shook up the country's medical establishment in the fight against SARS and became a hero. Hillary Clinton, the bane of America's Right, is universally popular; her memoirs were front page news. (Her husband is, too. No one gets the fuss whipped up by Monica Lewinsky's blue dress.)

Polarized Ideals

As the above suggests, China boasts two mutually inconsistent female "archetypes." Both are romanticized characterizations that, to this day, represent the

Fig. 3.2. This stereotype represents the traditional Confucian ideal of a loving and kind woman whose primary role is to protect her child. Provided by Mr. Song Jia Lin.

essence of womanhood. First, the Chinese woman is a Loving and Kind Angel who protects husband and child. Advertising often latches onto this one-dimensional ideal. P&G's Safeguard skillfully links germ elimination with a mother's urge to shield the family from harm. Maxam, a local skin cream, hired the wife of an actor known for portraying kind-hearted men as its spokesperson. She attests: "The best part of being a woman is feeling like a woman. My man is loved by the public for being a good husband. A woman also should be a good wife, soft and caring. Maxam lotion will make your skin as soft as your heart." In the United States, such traditional musings would be endorsed by Paleolithic reactionaries, but Betty Friedan would not be amused.

The other archetype is the Working Warrior, a modern-day Rosie the Riveter (see figure 3.3). She manufactures for the Motherland. She has strong ambitions. She is devoted to achieving both professional and national recognition. She's willing to forfeit femininity and even neglect her family. This aggressive impulse is fodder for many crudely simplistic (and, as discussed below, alienating) communications. In the mid-90s, Motorola launched a pager with a red casing. In their TV commercial, a female drives a sports car. Clad in crimson, she's a strutting, angular, hot-to-trot vixen, a professional who eats the competition—i.e., men—for lunch. (Such testosterone-injected creative is *too* aggressive, even for the most go-getting woman. That the ad was produced in the first place, however, is a telling signal of how competitive PRC women can be.) Strength vis-à-vis husbands and boyfriends is also striking. Pepsi launched its Lite variant with a bold tagline: "One calorie, unlimited attraction." Advertising featured a very confident woman, curvy and smart, who turns men into love slaves. She's the one pulling the strings. Well-built guys are boy toys, pretty puppets with dangling tongues. (The heroine's skillful cleverness keeps the ad from crossing the line. Women don't like their husbands or boyfriends to know they are, in fact, "whipped.")

It's critical to remember that China is not and never will be "individualistic." (Society's basic building block remains the clan.) The Working Warrior does have personal goals. But strength of identity remains inextricably linked to external approval. Chairman Mao decreed women *must*, not *can*, achieve. And he was very specific regarding what achievement would be condoned—i.e., accomplishments that contributed to the wealth of the nation and the Helmsman's hold on power. Real individualism implies a sense of self, even in the face of public scorn. Chinese admire Madonna (the singer) because she writes her own rules. She reinvents herself as she pleases, when she pleases. She controls not only her own image but also the paparazzi. However, she is never *emulated*. With the exception of moody chanteuse Faye Wong, a single mother fond of ni-

Fig. 3.3. The picture personifies the Maoist ideal of the female Striver, dedicated to contributing to the creation of a Socialist Utopia.

hilistic lyrics, China does not produce "pop rebels." And even Ms. Wong fled the PRC before having her baby.

The coexistence of The Loving and Kind Angel and the Working Warrior, two societally mandated paradigms, is awkward. They are poles apart, so fulfilling both is, to say the least, a difficult proposition. The Chinese woman is compelled to swing between mutually inconsistent objectives, achieving neither.

Recent Spiritual Pollution

It gets even more complicated. Over the past decade, a woman's identity has become even more jumbled. Driven by three factors, Western individualism is, for the first time, part and parcel of China's collective consciousness. First, American and European pop culture is everywhere. Glossy fashion magazines, from *Marie Claire* to *Elle,* are universal. Targeted to under-thirties, they proselytize self-fulfillment, perpetuating a fantasy of ego independence. Second, working women are encouraged to make money. They emulate entrepreneurs, mavericks with new ideas and unencumbered by conventional wisdom. Yue Sai, the ubiquitous cosmetics doyenne and Huang Hung, the Chinese *Seventeen's* publisher, are role models. (Ms. Yue and Ms. Huang are not Mainland citizens, by the way.) Such women fuel a mirage of Personal Liberation (one that, given China's Confucian core, can never fully materialize). Third, and most fundamentally, the single-child household created a generation of young women with a keen sense of self-importance. For as long as China has existed, children have been the bridge between hardship and hope. Today, finally, families invest hopes for the future (and future generations) in girls as well as boys. Young ladies are finally emerging from childhood brimming with hopeful pride.

However, despite these changes, challenges to social convention are still never truly accepted. Successful marketing balances aspirational individualism with Mainland conservatism. Nike produced an aerobics ad encouraging women to "do sports and empower yourself." The heroine wasn't controlled by "work, dates, shopping or milkshakes." They were "pushed" off screen. That was too much; the TVC, while not exactly offensive, was a dud. The subsequent print ads were better received. They projected individual "strength," albeit with a conformist payoff. Adroitly posed women appear above well-crafted headlines: "If you can 'maintain' this 'position' in the gym, just think what you can do in the real world." (Working out—i.e., lifting weights or doing aerobics—is translated as "body sculpting" or "body shaping." Not exactly the language of release. . . .)

The Master Conflict

The dream of "having it all" is, obviously, a glorious-but-impossible *balancing act*. Marketers can help women resolve internal conflict and achieve a better equilibrium.

INSIGHT APPLICATION

Let Her Succeed . . . Gracefully

Yes, put the woman on top but never sacrifice charm. She must never emasculate her man (or colleagues) with uncouth directness or a table-banging iron fist. In ads promoting self purchase (i.e., women buying for themselves), the Diamond Trading Company equates the stone with clued-in savvy; however, an understated and feminine "sparkle" also shines through. (See figure 3.4.) The diamond is not a "power tool." Procter & Gamble's Rejoice shampoo—a brand with a perennial 20 percent share—is all about uninhibited self-assurance, albeit one wrapped in gentle beauty (i.e., soft and silky hair). The mature professional's obsession with

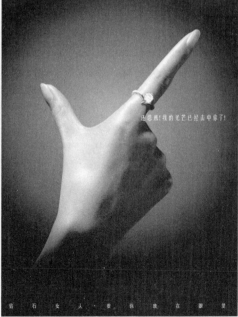

Fig. 3.4. A diamond represents the perfect combination of feminine grace and strength. Only in China.

all things cute and lovely—e.g., Hello Kitty, other fuzzy dolls, small animals, tinkling ring tones, white skin, black hair and slim figures—springs from her desire to wrap (i.e., conceal) an inner strength with feminine gentility.

Recognize the Importance of "Life Stages"

Few have what it takes to become a true *mei man* (complete and well-rounded) modern woman. So different ideals dominate at different times. The fresh college graduate is intoxicated with discovering "who I really am," so Siemens markets its "Minnie" mobile phone to the girl who wants to "go anywhere and do everything." After marriage, however, the Confucian in every Chinese woman compels selfless acceptance of responsibility. She should morph into a modern saint, the noble protector of the family and, most critically, of her child's future. Jin Sheng Insurance's recent TVC, for example, depicts an elegant, yet unemployed, mother accepting menial jobs so that her daughter can go to college.

Provide a Stamp of Approval

Dreams of self-driven individualism is a creeping phenomenon, only a *recent* byproduct of the infiltration of Western culture. As a result, most of a woman's self-worth is still derived from third-party endorsement. Therefore, irrespective of what socioeconomic segment is targeted, a product must elicit praise. Unilever's Fengcao, a rural market washing powder, delivers both "clothes that look like new" (i.e., effective stain removal) and community admiration (i.e., sanctioning her "performance" as a mom). Both Unilever's Knorr chicken essence and P&G's Sunlight washing powder advertising extracts the beaming satisfaction of life's toughest critic—the mother-in-law. DTC's *engagement* diamond copy projects a woman's *xing fu* (happy and prosperous) status shining into, literally, the admiring eyes of others.

Reassure Her of His Love

Marriage, too, is largely a social institution. Of course, romance is aspirational. But a truly successful union springs from and perpetuates a materially protected future, not a fluttering heart. (Taiwan's First Bank actually suggests that its retail services bind a man and woman together.) Since passion is not the core of courtship, women are insecure about (a) if he does, in fact, love her and (b) if he will keep her and the child's future safe. ("If he doesn't love me, will I lose him? Will I need to put work ahead of my kid? Will the neighbors treat me as a failure?") So position your product as a demonstration that he would go anywhere or do anything for her. Valentine's Day, now mandatory, is more "proof" of commitment than expression of love. (Translation: the price of the gift is more important than what's written in the card.) Unilever's Hazeline ginseng shampoo enhances the beauty of her long hair but, even more importantly, turns him into malleable putty, sheltered from the sensual temptations surrounding him.

The DTC's success in establishing diamonds as "love jewelry" is a smashing example of how Western aspiration and a Chinese worldview can be elegantly blended to produce a new cultural imperative. Since 1995, when diamond penetration for recently married couples was in the basement, a woman's need for security has been front and center in all advertising and promotional efforts. Diamonds as a representation of (aspirational) passionate love—the meat of all American and European copy—has been secondary in Chinese ads. Over time, the "safety" message has become less obvious, more skillfully integrated into the diamond offering, but it has never disappeared. The company's first ad, "Moongate," was spectacularly pragmatic. It depicts the wedding of a young couple who have grown up together; although they are clearly in love, the "don't worry he won't leave you" message is explicit. True, as incomes have risen and fears of famine have abated, romantic aspiration has become a bigger part of the sell. However, commitment, societal acceptance, and material ambition have always been played upon. The DTC's 2002 TVC, "Swimming," opens with an attractive couple walking toward a pool at a luxurious resort. She says, "Ah, the moon is so romantic." Proving his allegiance, he volunteers, "I'll go get it for you." Valiantly, he dives into the moon's reflection on the water's surface. Before he emerges, his hand appears with a huge rock, glistening in the moonlight. She takes the ring and pushes him away, ever so playfully. (See figures 3.5 and 3.6.)

Diamond penetration is approximately 80 percent in Shanghai and over 70 percent in Beijing and Guangzhou. It's almost 50 percent in Chengdu.

Abet Her Escape

Being a modern woman is a calorie-burning occupation. Around every corner, there's another role to fill and tightrope to walk. So alleviate her stress. The Lipton tea break should go beyond relaxation. It *soothes* and liberates her from the demands of others. An excursion to the mall is a *primal release,* not a

Fig. 3.5. Marrying commitment and material wealth with romance, this DTC engagement ring ad de_ a man who dives into the reflection of a moon and emerges with a big, fat rock. Note that the couple i_ never detached from society.

bargain-hunting expedition. A woman's apartment is both a place to live and a shelter from outside pressures. The convenience of a Little Swan dishwasher should "take her away" from taxing tedium.

To build a brand's equity and, hence, justify a price premium, know your target. Understand her fundamental motivations of behavior and preferences. Help her dream the impossible dream of being a perfect modern woman.

Fig. 3.6. In this ad for the Diamond Trading Company, the red string represents soul mates destined for each other. The maze symbolizes future uncertainty. The diamond means eternal commitment. A home run ad.

CHAPTER 4

THE MIND OF CHINESE MEN

THE ANXIETY OF DISORIENTATION

The Chinese character for "man" (男) depicts "power in the field." Angular and bold, the pictogram celebrates testosterone-fueled masculinity; it also suggests that men, while ruling the roost, are fully responsible for the material well-being of the clan. Confucianism, the Middle Kingdom's cultural blueprint, is rooted in double-edged patriarchy; men boast power but are constrained by the yoke of duty, both today and in the past.

CHINESE MEN'S CULTURAL ROOTS

Within the household, the markers of legitimacy have always been crystal clear. Men must *wu shi you wu er zhi yu xue* ("set your heart on learning by fifteen"), *san shi er li* ("be successful by thirty"), *si shi bu huo* ("have no doubt about yourself by forty"), *wu shi er zhi tian ming* ("know the mandate of heaven by fifty"), *liu shi er er shun* ("hear only the mandate of heaven by sixty"), *qi shi er cong xing suo bu yu ju* ("follow your heart's desire BUT without transgressing the norms"), and, from birth to death, *guan zong yao zu* ("honor and bring glory to ancestors"). Professionally, the "hierarchy of success" has always been extremely narrow and inflexible. Prior to Mao, merchants—i.e., money collectors—were scorned. Farmers were (barely) respected. Scholars were worshipped (in both the here and now and afterlife).

In dynastic times, the burden was heavy but, reassuringly, the path to success was meticulously laid out, ultimately within the control of the individual. Historically, a sharp mind was a man's greatest asset in his quest for greatness.

An oft-quoted adage dictates: "Those who excel in scholarship become officials; those who work with their minds rule; those who work with strength are ruled." A pithier one, *xue er tong bu,* states a golden rule: "Study *is* advancement." By mastering a finite body of Confucian scripture, an ambitious man could take the "palace exams" (supposedly in the presence of the emperor), enter the lofty ranks of the scholar-officials, and enjoy power, prestige, and wealth. (The civil servant exams were actually a series of increasingly taxing tests that weeded out anyone with any inclination to question Confucian convention. In ascending order of selectivity, they included: district exams for "Government Students," provincial exams for "Employable Men," metropolitan exams for "Presentable Scholars," and, finally, the palace exams for "Advanced Scholars.") Passing the test (or even taking it) was no cakewalk but still within the realm of theoretical possibility. True, not everyone is endowed with equal intellectual gifts but the ability to hone one's mind *is,* in large part, divorced from external variables—e.g., bad crops, stock market crashes, and airline delays. Furthermore, financial investment in decades of pre-exam education—in terms of both cash outlay and the opportunity cost of one less hand in the field—*did* preclude most from even dreaming of a better day job. Nonetheless, Chinese lore is replete with scholars-nee-peasants, local heroes who succeeded via academics. The path to success was conveniently, if restrictively, defined.

The 1949 revolution upset that apple cart. Scholars were dirt; books were burned. Merchants weren't scorned; they were shot. Success was singularly defined as a party career. One thing, however, remained the same; advancement in society hinged on "mastery," this time not of Confucian code but Marxist-Leninist-Maoist dogma. Creative thinking and "new" ideas had no adaptive value.

Then things changed radically. When Deng Xiao Ping embarked on his 1992 Southern Tour, he proclaimed, "To get rich is glorious," imperially pronouncing the acquisition of wealth as a man's newest and most worthy pursuit. The definition of success, always divorced from Western (self-driven) individualism, was as narrow and societally mandated as in dynastic China. A man's responsibility to his family was as absolute as ever. But the *means* of grabbing the brass ring—*chuan ye jing shen,* or an entrepreneurial, pioneering spirit—fractured, driven as much by serendipity as internal drive. Education, traditionally focused on "meticulous expertise," was no longer a nonrefundable ticket to greatness. In the brave new world, "high risk, high return" supplanted "no pain, no gain" as the guiding maxim. During the late '80s, legions of CCP cadres—modern-day Horatio Algers—embarked on business careers to find fame and fortune. However, for the first time, there were no signposts. There was no prescribed formula for advancement, no syllabus to memorize. The phrase *xia hai* says it all. Translated, more or less, as "out to sea," it refers to cadres who leave state jobs for the uncharted shoals of capitalism. More than ten years on, men, both inside the party and out, remain as disoriented as ever.

The concoction of prescriptive standards and diffused means of fulfilling them is a bitter brew. Contemporary Chinese men are filled with lingering anxiety and a nebulous loss of control. Marketers have an opportunity to touch their hearts by developing products and communications that dull the need to "cross the river by feeling the stones." They know where they want to go, but they are not sure of the right way to get there. This conflict between a penchant for order and an entrepreneurial imperative is profound.

INSIGHT APPLICATION

Project Status

The Chinese man is not confident of the road ahead. Status, therefore, is a crutch, a means of demonstrating (both to others and himself) the capacity to forge a successful future. Yanger apparel, a mid-priced brand, presents the "Yanger Man" as a savvy bidder at an upscale auction. Virgin Airlines positions its aromatherapy frill as the quintessence of personalization, effectively transforming a plane seat into a throne. *Hai Wang Jin Zun* tonic even draws a parallel between the strength of the drinker and the power of an emperor. Every communication should—preferably with a bit of grace—reinforce an individual's perception of himself as a high-potential stallion.

Give Him Tools

Capitalistic success is, in large part, determined by external variables. So an individual must seize fluid opportunities. Every product should be an enabler, a tool to extend his reach. Technology is not only a productivity enhancer but also a weapon, a means of snatching victory from the jaws of defeat. Siemens' GPRS-enabled mobile phone is more about "closing the deal" than "anytime, anywhere internet access." Motorola's business phones are "the choice of winning CEOs." Even Rejoice shampoo, a brand built around "the confidence that flows from soft and shiny hair," artfully connects "no dandruff" with "impressing the boss," one whose endorsement can be wielded on the business battlefield.

Either explicitly or implicitly, practically every auto on the road is positioned as an indispensable enabler, a pass key to a golden new era: Ford Fiesta ("invitation to the 'party'"), Ford Mondeo ("the world will look at you") (see figure 4.1), Buick Sail ("creating sparkle in your life"), Buick Excelle ("pursue success with your full heart and mind"), Buick Sedan ("calmness, wisdom, the will to go the distance"), Kia Accent ("reflect your inner heart, ambition and substance"), Honda ("the power of dreams"), BMW 7 Series ("reflect your leadership spirit"), Ford Maverick ("defeat ordinary challengers"), Lincoln Navigator ("drive presidential respect"), and Cadillac ("dare to be the first").

Release His Aggression

Confucianism is anti-individualistic. So, too, is its modern incarnation, Chinese communism. Regimented benchmarks of achievement imposed by a rigid social structure do not foster self-actualization. Instead, they breed repression. Consequently, a man relishes the release of pent-up frustration. Victory should be larger than life. Challenge should be heroic. ADSL (internet access) advertising compares the surfer's "unleashed power" to a gladiator's superhuman strength. Gentle patriotism can quickly morph into bold, ego-affirming nationalism, a

Fig. 4.1. The Ford Mondeo, the 2004 Car of the Year, positions the automobile as eye-candy, a head-turner on the road to success. More recent ads are a bit more subtle but still revolve around status as a projective tool.

projective conduit that compensates for some men's fragile identity. Coca-Cola's World Cup advertising features Li Tie, a new generation soccer star who spreads China's glory around the world. China Unicom paid almost $5 million for NBA superstar Yao Ming's endorsement. The advertising is crude (both strategically and executionally), but it still manages to draw a parallel between the heroic "national treasure" and Unicom's shining future.

Help Him Pass the Girl Test

Confucius said a man must provide for the family, and strong-willed Chinese women never fail to remind him of his sacred duty. To have a shot with a girl, he needs to demonstrate his ability to bring home the bacon. "Modern" Chinese guys marry relatively late, around twenty-eight or thirty. Before then, most can't afford to buy an apartment; sadly, a mortgage is the only way to demonstrate future dependability.

An ordinary guy struggles under the weight of responsibility; his wife or girlfriend rarely cedes an opportunity to remind him of his lot, sometimes to the point of emasculation. (According to locals, Shanghai husbands suffer particularly vigorous hen-pecking.) So, put him back on top. (Commercial sex— i.e., submission by the hour—is institutionalized and ritualized. To quote a short-lived McDonald's tagline: "What you want is what you get.") Eroticize the world outside his home. Vis-à-vis the fairer sex, make him feel in charge. The Schick man doesn't just "win" the girl; he "conquers" her. The China Southern flight attendant, unlike her American counterpart, gives the passenger an impression that his personal comfort, not his safety, comes first. Siemens has built its youth franchise on the premise of "being clever enough to catch her off guard." (Demonstration of intelligence is a huge turn-on. One of McDonald's most popular TVC shows a young man who pops the question by putting a diamond ring in a box of chicken wings. His girlfriend is amused, even charmed, but she still wants to know if she'll get her food.)

Leverage Friendship

It's a tough world out there. The disoriented modern man craves retreat; friendship is the ultimate sanctuary. Bonds that have stood the test of time— ideally dating back to childhood or, at least, high school—fuel the warmth of many alcohol campaigns (e.g., Rheineck beer, He Jiu liquor). Sedrin lager, Fujian province's leading brand, tackles friendship from another angle. It recognizes that most "newer" friendships (i.e., of "wine and meat") are, at the end of the day, about building a functional business network. Both are "trust enablers," transforming skittish acquaintance into robust (and practical) camaraderie.

Make Him an Expert

Finally, if he feels anxious about his ability to learn the professional ropes and conquer the business world, help him compensate by becoming a pro outside the office. From the lady-killer who has the body of Brad Pitt (e.g., Big Impression weight-loss tea) to the sailor who has tamed the sea (e.g., Suntory beer), local and international brands forge loyalty by paying tribute to the well-rounded, multidimensional man. From the chef to the golf whiz, from the literature aficionado to the racquetball champ, salute the man who at least appears to have more on his mind than the pettiness of corporate political intrigue.

In conclusion, Chinese men are caught between narrowly defined (monetary and professional) success and a broadly individualistic path to get there. The clash between means and ends leads to a diffused anxiety. To be successful in China, marketers must find a way of becoming a man's partner on the bumpy journey to greatness. (See figure 4.2.)

Fig. 4.2. To the man who strives for the highest level of success, wisdom—brought to you by Ballantine's—is the ultimate tool on the business battleground. The headline reads: "There's no need to flaunt it. Intelligence reveals itself."

CHAPTER 5

CONFORMIST INDIVIDUALISM AND CHINESE YOUTH

True or false? In the booming coastal cities of China, the new generation of youth—i.e., those consumers directly benefiting from the liberalized policies of the past decade—are becoming "Westernized." The answer is both true *and* false. In terms of lifestyle, there's no question. There has been an explosion of choice: the Internet; travel; a proliferation of fashion, leisure, and glossy entertainment publications; home ownership and modern, streamlined interior décor; multinational standards of employment and training; Nike vs. Adidas; basketball vs. soccer; bowling and go-cart racing (out); Ecstasy at the disco (still in); Valentine's Day (very, very in); premarital sex (coming in). Furthermore, Western-style *individualism* is, at least on the surface, a highly aspirational character trait. The "new generation," for example, reveres Han Han, a young and bold Chinese writer who decided to take up race-car driving à la Paul Newman.

However, it is important to separate a product from its packaging. Chinese youth remain deeply Chinese. Patriots boast of 5,000 years of history. The cultural blueprint of China is deeply etched in the hearts of every citizen. Ten years of economic liberalization will not dust it away.

CHINESE YOUTH'S CULTURAL ROOTS

Standing in Line

Confucianism, despite an inability of many to articulate what the creed actually is, thrives in contemporary China. As discussed above, Confucius preached the importance of virtue and loyalty and the five key relationships or *wu lun*—in order of importance: father and son, husband and wife, elder and young brother, friend and friend, and emperor and subject—which still hold sway among even the most "modern" youth. Cash is still given every month to parents (regardless of whether or not they need the money) as a gesture of respect. Very few single women are bold enough to ask for permission to move into their own apartment even after they have turned thirty. Trendy types still profess shock and awe at what they perceive as barbarous treatment by Western children toward aging parents; retirement homes are more shameful then penitentiaries.

What's more, the Confucian hardwiring in every "Westernized," dyed-hair head precludes even the slightest whiff of democratic impulse. Yes, complaints against the government are grumbled and protection of property is demanded. And, yes, thoughtful people grasp the abstract yet critical link between efficient allocation of resources and political structure. However, no one—save the "unrealistic" overseas Chinese in the United States—is clamoring for a representative form of government, and this is not just because people are afraid that they might be jailed if they did. In many ways, imperial political institutions still lord over the population. Reform will be triggered from within the power structure, not the "enlightened and open" new generation who read the Internet. Chinese are regimented. They exist in a rigidly defined and aggressively enforced hierarchical framework that has been constructed across millennia.

Standing at the Front of the Line

That said, Confucian youth are not passive. Stoked by an age-old emphasis on education as a means of self-advancement, trenchant ambition has always lurked behind the (safe) façade of an unemotional facial expression. And two *contemporary* phenomena make the clash between a conformist imperative and an individual's ambition even more uncomfortable: capitalistic reform and the single-child household. Both trends are nourishing the seeds of long-dormant *individualism*—that is, defining the ego independent of societal expectations. Indeed, the collision between "what I want" and "what they expect of me" can be fiery.

Capital Liberation

Capitalism is about more than the freedom to make money; it liberates individual initiative and, hence, a sense of self. The essence of capitalistic societies is respect for the entrepreneur. Chinese youth idolize Bill Gates for not only his immense wealth but also the confidence to reject conventional wisdom. By dropping out of college and introducing a new model of information technology, he rewrote the rules. He challenged "the way" and forged his own path. A pioneering spirit and renegade heart drives the entrepreneur. When a fresh graduate says, "I want to make money," he or she is talking about both a flush bank account and the freedom to bring home the bacon "my way."

My Own Kingdom

It is a cliché to say the single-child household policy has produced legions of plump, coddled, and spoiled Little Emperors. However, this draconian (and effective) strategy of population control has revolutionized the child's role in the family. Historically, parental love was a moot point. Children were resources. They were investments. A brood of loyal, strapping boys was a way of minimizing future uncertainty, the ultimate diversified portfolio. (By the way, as discussed, Confucian culture is patriarchical. Through much of its history, a girl had no value whatsoever and ultimately became the property of her husband's family.)

Today, however, the single child is a cherished investment, as "precious as a panda." The onus of elevating the financial, social, and education status of not only the immediate family but also the extended clan is on the shoulders of a child. To the singleton, his or her burden is a mixed blessing. On one hand, it is a heavy responsibility and results in millions of pre-teen neurotics with angst-ridden childhoods. On the other hand, it reinforces a sense of individual importance, one that, historically, never saw the light of day. Every child is a darling, a dumpling, the apple of every eye, a genius, a musical prodigy, and Harvard-bound. Like Pu Yi, the last emperor of the Qin dynasty, each is under the sadly mistaken impression that, in the world out there, he or she is really, really important.

Identity Crisis

When it's time for high school, things change dramatically. The babe in the woods sees the harsh day of light. He or she enters a land of ruthless competition and unyielding regimentation—school uniforms, marching in line, and group calisthenics. The child must thrive within an education system that prizes rote memorization and mathematical aptitude rather than conceptual, assimilative creativity. (In the United States, students write their first interpretive book report in the second grade. In China, no open-ended composition is expected before the ninth grade. Furthermore, there are two academic "tracks" in a PRC high school, Chinese and math. Unless a pupil excels in the latter, no one will consider him smart. The former is too subjectively nonquantifiable and, therefore, not as noble.) Then come the world's most unforgiving college entrance exams, job competition, and the battle to snare the "right" mate with whom a model family can be built.

The youngster is understandably confused. Before, he was everything; now he's nothing. Before, she was important; now she's an afterthought living in a small dorm with bunk beds stacked three high and six roommates. The single child, after crossing the threshold to maturity, looks up to the sky with consternation and exclaims, "Who am I?" A massive crisis of identity erupts. And to fill a barren ego, the quest for popularity beckons.

INSIGHT APPLICATION

Standing Out with Chinese Cool

Unlike the Japanese, who take genuine comfort in fitting in, the ambitious, individually driven Chinese want to stand out. And youth, emerging from a self-important cocoon, crave recognition. They want to be noticed for their hair, cool clothing, latest CD, skateboard, Hello Kitty collection, performance in school, dunking skill on the basketball court, and creative soccer moves. They want to be better-looking and more popular than their friends.

But in a regimented, Confucian society, the leading goose gets shot down. Standing out too obviously elicits ridicule, even scorn. Therefore, care must be taken to *subtly* attract attention. Loud clothing, loud voices, and loud mobile phone rings will alienate. If you want to attract attention, whisper, wink, and dress monochromatically with a flash of accessorized color. Walk with a glide that, only occasionally, departs from the conventional path. Don't flex muscles and say, "The beach is that way!" Broad physicality is boorish. American brashness is primitive. Direct assertion is uncivilized. A cute face is fine, but a sharp mind is sexy.

Conformist Individuality

Intelligence—and the agility to leverage it subtly—is the ultimate aphrodisiac and popularity generator. While desperate to be noticed, Chinese youth must move to the front of the pack with understated skill. There should be no gate crashing, no rebellion against familial or societal norms. Rules can be creatively interpreted but never broken. Quick-witted resourcefulness is a tool both during adolescence and on the battlefield of life. It represents working within the system, not against it. It is the key to standing out, albeit with peer endorsement. "Individuality" in the Western sense of the word—forging an identity independent of external approval—doesn't yet exist in China, despite a burgeoning youth culture. Individuality in the Middle Kingdom is a *twist* on the conventional. It is a reinterpretation of what is already acceptable. It is being in style, but with flair. It is effortlessly weaving around omnipresent and invisible barriers. It is "conformist individuality."

Smart marketers should help youth resolve this conflict between wanting to be noticed and to fit in. Here are five ways to achieve this:

Bring Out their Cleverness. A melodic ring tone on a Motorola cell phone shouldn't just sound nice; it should trigger a romantic dance between a guy and his girlfriend. A PDA should remind him of her Chinese lunar birthday, not just the normal one. A can of Pepsi should be the badge of the "Intelligent Generation." The dynamic dance steps of the handsome but superficial Aaron Kwok must be balanced by the poetic musing of chanteuse Faye Wong.

Facilitate Self-Expression among Regimentation. Yahoo! promotes its hyper-successful chat room as an outlet for revealing who you really are to an on-line community . . . anonymously. According to one twenty-something, "It's about letting out what you can't say at work. While you're on the Internet you don't have to pretend." Siemens' 1118 handset positions its multidesign covers as a way of "changing your own face" and "expressing today's mood." However, the zaniness of "letting yourself go" always happens in a group setting.

Release Repression. Due to a volatile combination of a restrictive social structure and aggressive individual ambition, Chinese young people are ready to explode. Video games, a passion worldwide, play a particularly cathartic role in China with larger-than-life action titles (e.g., Age of Empires, Romance of the Three Kingdoms) promising the repressed youth the ability to "remake the world." As one twenty-eight-year-old addict notes, "You can revise history to give China a second chance. When you've done it you get a sense of incredible achievement." Karaoke, an activity regarded with irony at best and derision at worst in the West, spreads like wildfire in China because it is the perfect antidote to repressed ambition. With a microphone in hand, a small voice of a little man can project to the rafters, but he is always protected by a lush musical score that at least partially covers up any errant tones or flubbed lyrics. In advertising, Schick depicts a handsome, sharp-jawed man "conquering the girl" as she collapses in his arms, appealing to men's desire to break out of their shell and be the hero. President instant noodles positions its large-sized packages for men who, though they now live in small apartments on a modest salary, will one day own a mansion and be a millionaire.

New Generation Nationalism. Jingoism thrives in an environment that both downgrades individualism and promotes achievement; frustrated personal ambition is displaced onto socially endorsed nationalistic expression. All Chinese are patriotic. But only the zealous youth are fiercely angered by an outsider's failure to recognize China's glory. Contrarily, street dancing erupts after any significant national victory—e.g., the 2008 Beijing Olympic and 2010 Shanghai World Expo bids or China's first man in space. Advertising often taps into such oversized national pride. Coke, for example, features soccer star Li Tie putting Chinese soil in a bottle and spreading it around the world. "Wherever you shine, China is with you!"

However, nationalism—ultra-sensitivity to outsiders' perceptions of China—can cut both ways. Even Nike, a true youth icon, ran into a bit of trouble a few years ago when it indirectly suggested that basketball hero Wang Zhi Zhi's skills rivaled those of NBA stars. The claim, according to Beijing focus groups, was "humiliating and unbelievable" and an example of "foreigners patronizing us." In late 2004, Nike was again in the news. A playful ad featuring basketball star LeBron James versus kung fu masters was decisively yanked off the air by the State Administration of Radio, Film and Television (SARFT). Thanks to Nike's strong brand image, the hubbub quickly died down.

Earlier that year, Toyota, a much clumsier advertiser, almost self-destructed. It ran a print ad with two stone lions—a symbol of Chinese strength—*bowing* to the Japanese car. The entire nation went apoplectic. Propaganda organs "solemnly protested" on behalf of the "dignity of the Chinese people," all 1.3 billion of them. Nationalism, by the way, helps the Party. Ever since the leaders abandoned the cryptoreligious pull of Marxist-Leninist-Maoist thought, the Communists' "spiritual" legitimacy hangs by a thread. On the shoals, "safeguarding the dignity of the people" comes in handy, so the government often whips up a nationalistic lather, often with Japan as the object of fury, as the protests in April 2005 over Japanese textbooks that whitewashed their wartime atrocities in China show.

Provide Escape from the Conflicts of the Changing World. Young people are confused about both their identity and rapidly changing environment. Although the new generation is perhaps the most optimistic cohort in history, it is stressed out. Temporary respites from competing social demands and a frenzied daily pace are essential. Teahouse chains are soothingly named "The Pond Sheltered from Wind" or "Woods Where Fairies Tread." Beer shouldn't "turn on the fun"; instead, it must create a mood of trust and relaxation. A recent TV commercial for Coke featured a white, clean, and well-lit Internet bar right out of Silicon Valley; location was elevated to the level of a heavenly retreat.

Decontaminate Corruptive Influences. Daoism and, to a lesser extent, Confucianism both stress the importance of an individual achieving a timeless harmony with the world and cosmos. Confucius speaks of a heavenly mandated social order while Daoism's Lao Ze emphasizes a balance between humanity, nature, and the universe. In both cases, new worldly influences are greeted with deep suspicion. In the brave new era of global capital markets, young folks are exposed to more "non-Chinese" elements than ever before and, hence, require "purification." Hello Kitty projects the inner wholesomeness of even the most modern female executive. The doll is targeted at adults, not little girls. Its advertising copy reads, "Hello Kitty, so soft and sweet. Cookies are what you like to eat. Perfectly beautiful in every way, seeing your face brightens my day." In a focus group, a twenty-eight-year-old woman sighed, "It hurts me when she gets dirty. I keep her in plastic bags."

Products positioned on a purity platform thrive. Bottled green tea enjoys growth rates that far exceed "sticky and heavy" colas—hence, Coke and Pepsi's aggressive move toward product diversification and localization. Platinum, a symbol of eye-catching luxury in Western markets, is compared to "pure and timeless porcelain" in China.

By recognizing the oxymoronic need for "conformist individualism," a marketer can greatly increase the odds of hitting the sweet spot of desire among one of the world's most exciting youth markets.

CHAPTER 6

THE "CHINESENESS" OF THE MAINLAND VERSUS HONG KONG AND TAIWAN

These next few sections are a diversion, outside this book's Mainland scope. But the question of the similarities and differences within "Greater China" pops up quite often—particularly in the form of, "How many commercials do I need to shoot?"

THE BIG PICTURE

Let's start boldly. Chinese, regardless of whether they live in China, Taiwan, or Hong Kong, are essentially the same. They are Confucian at the core. They share the same worldview based on a belief in fate, cyclical dynasticism, and go-with-the-flow Daoism. They have much in common in terms of broad social and business tendencies: filial piety (i.e., deference to authority figures, especially the father), comfort with/reliance on hierarchy; avoidance of the subjective; respect for mathematicians, disdain for humanities; round tables; strong personal ambition; a competitive worldview; reliance on fortune tellers and *feng shui;* intergenerational repression; commercial aggression individualistic suppression; fear of uncertainty; low crime rates; investment in education; high savings rates; imperial bosses, fear of bosses; fear of self-expression; binary ("yes or no?") questions, analog (circuitous) answers; no face-to-face conflict; respect for the natural order, relative environmental indifference; strong girlfriends ("iron flowers"), stronger wives, and fearsome mothers-in-law; a commercialized sex industry (with prices practically listed on menu boards); voracious consumerism; infatuation with neon; addiction to short text messaging (SMS) and on-line chat fixations; ultraviolent video games, cotton-candy pop music, Hello Kitty stickers, and kung fu flicks.

ECONOMIC DISCREPANCIES

Of course, the markets are structurally different. Most obviously, both Hong Kong and Taiwan are developed economies. (Hong Kong is finding its niche as a transaction facilitator—i.e., a go-between focusing on legal and financial services as well as logistics. Taiwan's forte is design/production of high-tech products.) China is still an emerging market. As a result, Taiwan and Hong Kong are years ahead in terms of brand familiarity and digestion of "challenging" campaigns. Although unfocused communication doesn't work anywhere, Mainland copy, no matter where and targeted to whom, must be dead simple. PRC audiences aren't "cognitively prepared" to process radically new ideas. People aren't willing to actively "figure out" creative advertising.

Second, despite its emerging status, China is a "scale" economy. Hong Kong and Taiwan are not. The result? The Mainland can afford mass media "thematic" copy—i.e., television and print brand-building advertising with sophisticated production values. Smaller markets tend to rely more on "tactical" (i.e., promotional) and "below-the-line" (i.e., non-mass media) programs. For example, Nike's Hong Kong marketing plan is dominated by "activation" efforts such as high school sponsorships, city marathons, and in-gym pushes. On the Mainland, those efforts, while still important, pale in comparison to the weight given to "Just Do It" television and print campaigns. (Due to the "tactical" nature of Hong Kong marketing, the city's range of point-of-purchase, outdoor, interactive, promotional, and event opportunities is impressive.)

Third, China's status as a *new*—as opposed to *emerging*—market also reinforces the need to stick to the basics—i.e., focus on *introducing* or *establishing* a brand's core proposition. Mainland consumers who reside in primary cities are familiar with fast-moving consumer goods (FMCG)—such as shampoo, soap, sanitary napkins, and soy sauce—brands. However, service brands are still foreign. (So is service.) Mobile networks, retail banks, credit cards, and investment companies are new advertisers. Likewise, luxury brands—from upscale cars to designer labels and watches—are largely undifferentiated. Together, they constitute a big blob of glitter. BMW, Mercedes, Jaguar, and even Audi are, for all intents and purposes, interchangeable. In Hong Kong and Taiwan, each has had the time to cultivate a distinct image.

HONG KONG: DESPERATE AMBITION

These "structural" differences are mostly self-evident, but what about psychological and behavioral motivations? Hong Kong, Chinese to its core, is both afflicted and powered by an economic-refugee mentality. The population exploded in 1949. In one fell swoop, millions of Mainlanders, desperate to escape Communism, besieged the city-state. Despite the presence of (an arrogant) British government and a well-oiled legal system based on Common Law, its people have never known security. The territory has lived on borrowed time, dependant on the kindness of strangers, be they Chinese or Western. Practically everyone over the age of thirty-five grew up poor in slum-like government housing estates, sometimes with families of 8 crowded into 120 square feet. "Honkies," as Hong Kong residents often call themselves, like their Mainland brethren, know how to *chi ku,* or, translated literally, "eat bitterness." All Chinese make it from one day to the next through sheer force of will. But, in Hong Kong, resources (especially land) have always been spectacularly scarce. Life was a daily struggle. Despite the territory's wealth (Hong Kong's per capita income is twice Taiwan's), it still is: Social Security doesn't exist, the gulf between rich and poor is enormous, its service-based economy is especially vulnerable to external shocks, real estate prices run hot and cold, people live in soulless skyscrapers—ant farms that dull the senses—and legal jurisdiction vis-à-vis the PRC is murky.

Hong Kong's collective insecurity belies extraordinary vigor. When things get grim—e.g., 1997's Asian financial crisis, 1997's Bird Flu, 2003's SARS epidemic, the aborted 1997–2005 Tung Chee-Hwa administration—Hong Kong steps up to the plate and defends itself. A Chinese adaptive instinct kicks in. (Even more admirably, the difficulties of the last several years have resulted in a new sense of community.) Hong Kongers are not visionaries or lateral thinkers but they are a resourceful, striving people. They play it one day at a time, conducting their lives *allegro con brio.* Therefore, relative to less harried Mainlanders, they are even more competitive, less obsessed with their global standing than the PRC (despite the Mainland's historic lack of linkages with the outside world), more "international," more confused about identity, more flexible, less long-term, more sophisticated, and less conceptual, more resourceful, and less revolutionary. In short, Hong Kong is a utilitarian roller coaster, a pragmatist's fun house. The city, like its brand landscape, lacks breadth, depth, and nuance but boasts snap, crackle, and pop. Just do it . . . quick, straight, and smart. Your advertising should, in a human way, reflect its citizens' impatient urge to progress in life or, in the words of Douglas Lai, SmarTone mobile network's CEO, to "move closer." But don't get hung up on anything philosophical (e.g., democracy). Keep it practical, close to the ground.

TAIWAN: CHINESE ASPIRATION MEETS AMERICAN DEFENSE

Hong Kong's history is a volatile mix of Chinese fatalism and refugee ambition. Taiwan's past is multifaceted, less black and white, and more politically charged. First populated by Austronesians, Mainlanders arrived, fleeing disaster, during the Ming and Qing dynasties. In the first half of the twentieth century, the island was colonized (and protected) by the Japanese. After Japan's defeat during the Second World War and the Kuomintang's (KMT) loss during the Chinese civil war, Taiwan was again flooded with immigrants. They were KMT refugees, more sophisticated than the Guangdong farmers who poured into Hong Kong during the same period. As the Communists' arch-enemies, Chiang Kai Shek and his ragtag army were embraced by an America obsessed with Red threats. The island prospered, first under dictatorship, then as a vibrant democracy. So what is Taiwan? How has its convoluted past affected its "Chineseness"? Less than one might think.

Taiwan's character is still entirely Chinese. The island has an isolation complex, not an identity crisis.

- First, and most obviously, Taiwan is an island. It is separated from the rest of Asia, and was (until recently) left to its own devices, culturally and economically.
- Second, until the late 1980s, the country was ruled by dictatorship, exacerbating an already reduced flow of information. (In 1984, the first McDonald's opened in Taipei. Hong Kong, a more globally connected city, discovered the Big Mac in 1975.) *Time* magazine was censored, sold with photos ripped from the pages. The arts scene was stifled and air-brushed into blandness. "Kuomintang capitalism"—i.e., the commingling of Party and financial interests in every sphere of business—spawned a bizarre blend of entrepreneurialism and kickbacks. Even the political scene was other-worldly and schizophrenic. On one hand, the KMT boldly insisted that it was the legitimate government of the Mainland. On the other, people lived in fear of invasion.
- Third, for the past one hundred years, first as a Japanese colony and then as a quasi-independent political entity, Taiwan has existed in limbo, neither a province of China nor an independent country.

Taken together, twenty-first-century Taiwan is an island in more than the physical sense of the word. A destiny-driven, insecurity-based, classically Chinese worldview cramps human interaction. Its people, individually warm and industrious, are "pure Chinese." They are protective safety seekers. (They are also projective status seekers.) For example, the leaders of the advertising industry surround themselves with lackeys whose loyalty is absolute. Talent matters less than obeisance. Taiwanese bosses, like their Mainland counterparts, rule by fear. They encourage factionalism as a bulwark against competitive power centers. The CEO—i.e., the emperor—wields absolute power. Only he maintains a holistic understanding of goings-on, so underlings have no choice but to curry paternalistic favor. Individualism, independent thinking, and rebellion against convention have no productive value.

The Chinese "protection" instinct, however, has been productively turbocharged by the island's "dynamic isolation." Taiwan has benefited hugely from its ambiguous national identity; it remains sheltered by the ideals and arms of America. Separation has made the island "safe" enough to embrace democracy and other reforms. (Rule of law has created a real sense of civility. On the street, there's no dog-eat-dog feeling. People queue up in an orderly manner. Taipei is dotted with lovely restaurants and bars, refreshing oases of humanity.) Taiwanese, like their increasingly organization-based Mainland cousins, are able to "experiment." They are adept at (collectively) demolishing dysfunctional "paradigms" and erecting new ones.

- The country is on the vanguard of a restructured advertising industry. Taiwan was the first to consolidate media buying and planning by pulling it away from creative agencies
- It has forged a new-fangled, high-tech partnership with the Mainland. (Taiwan is China's number two investor. Hong Kong is number one.) In recent years, Taiwan has confounded skeptics who insisted that it was doomed to become a hollowed-out IT sector. During recent years, patent applications have risen several fold. The country's industrial base is increasingly value-added.
- The island's economy boasts several sectors (e.g., broadcast media, financial services) that have, like magic, morphed from oligarchic dead zones to deregulated hotspots.
- With the exception of South Korea, Taiwan's shift from authoritarianism to free-wheeling representation in less than a decade has no historic equivalent.

The small island of Taiwan, in a quintessentially Chinese fashion, made the most of an opportunity—in this case, the window to the world opened by Cold War pragmatism and American idealism. Taiwan's political transformation bodes well for the ability of both the island and—eventually—the Mainland to amaze the world.

In the end, Hong Kong remains restlessly agitated, economically and politically insecure. As a result, it is not innovative but maintains a "dynamically short-term" orientation, a staccato anxiety. Taiwan, on the other hand, has benefited from an American aegis and, despite its mongrel political heritage, boasts a sense of self that has unleashed self-sufficient innovation. When push comes to shove, however, the Mainland, Taiwan, and Hong Kong are, first and foremost, Chinese, three components of a truly great Greater China.

PART II

THE
FUNDAMENTALS
OF
RELEVANT
CHINA STRATEGIES

CHAPTER 7

SOFT TOUCH AND HARD CASH

THE IRON LINK BETWEEN INSIGHT AND PROFIT

In the PRC, if marketers don't understand the motivations of the Chinese consumer, their products will die a quick and painful death.

CHINA'S GREATEST DANGER

Many economists believe that China's most daunting structural challenge is production overcapacity. Still bloated by the hangover left by a lingering command economy and saddled with commercial dregs churned out by state-assisted, walking-dead outfits, China is awash with goods. From televisions to mobile phones and automobiles, the PRC's industrial landscape is littered with the casualties of price wars and negligible profit margins. The central government, acutely concerned about maintaining social stability, struggles to sustain an industrial engine lifting the living standards of 1.3 billion people. Falling prices, however, will lead to layoffs. Sector-specific deflation, ultimately a result of "commoditization," is a curse on brands differentiated only on price, not quality or emotional appeal.

Matei Mihalca, an acquisitions expert working on the Mainland, believes the landscape's structural inefficiency has resulted in precarious balance sheets for many companies. "There are a large number of companies competing ferociously. They drive costs down to a suicidal level. Invariably, there's some protection from local governments, banks, or simply a moral hazard that keeps them alive." Most large local enterprises do have, to say the least, opaque book keeping practices, leading some observers to speculate that even the so-called power brands—Changhong, Konka, Midea, Gree, Aux, Galanz—are rotting with terrible financials. Appliance manufacturer Little Swan, for example, was recently acquired by a Nanjing-based conglomerate, SWT. The reason? Fiscal vulnerability and operational rigidity. In the West, when firms compete only on price, their profits sink, they go belly-up and then someone swiftly steps in and buys. However, the framework for the reconstitution of corporate activity isn't in place in China. Companies don't fail. There is no survival of the fittest, only survival. The resulting fragmentation is an important feature of corporate China, and there doesn't appear to be a *breakneck* trend toward a more consolidated market structure.

Companies that hope to escape fiscal purgatory have no choice but to end the vicious cycle of plummeting prices and surging red ink. They must: (a) build consumer loyalty, (b) forge a *sustainable* price premium, and (c) reinvest profits in future growth. Any manufacturer who thinks otherwise is doomed. The only way of escaping the market's ruthless jaws is to grasp the difference between "products" (i.e., things pumped out of factories) and "brands" ("friends" actively desired and preferred by consumers). The only way to build a brand is to invest in compelling communications rooted in a fundamental consumer insight.

All effective advertising, without exception, springs from an insight. A "brand vision"—i.e., a brand's long-term identity—is a combination of a unique product attribute and consumer desire. Most Chinese companies are skilled at highlighting the former; all too often, however, they ignore the latter, ending up with communications that are more about what manufacturers sell than what buyers demand.

WHAT'S AN INSIGHT?

Insights are not observations. Observations are records of what people say or do. Observations tend to be coldly statistical. (E.g., "Chinese women wash their hair, on average, three times per week. Japanese women use shampoo twice a day.") Or they can be aloof and journalistic, quoting what people say ("My life is stressed because I don't have enough time") without uprooting underlying causes of why they say what they say ("I'm stressed because I feel guilty about not being there for my children").

Insights, on the other hand, are fundamental motivations for behavior and preferences. Insights answer the question, "Why?" Why are Chinese men willing to spend a year's income on a new car? Why are most Chinese women unwilling to spend two days' salary on premium underwear? Why do insubstantial boy bands such as F4 intoxicate new-generation youth as equally well as Faye Wong's rebellious lyricism? Why are Shanghainese men so willing to buck against tra-ditional definitions of masculinity by assuming kitchen duty?

HOW TO DIG OUT INSIGHTS:
QUALITATIVE RESEARCH AND THE CONSUMER BUYING SYSTEM

Quantitative research, by definition, is incapable of unearthing a "golden nugget," an epiphany that elucidates buying behavior. Data are empirical—medians, standard deviations, and regressions to the mean. Insights, on the other hand, are *alive*. They connect with individuals' lives and, therefore, can be articulated only after talking with consumers, living with them, or actually leading their lives. They are the product of both qualitative, in-depth research and disciplined, analytic probing.

Insights allow a consumer to reach into communications. They transform profit-driven manufacturers into trusted partners, friends with whom heart-to-heart dialog can take place. They are the seeds from which full-bodied brands, not trademarks or logos, grow. They transform advertising from mind-numbing thirty-second propaganda pieces into communications relevant enough to linger into and beyond the thirty-first second. They are the roots of copy that actively engages consumers, the messages powerful enough to "buy consumers' time."

To repeat: insights are not observations. Observations record what people say or do. Insights are fundamental motivations for behavior and preferences. Yes, insights are gleaned from in-depth discussion with consumers and subse-quent analysis. However, a grasp of how consumers progress through buying decisions can provide a useful *structure* for information digestion. Such under-standing illuminates an individual's outlook as he or she moves from awareness of a need to handing over a credit card at the cash register. The consumer buy-ing system has six stages, as shown in the table 7.1.

Every product has its own buying process. Of course, they are not all the same; some are simple and others are complex. Soap versus new homes reflects different degrees of category risk and involvement. Unmarried females and mothers with kids (i.e., two discrete targets) have different needs satisfied by, say, pets. But, in all cases, a target's attitudes toward a given brand and/or cat-egory can be revealed via a grasp of the buying process.

HOW MANY INSIGHTS ARE THERE?

One. More precisely, for every combination of a single product category (e.g., SUV vehicles) and a unique market target (e.g., middle-income men who are

Table 7.1: The Consumer Buying System

Stage	What We Call It	What Marketers Call It	What It Is	An Illustration: Upscale Autos
One	Trigger	Category Motivation	A consumer's motivation for entering a category in the first place	Material display; comfort; demonstration of success
Two	Consider	Frame of Reference	All product categories that the consumer feels could satisfy the category motivator	Luxury cars, a limousine service, first class on commuter trains
Three	Search	Information Sort	Once a decision has been made to enter the category, how information on brand options is gathered	Internet, print, and television advertising, friends' recommendations, dealer literature, test drives
Four	Choose	Brand Discrimination	How an individual consumer differentiates between and ranks the importance of brand options within a given category	Price, "hand crafted interiors," "German engineering reliability," "streamlined chassis," "sex appeal"
Five	Buy	Point-of-Sale Impact	The intersection of preference and financial considerations, leading to a monetary transaction	"I was going to go for the Lexus but then the Audi dealer offered me a zero percent financing offer I couldn't refuse."
Six	Experience	Post-Purchase Reinforcement	How a consumer gauges satisfaction with his selection	"For a German car, it sure needs a lot of repair work. Thank goodness for the warranty."

bored with their daily professional routines), there is one fundamental motivator (e.g., escaping the boundaries of "my conventional existence" without "breaking the rules").

Another example:

- The category: insurance.
- The market target: Western young adults, most of whom do not buy insurance.

- The insight: "Life is an adventure. I am concerned about getting what I want from daily existence. I don't need to think about my health or tomorrow."

And another:

- The category: insurance.
- The market target: western older adults.
- The insight: "I am conflicted. On one hand, I am afraid of being helplessly alone when I am vulnerable and sick. On the other hand, I want to maintain the independence I've treasured since I was young."

And, finally, one more:

- The category: insurance.
- The marketing target: Chinese older adults.
- The insight: "I don't want my illness to prevent my children from focusing on my grandchild's future success."

As the above illustrations demonstrate, one category can play radically different roles in various consumers' minds. The product itself, often virtually identical, triggers different emotional urges depending on which consumer is targeted. However, each segment, properly defined, is motivated by a key insight. "Multiple" insights are illusions and signal:

1. A clumsily and broadly defined market target (e.g., all homemakers versus ones who resent leaving the job market or define themselves vis-à-vis husbands' success);
2. Confusion between insight and observation;
3. Confusion between related ideas within a single area.

A category leader, by definition, owns the category benefit within the broadest possible (meaningful) market segment:

- Cheese. Nutrition. Moms. Kraft.
- Sedans. Status. Upscale men. Buick (in China).
- Business computers. Networking. Purchasing department. IBM.
- Sports shoes. Self-expression (China). Youth. Nike.
- Sexual aids. Potency. Older men. Viagra.

So what can be done if a competitor already owns the category "driver"? As hinted above, the target should be narrowed and then the category benefit can be redefined. For example, cars mean status to all Chinese men. However, older men drive to celebrate achievement while younger ones broadcast their debut as legitimate "players" destined for future success. All women want beautiful hair. But less wealthy women want "natural beauty" while middle-class ones hope for "beauty that makes me look and feel like a star." All food must taste good and please the family. But working mothers must balance their "daily expression of love" with a convenience imperative. Stay-at-home moms, on the other hand, regard meal time as an opportunity to "achieve" or "impress."

GREAT INSIGHTS

Compelling insights touch the heart and resolve struggle. They probe the contours of the soul. Skilled marketers instinctively recognize that emotions are complex, often contradictory. We hope and fear. We look back for comfort and forward with ambition. Our passions of love and hate can be directed at the same individual. Self-esteem, a function of countless variables, fluctuates between confidence and self-deprecation, often during a single business meeting. In short, human desires run the gamut. Products emerge, standardized, from a factory. But we sell products to people. The best insights recognize conflict; they assuage anxiety caused by competing interests and instincts.

The Balancing Act of Women

For example, today's Chinese woman is conflicted, torn between polarized societal expectations of aggressively "holding up half the sky" and empathetically nurturing the family. These tensions are exacerbated by a tantalizing new aspiration: individualism. In short, she is caught between three seemingly incompatible goals, two of them imposed by a regimented social structure and the third by the individual herself. Marketers, consequently, should help her balance competing demands by allowing her to:

1. Navigate through "life stages," periods across which the force of individual motivations vary;
2. Achieve a marriage that is both "stable" and passionate;
3. Succeed without forfeiting graceful femininity;
4. Obtain "third-party endorsements" from role models;
5. Escape the conflicting demands of society.

The Anxiety of Men

Chinese men, on the other hand, are caught between a narrowly defined concept of success (monetary and professional) and a broadly entrepreneurial path to get there. In dynastic times, the standards of success were equally rigid but the path to success was meticulously laid out and ultimately within the control of the individual. Capitalistic reforms have splintered the regimented ladder to the top; success is now more a question of pioneering spirit than sheer determination. Once advertisers grasp that their primary goal is to assuage "testosterone-fueled anxiety," they can help a "new man" by:

1. Projecting his status;
2. Releasing his aggression;
3. Empowering him with coping tools;
4. Giving hints on how to "pass the woman test";
5. Reinforcing a sense of competent expertise outside work.

Middle Class Contradictions

Among the "new urban elite," China's millennia-old dynastic and Confucian culture has resulted in apparent contradictions that need to be carefully managed by marketers. The newly affluent are characterized by a mindset that blends an aggressive hunger for social and financial advancement and a rigid, hierarchical social structure that rewards conservatism. As a result, the Chinese psyche has always been torn between the two poles of ambition and caution. Chinese are torn by a desire to both *project* individual status and *protect* family welfare. They are motivated by both a dynamic and impulsive *now* orientation versus a stable and balanced *future* focus. Marketers can resolve middle-class tensions by:

1. Enhancing the salience of publicly displayed items;
2. "Activating" status so that it is a tool, "paying dividends" to facilitate forward momentum;
3. Ensuring that ambitiously aspirational items are also comfortingly accessible;
4. Positioning the home as a "fortress" of self-expression and escape;
5. "Presenting" the child as both an investment for the future and a proud reflection of family well-being;
6. Managing the trick of showing off while not appearing to show off (i.e., "can I help it if they happened to notice me . . . ?").

Mass Market Polarization

Unlike the middle class, China's great urban mass market has not directly benefited from the sweep of economic reform. Therefore, their lives are more fear-based, a struggle to get through each day without falling off a cliff. Daily existence is a grind, never-ending anxiety from which the Everyman and Everywoman seek transcendent release. So, the primal urges of China's mass market are polarized as well. Their hearts and minds are pulled in opposite directions: ensuring physical survival versus imagining—dreaming, hoping against hope—about a better tomorrow. To establish a bond with the urban mass, marketers should address at least one of these need states or, better yet, reconcile the two, turning survival into glory. This can be achieved by:

1. Establishing a brand of reassurance, the key not to advancement but continued existence;
2. Reinforcing the solidity of the family, a bulwark against chaos and the agony of ostracism;
3. Transforming lowly bargain hunting into a demonstration of quick-witted intelligence, the most precious adaptive personality trait;
4. Glorifying the mundane by celebrating even the most modest victory;
5. Regaining balance by indulging in a (larger-than-life) "fantasy of control."

INSIGHTS AND BRANDS

Insights hit the sweet spot of desire. From the consumer's perspective, they give a brand a clear reason for existence. A brand's long-term identity (or "brand vision") should be a seamless combination of user motivation and brand attribute. If the latter exists at the expense of the former, communications will resemble corporate PR, not consumer-driven advertising. (Some examples of successful brand visions appear in table 7.2 and in the following chapter.)

Creative expression, of course, reflects a brand vision that—one last time— is rooted in an insight. And great communications (i.e., copy consumers love and feel bonded with) is the key to long-term loyalty.

Table 7.2: Linking Insight and the Brand Vision

Brand	Market Target	Category Insight	Unique Brand Attribute	Brand Vision
Smarties Chocolates	All adult women	Release from stress	Bright colors	"Colorful Indulgence"
Nutrigrain Cereal	Australian young men	Physical fitness as key romantic "weapon"	Iron supplement	"Testosterone in a Box"
Mellow Bird Coffee	English low-income adults	Optimistic start to the day	Cheap price, weak taste	"Proud to be Mild"
Ford Escape SUV	Taiwanese businessmen	Escaping the monotonous convention of everyday professional life	Bold chassis, road "hug"	"Tough Car, Rugged Life"

CHAPTER 8

THE BRAND VISION

THE SOUL OF THE MACHINE

In the previous chapters, we established that a consumer insight is not an observation. In this short chapter, we reinforce the critical importance—in China and, for that matter, anywhere—of a compelling brand vision. In short, a brand vision is all about consistency of message. It is the seamless union of a product selling point and consumer insight. Despite the sweeping changes underway in today's PRC, a stable strategy—positioning—remains a vital competitive advantage on the Chinese battlefield.

First, there are very few brands—particularly local ones—that do not hopscotch from benefit to benefit every six months, with virtually no common thread on either a creative or strategic level. This is a gigantic wasted opportunity, a life preserver thrown out of reach on the media airwaves. Given the explosion of media, lifestyle opportunities, brand opportunities, and product selection, consumers are confused. Their minds are jumbled, overflowing with choice. Good times have never been so intimidating. Fully realized brands, essentially organizing concepts that "cluster" the product universe, are actively sought out by the titillated yet dazed new generation.

Second, coherent brand identities can save lots and lots of money. Although China's per capita income is still much lower than practically every market of note, media costs are frightfully expensive, particularly in the "primary" cities of Beijing, Shanghai, Guangzhou, and Shenzhen. (The lack of targeted television programming is the key reason that prices, on a cost per thousand basis, are the same as in London or Paris. When you buy into a prime show, you basically reach the entire population—young and old, hip and stodgy, rich and poor—whether you want to or not.) Consistency of vision is akin to getting to know a boyfriend or girlfriend better each time you go out to dinner. If your romantic life is a series of first dates, the amount you spend in restaurants will be greater than if you stick with the same lover. Media buying operates in much the same way as the spousal hunt. It is much more expensive to introduce a new message that builds on existing perceptions. There is a price gap between "launching" and "sustaining" media bursts.

Observations coldly record what people say or do. Insights, on the other hand, answer the question, "Why?" Insights shed light on fundamental motivations for behavior and preferences and illuminate basic psychological drivers. Therefore, they encompass desires far beyond the terrain of the product itself. A brand vision forges a strategic connection between the heart of a human being and a "thing" (i.e., the product) that is pumped out of a factory.

People are complex. They have anxiety, drive, and desire—sexual and otherwise. They are both nostalgic and resentful of the past; they are both hopeful and fearful of the future. They are pulled between practicality and impulse. Their egos are shaped by the tension between self-satisfaction and society's mandate. A product, on the other hand, is simple. It has weight and color and heritage and ingredients. A product (quite apart from a "brand") has a "cost of goods." It is a physical, heartless object, just a couple levels above beans or petroleum. As a result, a marketer's fundamental challenge is to position this "thing" as value-added, more than the sum of its parts. He or she must fashion armor to repel the devastating impact of profit's most potent enemy: commoditization. The brand vision, the iron link between product and people, is the lynchpin of sustainable, healthy corporate growth.

The brand vision is a product's long-term identity. It is not an advertising tagline, and it is not a benefit statement on a creative brief. Instead, a vision is the strategic soul of a brand. It does not change over time. The vision can mature, of course; it can grow; it can ripen, becoming richer and more multidimensional, just as people do. When Chinese parents name their child with one of two characters, they "stamp" the newborn with their hopes and dreams for his or her future, the first and most critical step in forging identity. A name never changes and personality stays consistent over time. Of course, as the child matures through adolescence, young adulthood, and old age, the individual evolves and outlooks shift. However, the essential character and drivers of a human being are fixed. The same must be true for a brand vision.

Let's take some examples. In Taiwan, Ford's Escape is the most popular SUV. Since launch, its vision has been "tough car, rugged life." While pithy, this four-word phrase is the brand's DNA, the invisible blueprint behind every television ad, promotion, auto show display, and test-driver premium. "Rugged life" is an encapsulation of the consumer insight motivating our market target, men who have achieved a degree of success by "safely" navigating a regimented, anti-individualistic social structure yet resist thinking of themselves as "conventional sell-outs." "Rugged car" is, obviously, the product component. It glorifies the bold chassis, superior drivability (i.e., ability to overcome obstacles on the road and haul heavy loads), and overall "maleness" of the model. When consumer desire and product point of difference are seamlessly merged into one thought, the result is an ownable, powerful, in-market position of unconventional masculinity, rooted in product performance.

In China, Nestlé's ice cream brand vision, "*sensational* escape," is the strategic core of the now-famous multiyear Ice Genie campaign, a communications program that has succeeded in decelerating the rise of Unilever's Walls, a juggernaut wielding a colossal media budget. On a functional level, ownable product attributes twist or "spike" non-discriminating creamy "sensuality" by highlighting Nestlé's unique combination of ingredients within individual variants. "Escape," of course, is a reflection of consumer desire. The PRC is experiencing relentless change and an explosion of lifestyle opportunities. The (optimistic) new generation, therefore, craves a break—just a moment of release—from the hyperkinetic merry-go-round.

A great brand vision—remember, we're not talking taglines here!—has three characteristics. First, it must be short, no more than four or five words (or eight Chinese characters). Within a corporation, various constituencies—marketers, the sales force, management, research and development, etc.—must focus energies on strengthening a brand's consumer franchise. Therefore, they should speak a common, simple language, not the jargon-laden prose of a marketing textbook. Since 1997, Unicharm's Sofy feminine napkin—number one in the market—has leveraged a two-word vision: "freedom protection." It's short, yes, but loaded with meaning. "Protection" underscores the brand's superior leakage prevention (versus P&G Whisper's absorption benefit) and its one-of-a-kind Side Gatherer barrier. "Freedom" springs from an aspiration of Chinese women to move ahead in life—even succeed in a traditionally male sense—rather than accept their current lot.

Second, to capture the flavor and personality of a brand, its vision statement must be not only short but also evocatively written. Australia's most successful breakfast cereal, Nutrigrain is "testosterone in a box," a daily dose of iron that fuels strength, masculinity, and victory. Until its recent decision to pursue a more therapeutic strategy, Cadbury's Halls mint candy's essence was a "refreshment assault," a taste so powerfully cooling it "knocks you off your feet and propels you into a world of surreal sensation."

Third, the best brand visions are unexpected. A vision, by definition, must combine consumer desire and product differentiation, but superior ones merge the dimensions in an unanticipated manner. An element of strategic surprise is invaluable in ensuring in-market distinction as well as owning a territory that is both relevant and resistant to competitive assault. Consumers will actively embrace a novel juxtaposition. The vision of the UK's largest low-priced coffee, Mellow Bird, is "proud to be mild." ("Proud" reflects the working class' demand for respect, despite its position at the bottom of a historically static social structure. "Mild," the functional component, is a clever way of leveraging the brand's weak taste.) "Proud" is big, bold, extroverted, confident, and buzzing with energy. "Mild" is soft, unassuming, modest, understated, and quietly resourceful. These two facets are rarely associated with one another, let alone fused as the core elements of brand architecture. But, in this instance, their marriage makes perfect sense, given the Mellow Bird's physical characteristics and the aspirations of its consumer franchise.

Within the diamond category, the Diamond Trading Company has achieved a 75 percent plus penetration rate in Beijing, Shanghai, and Guangzhou (up from less than 10 percent in the mid '90s) by ensuring that every promotion, product design, television campaign, and distributor activity reflects a vision of "eternal passion." "Passion" is transient, tempestuous, sexual, and immediate. "Eternity" is cool, conservative, civilized, and protracted. Yes, "passion" and "eternity" are strange bedfellows. But given the Chinese definition of an ideal marriage—a stable and harmonious union underwritten by romantic love—this unexpected combination hits the sweet spot of consumer desire.

A vision, although intangible and resistant to quantitative valuation, needs to be embraced by the entire corporation. It is more than a terse summary of an advertising creative brief; it should guide every dimension of a brand's existence from communications and pricing to promotions and product development. Every constituency must commit to the vision; resources must be mobilized to bring a few words to three-dimensional life—over time. Promoting and enriching a vision requires courage and discipline. An inspired and confident CEO will dedicate his organization to planting the seed of a brand's success.

CHAPTER 9

PORTFOLIO MANAGEMENT IN THE PRC

HOW AND WHEN TO EXTEND A BRAND

Building a new brand costs serious money in China, thanks to sky-high media costs and the proliferation of choice in virtually every consumer category. Consequently, owners of strong brands face the inevitable question of brand extension. How can one know whether or not it is appropriate to introduce new products under an existing brand name? When is it better to introduce a new brand altogether? This chapter will seek to provide some pointers on brand extension and portfolio management in China, using the Brand Vision as a criterion and guide.

THE ASIAN WAY

Much of Northeast Asia's success (and some current headaches) springs from economic models that focus on achieving economies of scale via aggressive horizontal and vertical integration. These models also signal implicit belief in risk diversification and maximization of potential revenue streams via supplying a wide range of goods (i.e., trans-category). This is best exemplified by Japan's *keiretsu*, somewhat similar to Korea's *chaebols*, which are modern incarnations of the Meiji era's *zaibatsu*—family controlled (and interlocked) conglomerates that fueled the country's industrialization during the nineteenth century. Without belaboring history, Japanese and Korean brands are gargantuan. (One of Hong Kong's most remarkable features is the presence of huge neon billboards on top of skyscrapers. They make the entire harbor look like a big shopping mall. The signage, however, shows only brand names [mostly Japanese], not benefit-driven visuals or even taglines.) Hitachi is both a trading company and a rice cooker manufacturer. Lotte sells chewing gum and operates department stores. Samsung produces both consumer electronics and semiconductors. (Only the Asian financial crisis prevented the company from further diversifying into automobiles.) Asia's industrial powerhouses of the late twentieth and early twenty-first centuries are built on the assumption that bigger is, in fact, better. Mega-brands rule. (Challengers do not.)

Chinese *consumers* are particularly willing to embrace brands that extend across disparate categories. China's largest companies, firmly guided and generously supported by the state, produce a huge variety of unrelated goods. For example, Chunlan manufactures both air conditioners and motorcycles. TCL sells everything from mobile phones to television sets. Maxam is both a toothpaste and a skin cream. In a 2003 study conducted by JWT, respondents indicated that they would have no problem accepting P&G baby food or milk, segments in which the company has absolutely no experience. There is, in general, a tendency to "delink" brand and category equity. Chinese have been conditioned not to trust brands that, until very recently, were pumped out of inefficient state-owned factories operating according to the edicts of a command economy. Size, in the minds of most, is still a surrogate indictor of the most basic level of quality: reliability. Given the high costs of launching brands on the Mainland, "extendability" can be wielded as a powerful platform for foreign companies to compete in a broader swath of categories than would be possible at home. This flexibility, however, can be abused. As a result, an important question remains: What are the principles of portfolio management?

CONSUMERS VERSUS MANUFACTURERS

This chapter is not an economic treatise on the microeconomic merits of scale versus (Western-oriented) specialization. However, it does strive to address the most taxing marketing issue that conglomerate-driven economies face: how to maximize efficiency by stretching a brand across products and categories without losing consumer relevance or appeal. While mammoth corporations tend to give birth to "reliable" or even "trusted" trademarks (e.g., Sony, Panasonic, Haier, Lenovo, TCL), they are very rarely fertile grounds for "loved" brands. Despite its need to export goods and alleviate the strains of overcapacity, China has never produced a McDonald's, Coca-Cola, or even Rejoice shampoo, all products with exceptionally strong consumer franchises.

Healthy brands offer a relationship between the consumer and manufacturer. They are the key to loyalty and, hence, higher price premiums. They are firmly rooted in a brand vision (i.e., long-term identity) that elegantly fuses the product's unique point of difference and the consumer's underlying need. They are the fruit of an empowered marketing team that has the know-how to address a compelling consumer insight, one that drives motivation and behavior. In short, beloved commercial icons "get" how a range of products fit into a consumer's life. Brands that extend across broad swaths of categories have a much more difficult time generating real consumer "velocity."

THE CHALLENGE: DIFFERENT STROKES FOR DIFFERENT FOLKS

Even within a single product category, customers' needs are often dramatically different and need to be satisfied differently. For example, carbonated soft drinks generally target three distinct market segments, each with unique consumption motivations. Kids look for fun, excitement, and sensory stimulation. Youth want something "cool" to make them popular with peers, and young adults are driven more by functional thirst-quenching refreshment. PepsiCo, as a result, markets three separate brands: Mirinda (kids), Pepsi (youth), and 7-Up (young adults).

Cognizant that "one size does not fit all," marketing-driven organizations leverage a range of different portfolio strategies. While Nokia relies on distinct mobile phone *models/variants*, Volkswagen has developed strong *subbrands* (e.g., Santana, Polo, and Passat). Rejoice, Head & Shoulders, and Pantene barely refer at all to their manufacturer, P&G. They are *stand-alone* brands.

THE OPPORTUNITY: ECONOMIES OF SCALE

As suggested above, creating distinct brands and subbrands is not cheap. (Media costs alone can be prohibitive.) To create one from scratch (e.g., Pepsi vs. Mirinda) is, naturally, more expensive than "stretching" an existing name (e.g., Nokia) to extend its appeal beyond its current franchise. In many cases, it can be done, but *carefully*.

For example, Citibank originally appealed to the mass market based on scale and presence ("The Citi Never Sleeps") but missed out on lucrative, high net worth individuals. But by later tapping into the insight that wealthy consumers demand special privileges and new services (e.g., no waiting, a personal banking manager, and private meeting spaces), the company efficiently launched an extension of the already-successful Citibank brand, CitiGold. In a different product universe, Lipton tea bags, used mainly by older, more traditional consumers, extended its powerful equity into younger (and more image-conscious) drinkers via Lipton Ice Tea. While the "Lipton yellow" unified the variants, Ice Tea now boasts a contemporary format and new flavors, some of them even carbonated.

Can your brand pull off a Citibank- or Lipton-like stretch? To determine whether its appeal can be extended to cover new products, three questions should be asked:

1. Is your trademark being forced to appeal to consumer segments with different category relationships/motivators?
2. What is your brand's "heritage" and is it relevant to an expanded product universe?
3. Are your new products targeting consumers within the same basic socioeconomic class?

TO STRETCH OR NOT (I): CONSUMER-CATEGORY RELATIONSHIP

A portfolio should be developed from a consumer—not manufacturer—perspective. As a first step, any multiproduct manufacturer must assess whether different consumer segments have different category relationships. If schisms are fundamental, the brand won't stretch.

Both China Unicom and China Mobile are obsessed with the adoption of the Code Development Multiple Access (CDMA) versus Global System for Mobile (GSM) network platforms and, in effect, have been investing hugely in establishing the two as different "products." But the vast majority of China's 300-million-plus mobile subscribers couldn't care less about whether they are using CDMA or the GSM communications. Customers care about their lives, and different customers have different needs—price versus service, local vs. national vs. international coverage, voice vs. data/SMS, and so on. The CDMA vs. GSM "brands" are artificial force fits; they don't reflect different segment drivers.

Likewise, shampoo consumers are not a monolithic block, and manufacturers bow to this reality. P&G is not a "brand" at all; rather, it functions more as a seal of quality reassurance. Head & Shoulders is targeted to the dandruff-avoider while Rejoice's core audience is men and women who want beautiful, soft hair. In retail, Lawson caters only to convenience-seekers (one small shop on every corner); Carrefour is targeted strictly to consumers who care about choice and price (one megastore in every district).

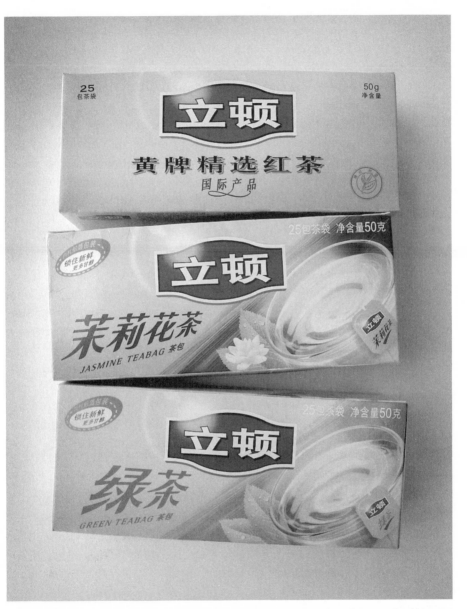

Fig. 9.1. Common graphic elements unify all variants across a power brand's range, in this case Lipton teas.

TO STRETCH OR NOT (II): BRAND HERITAGE

A company's historic equity will also determine the extent to which a brand can be extended. A basic example: Nike is a sports shoe MNC. While sports accessories and lifestyle apparel rest comfortably within the brand's footprint, high fashion certainly does not.

Within the information technology industry, IBM, Compaq, and Apple seem to grasp consumers'/customers' perceptions of their core competencies. IBM, boasting complex and "corporate" technology credibility, evolved from mainframes to servers/workstations and, only in the 1980s, desktops and laptops. Even today, IBM's service-driven position—"Solutions for a Small Planet"—is built around heavy-duty technology; PCs are no longer even part of their business, now that they sold off the entire division. Compaq, on the other hand, is first and foremost an end user (i.e., PC) brand. Yes, like IBM, Compaq sells servers, but, unlike IBM, it lacks the technological heft to penetrate the mainframe market and doesn't attempt to do so. Furthermore, Compaq has diversified into consumer-friendly handheld palmtops, territory "Big Blue" dares not enter. Both companies know who they are and what they can become.

Apple exudes an even more (digital) lifestyle equity. As a result, its "i" sub-brand (iMac, iBook, iPod, iPhoto, iMovie) can effortlessly weave throughout a stylishly contemporary target's home and play spaces. Its business applications are limited to creative-intense industries such as advertising, graphic, and product design.

Few high-tech companies strive to focus on both business and consumer markets, but the ones that do (Motorola, Acer) spin off sub- or stand-alone brands (Benq, Moto), despite heavy investment in the latter's creation.

TO STRETCH OR NOT (III): PREMIUM VS. MASS

Upscale products focus on high-margin per-customer revenue while the mass market is driven by low-margin scale. Divergent models are a reflection of fundamentally divergent *consumer* mindsets. Thus, the same brand will rarely appeal to both mass and premium segments.

Mass market Volkswagen is rooted in sturdy, reliable German engineering. Of course, a rather "nuts and bolts" core does not restrict the company to producing box-like utilitarian tanks. Indeed, Polo, Jetta, Bora, and Passat—all much more dynamic and youthful models than one would expect from "the car for the common folk"—leverage a very dominant Volkswagen heritage. However, to entice upscale consumers, the Audi logo makes its entrance, and the familiar circular VW logo fades into the woodwork. Toyota's Lexus brand springs from the same logic. In mobile phones, Nokia taps the ultra-premium niche with Vertu while Siemens used to push Xelibri.

BEYOND THE BRAND NAME

It's worth mentioning that once a decision has been made regarding how far to "stretch" a brand, care should be taken to ensure that a common vision unites the product portfolio. This Holy Grail can be achieved via a variety of elements from across the marketing mix. In no particular order, they include: usage of celebrities (e.g., across all Lux product forms), dominant graphic "signatures" for the products themselves (e.g., the curves of Apple computers and its "i" sub-brand range, the BMW radiator "grill," Nokia's shield-shaped face), packaging consistency (Lipton's yellow background and red logo [see Figure 9.1] and Marlboro's inverted triangles), "characters that integrate brand communications" (e.g., Colonel Sanders, the Singapore Girl, the Michelin and Marlboro men), and, critically, a consistent corporate/visual identity that covers the gamut from advertising, promotional material and internal communications (e.g., IBM's blue strip, the Dove silk ribbon, iPod's black silhouette).

Portfolio management requires a balance between achieving economies of scale through brand extension and accepting that a good thing can be taken too far. Brands are not putty. If you pull them too far, they might snap. Chinese companies such as Lenovo, Konka, and TCL are only now beginning to come to terms with the trade-off. But, with an eye on the consumer, savvy marketers optimize the value of a company's most valuable intangible asset—brand equity.

CHAPTER 10

ANTICIPATING THE PECULIARITIES OF CHINA'S MEDIA SCENE

Unlike our sister company, MindShare, JWT is not a media house. We earn revenue from developing advertising, not buying and planning television, radio, print, and outdoor schedules. However, the oddities of the PRC's media landscape are of great interest to many companies, particularly those who have not yet launched their products. The following briefly address the questions we are most frequently asked by clients.

WHAT MEDIA SHOULD I CHOOSE?

Television—with its sound, color, movement, ability to "break through" clutter and forge a brand's identity—is an indispensable tool in new, untamed markets. Despite the growth of mobile phone and Internet usage in the PRC, China is still a mass market. "Narrow casting" and TiVo do not pose a threat to mainstream advertising agencies. The thirty-second television commercial still rules and, contrary to conventional wisdom, it will continue to rule long after today's young generation ceases to be the New Generation. Other traditional mass vehicles—e.g., print and newspaper—are also critical components of most plans. The Middle Kingdom's media terrain remains "retro" for two reasons. First, newer, nontraditional choices are still in their infancy. Database-driven "customer relationship marketing" (CRM) is an unfulfilled promise, largely because target consumers' names, addresses, and telephone numbers cannot be identified. Most companies must generate their own "lists" from scratch. And other "below the line" tools such as retail management and sophisticated event management have not achieved critical mass. Why not? There's a limited pool of seasoned talent. To boot, distribution channels are highly fragmented.

More fundamentally, consumer choice, while still a new phenomenon, has experienced a Chinese Big Bang. The marketing universe is dynamic but unformed. In most cases, "equity drivers"—intangible associations that reinforce consumer loyalty and a sustainable price premium—have not yet been defined. Brands are organizing concepts that alleviate this disorientation. Print is important, too; it is "high involvement," ideal for fleshing out the details that support a brand proposition. (In all markets, newspaper is used primarily for promotional/tactical purposes. In China, reproduction quality is still a problem.) Is it impossible to forge a brand without mass media? No. For example, Nestle has done just that with its 1 renminbi (RMB) chocolate wafer (see later section). But if a marketer relies too heavily on "below the line," he or she faces an uphill battle.

IS MEDIA EXPENSIVE?

Yes, it is expensive. On a cost per thousand basis (CPM, or expenditure required to reach 1,000 people), television prices are similar to those of many Western cities, despite dramatically lower disposable incomes (Beijing is especially expensive.) Overdelivery is the culprit behind this. PRC television does not have many programs that attract distinct audiences. There is no Chinese equivalent of *Sex in the City*, a multiyear series that developed a narrow but passionate following within the Blue State (female) urban elite. In the United States, *Will & Grace* is popular with younger, wealthier, more liberal adults; *Everyone Loves Raymond*, on the other hand, attracted a more conservative and less wealthy audience. Constrained by all-powerful censors and usually limited to a maximum of twenty-four episodes, Chinese programming is bland, a blur of politically correct shows that neither provoke nor intrigue. China's cable menu is not yet "nichified." There is no History Channel, no Lifetime, no Nickelodian, and no ESPN. TV fare regresses towards the mean, resulting in tremendous waste. Although you may be targeting only college-educated men aged twenty-five to thirty-five, your advertising will also be seen by their fathers, sisters, and wives. And, unfortunately, you will be charged for every eyeball. (Print titles *are* quite varied and appeal to well-defined segments. However, local/regional buys are impossible, resulting in geographic—as opposed to demographic—overdelivery.)

Finally, despite the proliferation of television channels over the past decade, China remains a seller's market. Demand for airtime is constantly on the upswing, with real annual growth rates in the 15 to 20 percent range. To boot, during the past five years, all television stations *within* key cities have centralized sales. The Shanghai Media Group (SMG), a media powerhouse consisting of twelve television channels and numerous print publications, is a monopoly.

Yes, media is expensive. If funding is not sufficient, launches should be: (1) reconsidered or (2) conducted as a test market in two or three second-tier cities. Hangzhou, for example, shares many of Shanghai's demographic characteristics. But, due to its relatively small population, airtime is a fraction of the price.

HOW MUCH WILL IT COST TO ADVERTISE?

It depends on which and how many cities you want to hit. A solid (but not extravagant) one-year plan that covers the three "primary clusters" of Beijing, Shanghai, and Guangzhou will require an investment of anywhere between four and six million dollars. (These figures apply to ads for consumer goods, not business-to-business products.) The specific amount will depend on the use of secondary media such as print and outdoor. (Caution: bus shelter space is high-quality but very expensive, sometimes almost as much as TV.) If you extend coverage to include ten to fifteen relatively wealthy but smaller coastal cities such as Qingdao, Dalian, Xiamen, Hengzhou, or Suzhou, count on an incremental $1.5–$2.5 million. If coverage expands to more than twenty-five or thirty cities, it is time to consider using national channels (Chinese Central Television) in at least some of your buy, increasing the total tab to at least $10 million. (P&G, a company boasting deep distribution and an expansive sales network, became CCTV's largest customer in 2005.)

China's television market consists of three, not two, tiers: national, provincial, and local. In America and most European countries, there are only national and local options. Identifying the optimal mix or balance between three levels is a sophisticated analytic undertaking and must be managed by specialized buying and planning companies such as MindShare, Zenith, or Starcom. Failure to do so will result in inefficient media strategies that literally waste millions.

WHAT ABOUT THE MEDIA BROKERS?

They are ubiquitous and can negotiate great bargains and have unbeatable, deep, local connections. Brokered deals, usually greased by kickbacks, offer discounts of up to 70 percent versus listed prices ("book rates"). International media agencies obtain discounts of only 20 to 30 percent.

That said, two very important risks must be considered before playing the brokerage game. First, there are no *national* brokers. Their local deals *can* be quite efficient, but multicity or national buys should be handled by a reputable media network. Second, brokered discounts are calculated based on the number of times a commercial appears on television. Marketers have very little control over when, where, or how a spot appears. This explains the frustrating phenomenon of the same ad appearing many times during one commercial break. In short, it is not difficult to make an empirical case that a professionally planned schedule saves money both short- and long-term, hence the breakneck growth of Western media outfits.

WILL CHINA'S MEDIA ENVIRONMENT LIBERALIZE?

No, it will not liberalize. It is true that, according to WTO stipulations, China must increase the number of foreign films allowed in local theaters. In addition, the State is no longer subsidizing many money-losing small local and regional newspapers, mostly Party mouthpieces. And major media vendors such as Chinese Central Television (CCTV) have recently adopted practices such as open bids and compensation to advertisers when programs do not achieve ratings projections. However, as long as the Communist government remains in power, control over mass communication will remain strictly controlled, despite the presence of an "international" patina. There may even be a trend toward further consolidation, particularly in television negotiation. Yes, print titles will continue to multiply but nothing provocative will appear at newsstands. The China edition of *Maxim* will be a tame affair. *Newsweek*'s new Mainland version is laughably apolitical. Furthermore, it is hard to imagine how media companies such as News Corporation, Viacom, or Time Warner will ever be permitted to operate even quasi-independently. Instead, their presence will be constrained, limited to bland coproductions or spin-off events such as Star TV's Channel V Music Awards. (A few foreign media outlets such as Star TV's Phoenix channel have obtained the rights to air in Southern Guangdong. But these deals are little more than PR coups. They are allowed only because the province already receives spicy "spillover" programming from Hong Kong. The door to the Mainland is, and will remain, closed.)

WRAP UP

In conclusion, as you prepare to stake a claim to the Mainland's bounty, please remember:

1. China is still a mass media market. Brands are new and alternative marketing tools are relatively undeveloped.
2. Relative to other emerging markets, media is expensive. This is unavoidable and largely due to wastage that occurs when spots are aired in nondifferentiated programming.
3. If you do not have enough money for a multicity or national plan, consider a test market launch before investing in larger, more expensive cities.
4. Avoid media brokers unless volume is dominated by a few key cities.
5. Resign yourself to a future of heavy regulation, strict censorship, and monopolistic or oligopolistic prices. The Party will not allow meaningful liberalization of the media sector.

CHAPTER 11

HOW TO LEVERAGE THE GLORY OF BEIJING 2008

For foreign enterprises, the Beijing Olympics represent a very big opportunity. There is not much faith in the government's ability to throw a party devoid of Orwellian overtones, not to mention local corporations' willingness to "de-politicize" marketing units prior to the Games (see chapter 14). However, if MNCs implement a long-term, market-driven strategy, 2008's potential is huge.

Two questions spring to mind. First, how does a savvy company avoid pouring its advertising and promotion budget down the drain in the midst of what is sure to be the most orgiastic, cluttered spending extravaganza in commercial history? Second, are the Olympics important to Chinese consumers and, if so, why? To address the first question, we must begin by answering the second.

DO THEY CARE?

The Chinese care enormously about the Games. Public support for the Beijing Olympics runs deep, and it is universal. The recent political slugfest in New York over a proposed stadium *cum* 2012 Olympic arena was, to PRC apparatchiks, a petty little affair. Beijing is *literally* being rebuilt, and the entire public is cheering, despite a traffic situation that would turn even the most ardent Jets fan into a twitchy mass of putty. 2008 is more than modern China's debut on the world stage. It is more than an acknowledgement of the nation's rightful place as a budding superpower, soon shoulder to shoulder with the United States, astride the globe. It is even more than a confirmation of a new glorious era, the end of the eclipse that has enveloped China since the Opium War.

As discussed earlier, "culture," not Buddhism or Communism, remains China's spiritual adhesive. It transcends any doctrine or "ism," for it ensures survival. The rise of an Olympics-worthy China validates the Middle Kingdom's entire worldview and confirms, in no particular order, the ebb and flow of history, the cyclical essence of *yin* and *yang*, as well as a fresh Mandate of Heaven. Beijing 2008 represents a vindication of Han culture.

Therefore, a successful Olympics—i.e., positive PR in both media and political circles—will yield a confident China, one less inclined to stir up trouble abroad. A country's most potent asset is a strong national identity. From the Philippines' destructive "crab mentality" (*schadenfreude* elevated to a boardroom blood sport) to the swath of authoritarian Southeast Asia still burdened with postcolonial resentment, an insecure country is an unproductive country. After the Olympics, China will be haunted by fewer demons. The PRC, never an expansionist power, will finally smile, brightened by a belief that the external world, at least for the next few decades, poses no threat. At last, a confident Middle Kingdom can emerge from its self-protective cocoon. It will look up and out, no longer toward shielding itself from indignity or worse. It will become a modern member of the international community, no longer baring the teeth of a frightened mother bear. (We hope.)

The unloading of historical baggage will ensure Chinese consumers' *huge* emotional investment in the Games. They will actively embrace MNCs who boast *integrated, insightful, China-centric* sponsorship strategies. Chinese ego repression ensures that individual identities are linked to national pride. All strands of Chinese culture—Confucianism, Legalism, and Daoism—deemphasize the individual. Yet both Confucianism and Deng Xiao Ping's "to get rich is glorious" mandate put a premium on (state-endorsed) achievement. The vast majority of Chinese, particularly younger and wealthier ones, are caught between two mutually exclusive goals: standing out and fitting in. Chinese ambition is restrained by convention. Individual identities are smothered, burdened by layers of suppressed expression. In this context, Brand China—i.e., nationalism—is seized en masse as the ultimate identity surrogate. Therefore, the Olympics reflect not only the nation's potential but also "my own greatness." Beijing 2008 will be epic motivational therapy. It will touch Chinese individuals at the deepest, most personal level. It is, therefore, a much better tie-in vehicle than *Star Wars: Revenge of the Sith.*

HOW TO CONNECT

So how can the Olympics best be leveraged? Marketers must tap into the emotions that will swell in advance of, and throughout, the Games. Avoid the limpness signaled by the phrase, "Official sponsor of Beijing 2008." The Olympics can make your brand "a friend of China," the best designation of all. Here are six ways to do this:

Don't forget China

2008 boasts two massive audiences: Chinese (Mainland, Hong Kong, Taiwan, and overseas Chinese) and global spectators. Perennials like Visa tend to run the same campaigns everywhere and now elicit yawns. Your global Olympic strategy, even if you're a global Top Olympic Promoter (TOP) sponsor, will require tailoring—even radical reconstruction—to achieve the optimal "China effect." The Games celebrate humanity, a relevant calling everywhere. But, in China, they're also about super-sized nationalism and personal self-esteem.

Don't go soft and fuzzy

Do not get overly sentimental about the Games. Applaud achievement, victory, stars, and advancement. Embrace forward momentum. Kindness and dignity are lovely but, in a land where human rights are an abstraction, messages must hit home hard. Chinese revere (and fear) *winners*. (Losing members of the Olympic team still feel obligated to apologize to the Motherland for their inadequacy.) Directly link your product to the conquering spirit of victors. Olympics celebrate heroes, not dreamers. Health clubs shape your body for success, not life enjoyment. Yili milk doesn't just make you fit. It enables you to swim faster and study harder. It is a pity the Chinese do not like cold cereal. "Wheaties. Breakfast of Champions" would be a hit. (And cosmetic surgery, by the way, bolsters marketability during job interviews, not self-esteem.)

Do not underestimate local companies

Although PRC enterprises are sports marketing neophytes, a nationalistic impulse is second nature. Lenovo, Li Ning (the leading local athletic shoe brand), and Haier, not to mention legions of less familiar companies, are preternaturally clued into the power of Chinese pride. Their tactics may be crude and their advertising less than polished. However, they pull heartstrings. China Mobile, for example, recently positioned its mobile network, including state-of-the-art 3G services, as "in touch" with the hopes of all Chinese, "spreading new joys" to every corner of the country. Who was the spokesman? Liu Xiang, a famous sprinter and the first Chinese track and field gold medalist. In the run-up to 2008, he and other Olympians will surely be back.

Don't get locked out

If you are not a global or local sponsor, try a little ambush marketing. Sure, you won't be able to show the rings, and your packaging will be naked. But no one owns the Olympic spirit. So turn limited exposure into moral superiority. Scoff at crass commercialism! Sneer at rats following a Pied Piper! During the 1998 Indian cricket championship, Pepsi scored a home run by tweaking Coke's shallow appreciation of Indian teams and stars. Nike, not an Olympic sponsor, associates itself with individual athletes, ones that personify the brand's values. During the 2004 Games, it signed up Liu Xiang, the obviously very busy and now very wealthy sprinter. In a quickly shot TVC, Liu was transformed into a champion of Chinese aspiration, an understudy finally sent up to the show. The copy teased: "The strength of Asian muscle is second rate. Asians can't become world-class sprinters. Asians don't possess the aura of winners. Stereotypes are made to be broken. Congratulations, Liu Xiang!" Nike, a company that never paid a dollar to the IOC, was perceived as the company "most associated with the Olympics."

Don't ride one trick ponies

Olympics are usually quadrennial supernovas, lighting up the sky with a brief flash of brotherhood. But the spirit of Beijing 2008 is an invisible force that, even today, permeates every dimension of national purpose. The Games are already upon us, rallying the nation to reach for the stars. Clever marketers should orchestrate a multiyear, integrated "Olympic build," regardless of sponsorship status. Nike, for example, has crafted a four-year plan that encourages both soccer/basketball participation and Olympic pride. As 2008 approaches, Olympic excitement ("Show the world!") will become an increasingly dominant theme, but, even today, the company is pushing consumers to "get ready" by embracing a sportsman's spirit. TOP sponsor Adidas, a more "technological" and less emotionally irreverent brand, has also formulated a multiyear, integrated Olympic platform. It has taken the route of becoming the Official Sportswear Partner of the Beijing 2008 Olympic Games and considers itself as "The Olympic Brand having supported more Olympic athletes and more Olympic Games than any other sports brand dating back to Amsterdam 1928." Its strategy involves combining the Adidas brand values of passion for sports for athletes of all levels with the Olympic ideals. The company has also formulated a multiyear integrated Olympic platform. According to Erica Kerner, director of the Beijing 2008 Olympics Program for Adidas, "We're confident that, by

2008, there will be no question which brand helps the Chinese run faster, jump longer and aim higher." (Tactical sidebar: long-term planning requires a long-term budget. Carve one out early.)

Don't be a carpetbagger

Chinese are nervous about 2008. Multinational sponsors (i.e., official ones) can enhance relevance by highlighting how their goods and services will increase the chances of success, both operational and athletic. Lenovo, the first Chinese TOP sponsor, should enhance its technology credentials by stressing how its information technology products "make the Games run smoothly." Kodak should position its digital imaging as "instantaneously transmitting China's triumphs." Visa should replace its stale "accepted everywhere" claim with a message of "enabling more people to discover China's greatness."

In conclusion, the Chinese have more at stake in a successful Olympics than an expanded subway system and a few new stadiums. The Games represent an affirmation of everything China represents and will become. As 2008 nears, MNCs should signal respect for the bold aspirations of the nation and its people, riding the Games as an express train to the heart of desire.

PART III

ON THE
GROUND
LESSONS:
WINNING
AND
LOSING
IN CHINA

CHAPTER 12

INTO THE SHALLOW END

TEN EASY TIPS FOR GOOD CHINA ADS

Although some of these points have been covered in previous chapters, this section serves as a handy consolidation of ten key ways to successfully sell to the Chinese.

BUYER BEWARE

Within the advertising industry, it is quite clear that the more we generalize on "effective copy," the more we end up with platitudes. The rallying cries of any ad agency (including JWT) make a long list: "create likable advertising to maintain consumer loyalty"; "don't forget the big idea"; "base your strategy on a compelling point of difference," and so on. While true enough, they are no-brainers. As "tips" become more pointed—more insightful, more penetrating—they become more nuanced and, therefore, less conducive to algebraic application. Advertising, despite recent strides in quantifying effectiveness, remains more an art than a science. The Holy Grail—copy that's *guaranteed* to drive sales—will never be found.

China, in particular, is brand management's Great White Hope. But the landscape is raw and untamed. Commercial laws are made and thrust aside. Consumers are disoriented. From a (smart) marketer's point of view, "China" doesn't exist. The myth of "1.2 billion consumers" exploded long ago and has been replaced by the reality of a market vertically segmented by different levels of price sensitivity, ranging anywhere from "high" to "stratospheric." Sales agents bow only to cowboy justice. Infrastructure and distribution are still primitive (though improving); getting a product shipped from Chengdu to Guangzhou can be a horrific nightmare that even Stephen King would have a hard time dreaming up. Unlike the United States, a market that bows to rational, quantifiable "evidence," China is a country without a functioning legal code. Everything is held together by malleable, ephemeral *guanxihu* (relationships). Infrastructure remains underdeveloped. The regulatory environment never ceases to present head-spinning surprises.

As we wade into murky complexities of "Chinese culture," the roadmap is even more Byzantine—north vs. south, coastal vs. inland, urban vs. rural, young vs. old, middle-class vs. everyone else, et cetera vs. et cetera. The Chinese consumer is in flux; she is diverse; she will rebel against the superficial generalization.

And yet, contrary to conventional wisdom, China isn't a tapestry. Its people are relatively homogenous, bound for thousands of years by a near-sacred belief in the supremacy of "Chinese culture." There *are* commonalities and trends that provide helpful clues to making relevant, penetrating, powerful advertising for "the masses." So, here they are:

TIP #1. DON'T ANGER BEIJING

The Chinese power structure, especially its Beijing-based epicenter, is still deeply suspicious of advertising, a feared source of spiritual pollution. Censors leverage ambiguous regulations to reject what someone does not happen to "like." True, the "dos and don'ts" have been promulgated, but they're in Chinese and loaded with inconsistency. As a result, start the censorship-approval process early, as soon as you have a storyboard.

The government's wariness is only one dimension of Beijing's ultrasensitivity. The city's consumers are also easy to offend. They consider themselves the intellectual elite and are extremely proud of Chinese culture and heritage. Copy that is perceived as condescending or an insult to national pride will backfire. Reference to "America" or, for that matter, "the West," will probably alienate. Northerners will also pick apart your ad to find "the lie," and delight in outfoxing the mouthpiece of a multinational juggernaut.

TIP #2: KEEP IT SIMPLE IN SMALLER CITIES AND RURAL AREAS

Companies such as Unilever and Procter & Gamble have only recently started focusing on "tertiary market clusters." Before that, this advertising landscape had been a wasteland. Rural consumers have little experience digesting "creative." The 800–900 million Chinese citizens living outside the primary and secondary coastal cities do not yet regard "products" as "brands"—i.e., with distinct benefits, equities, and emotional associations. A rural shopper is more likely to select Lux shampoo due to its "pretty package" rather than a belief that "my hair will be smooth and silky like a movie star's." Of course, lack of consumer sophistication is no excuse for developing an empty ad—all copy must have a point, a focus. However, your message must be basic, even concrete, and incorporate a clear expression of why a product will make a difficult life easier. Abstract creative (e.g., esoteric puns or metaphors) should be avoided at all cost, or your investment will evaporate as soon as it airs.

TIP #3: TEACH THE OLD

This "tenet" begs the question, "How old is old?" Well, no statistical approach will provide an answer, but it is fairly clear that people are "older" in China than in the West. People older than forty have experienced (perhaps as children) the shocks of Liberation, the Great Leap Forward, and/or the Cultural Revolution. Many have not directly benefited from the economic strides of the past eight to ten years and, as a result, their orientation is quite traditional. These battle-weary people often view advertising as only a necessary, but slightly evil, source of information. On the other hand, younger age groups are predisposed to Western-style creative. Indeed, those under thirty-five actually enjoy advertising. It's entertainment. However, their parents, uncles, aunts, and grandparents want you to get to the point—quickly. They simply do not have the time or inclination to treat commercials as a diversion.

TIP #4: AMUSE THE YOUNG WITH CHINA COOL

Chinese youth, on the other hand, like hipness and love brands. Teen-agers and young adults, the most savvy and sought-after target in China, suffer from what we call "The Little Emperor's Syndrome." Raised in single-child households, they were pampered, fawned after, and the center of their family's universe. The apple of every eye, a Chinese child enjoys emperor-like status, until he or she hits puberty. Then they are pushed into a rough-and-tumble world. They forfeit their "I'm in charge here" position. Instead, they become cogs, bit players in "the system." For the first time, they deal with anonymity. At school, they wear uniforms, compete for university entrance, dream of grabbing a rare Joint Venture job. Therefore, Little Emperors want to be noticed. They look up to the sky and scream, "I exist! I'm special!" But, they must balance "recognition of individuality" with the key driver of teen-age "success"—peer-group acceptance rooted in mandatory social conformism. So Chinese youth are ultraconservative. Individualism is *never* an end in itself. It is a means to a higher goal: having all your friends think "you're popular." It is a delicate balance.

"Youth Cool" is a personality style. It is a subtle approach to life, a hip "tone and manner" that never rocks the boat. It is really an *illusion* of individuality, a *twist* of the expected and conventional. It is "hot on the inside, cool on the outside," "monochromatic with a burst of color," or "skills, not words, doing the talking." Chinese cool is the antidote to anonymity, the route to being admired. And the most aspirational brands—the Nikes, the Pepsis—project this attitude. A commercial's hero, always good-looking, should demonstrate clever resourcefulness and *understated* individuality. He should wear what is "in" but avoid even a whiff of rebellion (e.g., spiked hair, explosive 60s-style colors). And, most critically, every teen ad must suggest peer-group appreciation of a character's coolness. A teen-ager wants to see an idealized version of himself or herself on the screen; they want to project themselves into the action. Make your images the quintessence of "China cool" but keep them social and conformist.

TIP #5: SHOW THE PROMISE, NOT THE PROCESS

This "rule" is a coda to our "teach the old" principle. Brand differentiation is an acquired skill, and new Chinese shoppers need all the help they can get. So don't bog down your message with elaborate computer-generated demos that flash wordy "reasons why." Make your copy benefit-focused. Answer the question, "Why should I buy this stuff?" The answer can be emotional ("people will think I'm a success") or functional ("my teeth will be white") or somewhere in between ("people will think I'm a success if my teeth are white"). But it must be clear, simple, direct, and result-oriented. Of course, a good "support point" is always helpful ("your kids will grow tall *because* our yogurt is rich in calcium"), but make sure your reason to believe links to the benefit.

TIP #6: TELL MOM THEY NEED HER

Despite Mao's famous saying that women hold up half the sky, even "liberated" females consider their role inside the home paramount. In the West, working mothers struggle with balancing career and family satisfaction. In China, the battle is much less fierce; the kid wins, hands down. Mom's aggressiveness in protecting family interests can be best understood within a historical context. Until recently, living standards throughout *all* of China were so low that basic physical needs could not be assumed. Mothers warded off daily dangers thrust upon the family by poverty. They "defended" children against malnutrition or social alienation; her main role was to defeat "the bad." Today, that instinctive "fear of invasion" still exists. So, to bond with your female "head of household" target, tell her she is really, really needed. Without her, there would be no family harmony. Without her, the doctor would pay too many visits. Without her, the family would lose face. Without her, there would be germs on the soap!

TIP #7: DON'T SHOW REAL LIVES

We call this "accessible aspiration." Daily life in China is an obstacle course, and viewers don't need any reminders of their problems. Make every woman a *xing fu nu ren* (a woman blessed with complete happiness—material, professional and romantic). Men should be "on their way up the ladder." Families should glow with "Leave It to Beaver" serenity. True, it is a fine line; dad should not drive home in a new Jaguar. An out-of-touch and unrealistic promise will be forgotten or disliked. But individuals' hopes for the future, achievable or not, should be glorified on film. Call it sanitization. Call it simplistic. It works.

TIP #8: BE CONFIDENT BUT NEVER, EVER BRAG

In a Confucian, hierarchical society, it is not polite to boast. In fact, it is offensive. And it is illegal (really). You can *imply*—but don't actually *say*—"my brand is bigger and better than that brand." If your claim is too competitive, you will antagonize your franchise, assuming you get your ad through the censors in the first place.

TIP #9: BIG IS BEAUTIFUL

"Ah," you say. "The advertising guy is worried about his commission." While I admit agencies charge up to 17.65 percent on production costs, a top-quality ad signals corporate credibility. They stand out. They reassure. Frankly, there's a lot of really terrible-looking copy still on the air. If your ad doesn't sparkle, people won't exactly turn away from the screen in disgust. On the other hand, if a spot has top-rate production values, it will get noticed.

TIP #10: WHEN ALL ELSE FAILS, USE A BABY

Chinese worship children. The cuter and smarter, the better.

CHAPTER 13

MISSING THE POINT

WHY MULTINATIONAL CORPORATIONS FAIL IN CHINA

All the strategic insight in the world is useless if multinational corporations (MNCs) fail to understand the operational realities and business potential in China. So, when we assess the viability of long-term partnerships with MNCs, we force ourselves to ask five questions. (Please see chapter 14 for further elaboration on multinational challenges/strategies.)

HAS THE CHINA VOLUME POTENTIAL BEEN OVERSTATED?

The glittering panorama of the Bund, a riverfront avenue boasting colonial Shanghai's finest architecture, is seductively impressive. But, behind the façade, things get gritty. Penetration levels are low; for example, only 3–4 percent of babies wear disposable diapers. And limited disposable income places an iron lid on household consumption. The Shanghai Carrefour at Wuning Lu once boasted the world's largest footfall—and the smallest per-person sales. Although China now has over 300 million mobile phone subscribers, the average revenue per user is less than $15, compared with $80 in Japan.

The only way to overcome a low-volume ceiling is by "standing in front"—i.e., grabbing the category benefit and effectively "owning" a fundamental motivator to get a big slice of a small pie.

IS A "GOLD RUSH" CORRUPTING DECISIONS?

Competition is pervasive and ruthless. The PRC, awash with overcapacity, is plagued by supply-driven commoditization and falling prices. The annual demand for TVs in China is 35 million sets while the capacity is 50 million. Most consumer durables have low utilization—e.g., refrigerators (51 percent), washing machines (44 percent), or air conditioners (34 percent). FCMG goods are often trapped in the same vicious cycle. In 2001, there were 278 shampoo brands. By 2005, that number had been culled to 201.

To establish a profitable foothold, MNCs can adopt one of three strategies: (1) acquire local business to build scale/distribution rather than investing in new capacity, (2) form strategic alliances, or (3) step up imports or outsourcing.

ARE PRICE POINTS TOO *HIGH?*

Multinational companies often fail to recognize that a majority of the population is poor. For example, in most countries, Pantene is priced at market average; in China, it's up to 40 percent above. Ariel detergent foists a premium of 100 percent on a penny-pinched public; its share is under 5 percent.

In the face of cutthroat prices, MNCs are launching "second tier" brands as volume generators. P&G carries both mass market Tide (global name but cheaper cost of goods [COGS]) as well as premium Ariel. Within Nestlé's culinary portfolio, Maggie (190 price index and 6 percent share) skims the surface while Taitaile (88 price index and 43 percent share) bites out the major chunk. Similarly, Colgate Palmolive has leveraged a powerful brand by extending the equity of Colgate Total to embrace no-frills Colgate Strong and Colgate Herbal (combined share of more than 25 percent).

IS A PRODUCT COMPATIBLE WITH CONSUMER DEMAND?

In a land of instant noodles and health tonics, too many global giants impose Western tastes on a Chinese public. Cheese, ice cream, chocolate, and breakfast cereal are simply not natural fits with local preferences. Instead of pushing water uphill, MNCs are moving into local product categories either through acquisition (e.g., Danone and Wahaha AD calcium drink) or introduction of familiar concepts under global brand names (e.g., Heinz Babao congee, Knorr MSG).

ARE ABOVE-THE-LINE COSTS UNAFFORDABLE?

Due to high media rates, heavy clutter, and difficulty in reaching discrete targets (i.e., unavoidable media "wastage" or "overdelivery"), building equity is expensive. Advertising-to-sales ratios in China are high. Regrettably, this is a fact of life and must be confronted with deep pockets or a (realistic) tactical approach encompassing below-the-line, *gradual* distribution expansion, or brand extensions.

CHAPTER 14

CULTURE, CORPORATE STRUCTURE, AND THE ELUSIVE POWER OF LOCAL BRANDS

A NEW THREAT

Western multinationals have long approached the Chinese landscape tinged with both fear and titillation. The perceived upside of aggressive investment is simple and has remained the same for a decade—the promise of dominating the world's largest market of the future. The risks, however, are many and varied, lurking like bandits off the highway. Traditionally, these "threats" have been articulated in operational terms—cratered distribution (getting better); arbitrary, politically tethered, and provincially biased courts (getting a bit better but still light years from impartiality); lack of skilled local management (definitely getting better, despite a cultural fear of breaking from the pack); and so on. But, in the face of all these problems, we take heart in local consumers' preference for the reliability, innovativeness, and "coolness" of Western products.

However, just when we hoped we might be able to navigate through the operational shoals of the market, along comes a new terror: The Chinese Brand. Nimble local competitors are appearing in every corner of the competitive battlefield—mobile phones (Bird, TCL), appliances (Little Swan, Haier), televisions (Konka, Changhong, TCL again), insurance (Ping An), low-priced autos (Brilliance), and an infinite number of hair care products.

A NEW OPPORTUNITY

In the early '90s, Western advertising agencies entered China primarily to service MNC clients. Over the past three or four years, however, we have awoken to the necessity of broadening our appeal to the emerging local players as well. For example, four years ago, JWT did not receive any revenue from domestic clients. Today, 40 percent of our income is generated by local brands that some in the West may have heard about (e.g., Haier, China Mobile, Lenovo computers), as well as less "familiar" ones (Fuijian province's Xuejing beer, Inner Mongolia's Yili dairy and Mengniu dairy, and Guangdong's 999 pharmaceuticals). There is a brave new world out there.

Clearly, the impact of WTO-stimulated efficiencies, an export-led economy, and a macroeconomic policy designed to wring overcapacity from an inefficient production base is enormous. Local companies are discovering the benefits of "the brand." Cutting-edge players now know the difference between a mouse and Mickey Mouse. For many, this is no deathbed conversion; more and more are practicing what we preach.

On the most basic level, many local brands boast acceptable "performance" and are not actively resisted. Furthermore, several nimble firms leverage communications rooted in genuine consumer insights. Both Yili milk and Liushan shower gel, for example, tap into consumers' comfort with natural ingredients. Skyworth television has emerged from nowhere with "healthy TV"; although bizarre to Western ears, the concept appeals to the Confucian imperative of "protecting" the family. And Diaopai detergent's "Why use a lot when you can use a little?" positioning elegantly blends hardheaded value with warm-hearted empathy for the plight of the laid-off state-owned enterprise worker. Finally, over the past two years, local companies' new product development has become increasingly aggressive. From Sanyuans' three-in-one breakfast beverage ("nutrition made easy") to Suyixian's MSG-free vegetable bouillon ("worry-free deliciousness") and Haier's "personalized" mini-refrigerator targeted to American college students, Chinese enterprises have discovered that innovation lifts profit margins.

Yes, at long last, local corporations are waking to the call of the market. But, as they say, *yi bu yi ge jiao ying,* one step at a time (or more literally, "one step, one footprint").

CAUTION: SLIPPERY WHEN WET

For every local manufacturer that "gets it," there are fifty that do not. It is important not to confuse brand awareness with brand equity. Brand equity equals affinity. A healthy, vibrant brand carries images and associations that translate into long-term preference and "intangible" assets. According to BrandZ, WPP's proprietary research initiative designed to assesses local and MNC "brand velocity," many domestic trend shapers—e.g., Haier, Lenovo, and Wahaha beverages—have scale but surprisingly shallow consumer loyalty. This is due to local manufacturers' mercantilist modus operandi, underscored by advertising that is frequently incoherent and laden with basso profundo SOE-style propaganda. *The Economist* summarizes the jarring coexistence, driven in large part by both political and cultural values, of impressive scale and unimpressive innovation-driven brand depth: "The contradictions of [telecom manufacturer] Huawei are mirrored to some degree by all the country's emerging multinationals and ultimately reflects those of China itself. The economy is still in transition between dirigisme and free markets. Its political system can harness enormous resources but, ultimately, undermines its own objectives in a paranoid desire to retain control."

The rise of globally competitive and world-class Chinese consumer goods companies is inevitable, but in the distant future. Most savvy Western companies have time to prepare themselves for the emergence of true local brands.

Local companies that hope to remain viable for five, ten, or fifty years have no choice but to end the vicious cycle of plummeting prices and surging red ink. They must: (a) build consumer loyalty, (b) forge a *sustainable* price premium, and (c) reinvest profits in future growth. Any manufacturer who thinks otherwise is doomed. The only way of escaping the market's ruthless jaws is to grasp the difference between "products" (things pumped out of factories) and "brands" ("friends" actively desired and preferred by consumers). The only way to build a brand is to *invest* in compelling communications that deepen over time.

As discussed earlier, all effective (i.e., "international standard") advertising springs from an insight, a firm grasp of consumers' fundamental motivators for behavior and preference. A "brand vision" encapsulates a brand's long-term "identity"—it's the difference between a burger stand and McDonald's, or bits of tobacco rolled in paper and a Marlboro. It is a combination of a unique product attribute and consumer desire and is the key to loyalty. Most Chinese companies are skilled at highlighting the former; all too often, however, they ignore the latter, ending up with communications that are more about what manufacturers sell than what buyers demand.

However, there are structural barriers, most of them rooted in cultural imperatives, which will slow the rise of the Chinese brand. (We will see in the following chapter that the healthiest local brands are found in relatively simple organizations. The large-scale behemoths admired by Conventional Wisdom—e.g., TCL, Haier, and Lenovo—are not embraced by consumers. When companies compete in a broad range of categories, profit centers multiply. Interdepartmental struggles fester. The entire corporation becomes less efficient and more political. This, in turn, fosters an environment filled with politics, tight lips, and insecurity. Brands are intangible, unquantifiable abstractions. Healthy equity, the manifestation of confident, unified leadership, does not thrive within a fear-based culture.) These barriers are:

Senior Management Is Not Market Driven

The large state companies are still heavily influenced by the Communist party; even if the CEO is not a Party member (which is rare), the CCP is always fully represented—indeed, dominant—when critical *business* decisions are made. Having an eye focused on the market and an ear tuned into the Party line will always result in decision-making schizophrenia. State enterprises suffer from chronic structurally conflicting goals. Very often, precious little progress has been made in rectifying this situation, for obvious reasons of stability and/or self-interest.

For example, on a microeconomic level, the automobile industry has long been a bastion of local protectionism; every province seems to churn out its own model, often at huge losses. The market simply can't absorb the number of (shoddily produced) vehicles flooding the hinterlands. However, a political fear of "social instability" turns even the most market-savvy manager into an official deaf to the dictates of supply and demand. The net result, of course, is chronic overcapacity, vicious price wars, and underemployment; post-WTO market liberalization threatens to only make matters worse, at least in the short-to-medium term. The television industry is suffering a similar production-led glut.

Poisonous corruption also results from the lure of command-economy "booty" trumping the discipline of free-enterprise incentive. The Party's intention to release all but "strategic" industries from central government control to the purview of the provinces and municipalities has raised the eyebrows of many foreign observers. Will bureaucrats resort to bargain-basement pricing to siphon state assets and line their own pockets? Or will they rely on market principles to fairly value assets and sell companies to buyers with a valid business proposition?

Internal corporate politics also pulls decision-making away from the mandates of a consumer orientation. JWT believes it lost the TCL television account as a result of a struggle between two management adversaries; the victor planted tactically-driven sales managers in all key marketing positions.

There Is a Lack of Communications between Senior Management and Market-savvy New-generation Types

China is a very Confucian society where respect for hierarchy is deeply (and, at times, imperceptibly) engrained in even the most individualistic-looking and -acting younger people. In many organizations, the "big boss" exudes a mysterious, cult-like charisma and his directives are rarely openly challenged. A "behind the curtain" decision-making secrecy only exacerbates the situation. (Again, Chinese are "protective" people who accept authority unconditionally. An old-style or "typical" Chinese boss "leads" by issuing ambiguous instructions and creating adversarial power centers beneath him. Both tactics are designed to stir up fear and nip in the bud the emergence of competitors.)

The companies with the most inaccessible and nontransparent leadership tend to be those in which the hierarchically rigid Communist Party still maintains a high degree of operating control. From experience, it appears that the Big Four banks are particularly burdened by layered—even Byzantine—decision-making for two reasons. First, as just mentioned, the leadership culture rewards "conservative opacity." Second, these companies have no incentive to operate according to the laws of supply and demand; instead, their primary role is to manage allocation of capital in a manner that ensures maintenance of high-priority state-owned enterprises and "social stability."

Advertising agencies frequently bear the brunt of feckless capriciousness. Effective product communications can only emerge from streamlined decision-making. At critical junctures—strategy approval, storyboard or layout buy-in, and final creative material release—all key players have to be in the same room at the same time. However, imperial senior management is loath to participate in "lowly" advertising discussions and often renders broadcast-or-no-broadcast judgment only after hundreds of thousands of renminbi have been spent on finished copy. Given the subjective nature of creative evaluation, top management's aversion to direct discussion with junior marketing lieutenants results in loss of time and quality. Sometimes, yes, the corporate chieftain does participate in communications discussions. But he often holds court with dozens of lackeys sitting beside him, each offering a politically correct, watered-down point of view.

Sales Department Trumps Marketing

Very often, sales teams are responsible for profit and loss. The sales force, by its very nature, is focused on short-term gains. A legitimate marketing department's ultimate mandate is balancing a sales-now battle cry versus a quieter plea for lingering equity. Until the marketing function emerges as an *empowered and strategic* center of gravity (equipped with a real budget), patient and step-by-step investment in brand loyalty will be a pipedream.

This barrier is frequently most daunting in white goods categories. Unlike in most multinational companies, local sales teams are not only responsible for profit and loss but also are structured along very narrow product lines resulting in a proliferation of discrete profit centers. Decentralized sales-based profit and loss (P&L) is both strategically unmanageable and politically "Balkanized," strained by warlordism at even the lowest level of the organization. Electronics and appliance distribution networks are notoriously fractionated; they are the PRC's most vertically integrated. The manufacturer frequently owns retail outlets—either outright or through joint ventures. This configuration reinforces a (short-term) sales approach at the expense of (long-term) brand building. The marketing department operates more as a coordinator or "service center" supporting sales; indeed, it becomes an in-house advertising agency capable only of churning out reams of low-quality, strategically bankrupt promotional material that, at best, push product out the door at fire sale prices.

Guanxi-obsessed sales kings also dominate the automotive landscape. ("Guanxi" are personal relationships that fuel many business transactions in China.) Across dealer networks, red packets stuffed with kickback cash count much more than brand equity. Both long-term consumer loyalty and superior road handling are irrelevant. Western companies without a controlling interest in production and distribution joint ventures don't stand a chance. Mazda's local partner, FAW, commands a 70 percent stake. It's a safe bet that the brand's "Zoom, zoom!" strategy, so successful in Japan and Europe, will be implemented in the PRC only after months (or years) of arduous negotiation. Advertising, if the forces of "localization" prevail, will be handled regionally, greased by a constellation of unaligned bucket shops, each with a small piece of the action.

Relationships with Advertising Agencies Amount to Cheap Quick Fixes

Pitches occur for each and every creative assignment, making it impossible for a multiyear agency-client partnership mentality to take root. A "brand" is the manifestation of a long-term dialogue between manufacturers and consumers. Advertising agencies—at least the professional ones—should be chartered with nurturing this relationship; however, very few local entities earmark yearly budgets to sustain an ongoing alliance with communication specialists. Furthermore, agencies are usually paid at extremely low rates, often out of production monies (the funds set aside for actually making a print or TV ad), not on a long-term fee. The result? Cheap, shoddy communications that, on a per-job basis, maximize short-term gain.

(As a benchmark, international advertising agencies usually charge medium-sized clients—ones that might produce two television and print campaigns per year—around US$300,000–US$350,000. This fee is paid over a one- or two-year time frame; stability of the relationship is protected by contractual exclusivity. Many local clients resist compensation of more than US$50,000. And multiproject arrangements are the exception rather than the rule.)

On a More Nuts and Bolts Level, There's a Lack of Understanding of How to Measure the Success and Depth of Brands

Equity doesn't appear from thin air; rather, it is "constructed"—meticulously—over time. The essence of a brand is abstract; indeed, proof of its existence is tantamount to the emotional response it elicits from consumers. However, tracking, analyzing, and projecting the richness of a brand's "magnetic pull" is eminently concrete and requires familiarity of, and respect for, marketing and measurement tools. The blind spots run the gamut from how to conduct relevant research to how to determine what a creative brief should achieve (i.e., concept tests). The difference between monetarily cheap media buying and effective media planning is ignored. The value of focus groups, Usage & Attitude studies, pre- and post-copy testing, as well as other research tools, are scoffed at. Until marketing is viewed as a science, an organ vital to a brand's success, the knowledge required to sustain equity will never be formalized. (Note: for the first time, JWT *is* sensing a real desire to get a leg up in absorbing basic marketing concepts. But even an infinite stream of "knowledge" will be meaningless unless the aforementioned structural issues are resolutely addressed.)

CHINA: AN OLYMPIC BRAND?

And then there's Beijing 2008 again, perhaps the most ambitious brand-building exercise in history. Beyond generating income from corporate sponsorships, the Middle Kingdom wants to leverage the Olympics as its "debut" as an up-and-coming superpower. It is seeking the ultimate multinational endorsement: a worldwide stamp of respect. China is prepared to pay a pretty penny for this recognition—hundreds of billions of dollars.

As discussed in chapter 11, a powerful mix of benign patriotism, angry nationalism, and the ruthless quest to extend the legitimacy of the Chinese

Communist Party has intoxicated both the nation and the political establishment. Furthermore, a quest for hard, cold cash—and lots of it—has ignited Olympic dreams. The nation's Olympic marketing objective is to position China as a blockbuster product, a New Horizon travel destination and investment magnet. On top of this, hundreds of local enterprises will "borrow Olympic equity" to upgrade perceptions of their own products via Olympic-themed events, sponsorships, and PR.

There's nothing wrong with either objective. Politicians have always used the Games to bolster the appeal of a host city or country. By trumpeting sparkling Olympic infrastructure and the worldliness of its citizens, both Tokyo (1964) and Seoul (1988) "launched" themselves as modern commercial and cultural centers. What's more, for the past several decades marketers from General Electric to Visa to Samsung have been ruthlessly aggressive in marrying product promotion and Olympic ideals.

Can China leverage the 2008 Games to enhance international perceptions of the country and its goods? Will the Olympics be harnessed to transform perceptions of the PRC from a producer of low/mid-priced commodities to a nation that practices international standards of product development? We certainly hope so. But, in reality, the jury is out. The real question to ask: Is there enough time for "bureaucratic China" to fade away so that "dynamic China" can step boldly onto the world stage?

The outside perception of the PRC is, at best, murky. In the eyes of many, China is a land of gray concrete buildings, expressionless faces, backward facilities, dirt-cheap laboring hordes, and dusty tourist attractions. Beijing 2008's marketing arm, working in conjunction with the Ministry of Tourism, should use the Olympics to reposition the country as full of visual delights, bursting with humanity, modern yet historic, and multidimensional. It needs to develop a multiyear plan that seamlessly integrates the tactical and commercial opportunities presented by the Olympics with the broader objective of elevating the image of China around the world. In short, China needs a "brand vision" and a "big creative idea" that can be woven into all globally targeted communication. Unfortunately, politically motivated, short-term-oriented cadres, divorced from the realities of how the rest of the world perceives the motherland, clog the Olympic machine. Likewise, to my knowledge, there is no corner of the tourism sector dedicated to projecting a cohesive, animated image to the world's traveling set.

What will visitors experience when they arrive in Beijing? Will attendants be warm or will they be robotic in a heartless, Pudong Airport kind of way? Will the city be festooned with creative decoration or can we look forward to thousands of already-ubiquitous cheap, white plastic pots containing one of four plant types? Will the opening ceremony be a rousing release of national passion or an Orwellian propaganda spectacular? Will the awe-inspiring zip, zing, and pizzazz of the Chinese people be overshadowed by an insecure government apparatus paranoid about lost face? Will an instinctively self-protective China open its doors to the unfamiliar, or stage a well-rehearsed Beijing opera sure to leave most of us cold? Time will tell.

On a microeconomic level, the vast majority of enterprises are still not equipped to translate Olympic goodwill into momentum in the supermarket. Again, very few state owned enterprises (SOEs) or listed companies are structured to build brands. Lenovo, China's ambitious computer manufacturer, IBM raider, and "Top Olympic Sponsor," is having an awkward time figuring out what do with both billion-dollar investments. (They are still "brainstorming" or consulting their marketing masters in New York.) In early 2005, observers were still wondering who, exactly, was in charge of managing the money pit. (Rumors are rife that Lenovo, not a SOE but a leader of a "strategic" industry watched over by the central government, was strong-armed by the CCP into achieving global-sponsor status.) Developing communications that (a) integrate product and Beijing 2008 in a manner relevant to consumers and (b) are approved by the highest level of Oz-like corporate bureaucracies is, to put it mildly, challenging. So even if, on a national level, the Olympics are a success, it may not boost consumer perceptions, inside or outside the PRC, of Chinese goods.

Ultimately, the root of the problem with both the Beijing 2008 Olympics and corporate management is the same. Politics trump commerce. When the Party is involved in all aspects of business, Olympic or otherwise, one eye will always be on the market and the other firmly fixed on individual, self-protective interests. Rational and efficient allocation of resources—what is needed to build brands—becomes exponentially more difficult. China is already changing. But its evolution will be gradual. Many doubt the years between now and 2008 are enough to "wow" the world.

In summary, in most industries, especially those not yet affected by the WTO, the rise of local brands is still a relatively superficial phenomenon. There are fundamental operational, structural, and political barriers that preclude energized brand "velocity." But as the next chapter demonstrates, China's capacity for a Great Leap Forward of the positive kind should never be dismissed. MNCs may have just a few years to shield themselves from what might be a threat of epic proportion.

CHAPTER 15

CHINESE CONSUMERS, CHINESE BRANDS, AND THE MNC LEARNING CURVE

Local brands—three-dimensional vessels carrying intangible equity—did not exist prior to the late 1990s. Of course, local trademarks littered (state-owned) supermarkets and corner stalls. Today, they are an increasingly high-power threat, one that multinational competitors ignore at their peril. They now control almost 50 percent of the shampoo market, up to 25 percent of mobile phones (albeit mostly in secondary and tertiary cities), and are even making inroads in midtier automobiles (e.g., Cherry). Tactically ruthless, they are a school of piranhas smelling blood in the water and instinctively detecting weakness in the primordial soup that is China's brand universe. They will chew the flesh off of MNC players trying to survive off quick, shallow liaisons with (increasingly savvy) consumers. Less than a decade ago, local "trademarks" were laughably inferior, fodder for self-denigrating (yet nationalistic) Chinese patriots. Yet, as we pass the midpoint of the twenty-first century's first decade, Shenzhen-based TCL is (painfully) digesting its recent Thompson television acquisition and Lenovo has—in one breathless, bold stroke—purchased IBM's PC division. As this book went to press, Haier had made a (failed) bid for the quintessentially American appliance brand, Maytag. And the United States Congress was wringing its hands over CNOOC Ltd.'s aggressive attempt to take over energy producer Unocol. No one is snickering now.

THE WHITE SPACE

Local names such as Lenovo (computers), Haier (appliances), Wahaha (beverages), Tsing Dao (beer), and Bird (mobile phones) have exploited the blind spot of even the most eagle-eyed multinationals. The cool brands—yes, foreign brands are still hip—are too expensive. Understandably, CEOs from San Francisco to Tokyo are intoxicated with the emergence of a Mainland middle class, one fueled by exponentially rising disposable income. But even a cursory look at the China Statistical Bureau's crudely manipulated data reveals an unassailable truth. Living standards of the rich, the top 10–15 percent, the urban elite, call them what you will, have improved at a much healthier clip than the circumstances of the bottom 85 percent. (For the past decade, the top quintile has enjoyed annual income gains of almost 10 percent. The wages of farmers, on the other hand, were stagnant until very recently.) Pepsi, Unilever, Nike, and Microsoft harvested small ponds of overgrown fish, juicy catches fattened by Deng Xiao Ping and Jiang Zemin's dog-eat-dog growth regimen. Even today, MNCs boast high prices relative to competition. In fast-moving consumer goods, categories where achieving scale is a critical precursor to healthy profits, foreign/JV goods are much pricier than local counterparts. Shampoo is 50 percent more expensive (and this is after both P&G and Unilever slashed prices to compete against down-and-dirty Slek, et al.). In skin care, a category dominated by local brands, foreign ones (even "upper mass" Olay) have a 250 percent premium. International feminine hygiene brands such as P&G's Whisper or Unicharm's Sofy are 71 percent more expensive than the average Chinese stock keeping unit (SKU). But they have been often relegated to a rarified, "nichified," aspirational yet unaffordable plane.

Multinational companies, fixated on the pyramid's tip, have left the "base of the temple" uncovered. (It is here, by the way, where clout with distribution networks and retailers is forged.) Local brands have taken advantage of Westerners' narrow worldview to target our blind spot. They have across-the-board momentum in some categories (telecoms and personal care—shampoo, soap, skin cream, sanitary napkins, cosmetics, fashion, food/beverages). Meanwhile, local players already dominate the appliance (Haier, Konka, TCL, Chunlan), furniture, and intimate apparel industries. (The latter group consists of goods consumed out of public view. Please see chapter 1 on the Chinese middle class.) In China, figures can lie. Reported rises in market share are often flights of fancy. However, distortions are not gross enough to mask an uncomfortable truth: Chinese brands are not strong but they are getting stronger and are here to stay. As a Western firm, if you are lucky, they will disintegrate into irritating background buzz, targeting the fringes of the consumer universe. If you are not, they will coalesce into juggernauts to smash your company to smithereens.

THE CHEAP PRICE

Fortunately, your death knell has not yet rung; there is not a single local brand that consumers actively prefer. We must never confuse equity—perceptions of functional superiority or relevant "value benefits" that translate into long-term loyalty at a higher price—with awareness. The vast majority of Chinese—at all income levels—still favor Western brands. Youth dream of Nike but buy Li Ning. True, local brands are ubiquitous and have achieved universal awareness largely by leveraging two hugely important competitive advantages: (1) control of, insight into, or ability to manipulate prehistoric distribution channels and (2) massive media investments that are often state-funded and usually irrationally allocated. Despite this, few hearts are touched. According to BrandZ, Chinese companies have failed miserably at converting "presence" into "bonding." For example, in white goods, both Little Swan dishwashers and Chang Hong televisions boast universal recognition, even in tertiary cities. However, relative to competitors, they are saddled with negative affinity. In other words, buyers actually *resist* purchasing them. Even European Electrolux, a little-known international player handicapped by both modest television spending and a cratered retail landscape, is more aspirational than any indigenous brand. The story is similar within the health care category.

Nao Bai Jing, the health supplement brand responsible for history's most brutally incessant and sensorially merciless TV campaign, is a household name. So is omnipresent Ang Li tonic. It, too, is barely endured. Wyeth's Caltrate and Centrum, on the other hand, have quietly become image leaders. And, despite China's rapid emergence as a beer-swilling nation (not to mention the widespread availability of local brands such as Tsing Tao and Reeb), American king Budweiser boasts a much richer relationship with consumers.

Local brands have succeeded at achieving on-the-ground scale. While this coup is nothing to sneeze at, for the most part, they are mere clones of their international counterparts. In many cases, there is functional parity but, like the Tin Man, no heart. They offer nothing more than basic reliability and low, low prices. Financially, pocket-book equity is not a pretty picture:

- Da Bao skin cream deludes itself by believing the brand represents "dreams of beauty." But its price is 17.8 percent of the average international brand.
- Wahaha's "premium" calcium-enriched dairy drink did not achieve in-market lift-off until its price was lowered to one RMB per bottle.

- Due to vicious price wars between "commodity brands," the entire television industry is on state-mandated life support. (At current market prices, production capacity is 150 percent of consumer demand in value terms.)

Few local enterprises keep one set of reliable books; in fact, most keep two or three sets, depending on the audience. Accountants are exotic. However, it is safe to assume, given the Mainland's obsession with fixed capital investment, profit margins are frighteningly unsustainable. Due to both apathy and bargaining prowess, Chinese consumers will not hold up half this sky indefinitely. Smart organizations know they must restructure, refocus, and reposition or die. As we discuss later, a few are doing just that, and successfully. However, even at this late hour, with China's financial infrastructure finally embracing real market reform by loosening interest and exchange rates, most marketing managers put up a good front but are feeble equity builders.

The next section discusses, in terms of consumer communications, what is still going wrong. (These weaknesses are driven by both a failure to grasp the link between brand equity and profit as well as corporate structural and cultural barriers. Please see chapter 14.)

CHANGE THE CHANNEL, NOW!

Local brands, as a whole, are burdened by three communications barriers. Unless they are removed, meaningful affinity will be impossible to achieve. First, marketers confuse brand awareness with three-dimensional equity. Second, advertising is usually only one step above an annual report, more rooted in corporate credentials than a relevant, single-minded proposition. Finally, most brands' messages are alarmingly inconsistent and incoherent.

Awareness vs. Equity

Except for P&G, local companies far outspend MNCs in television, print, and newspaper advertising. Even after adjusting for the 60 percent–70 percent discounts offered by fly-by-night local brokers, it is not abnormal for a large local brand to spend $75–$100 million. Stunningly, an aggressive national media schedule (albeit efficiently planned by reputable media specialists) can be achieved for around $10–$25 million. Chinese marketers, always reassured by gargantuan projections of status, are hooked on screaming their brand name, loudly and frequently, across the airwaves. Despite recent advertising to programming restrictions, commercial breaks are interminable affairs, rendered even more painful by looped TVCs, the same ones playing seven times in one eight- to ten-minute "pod." To boot, these "bulk buys" usually support creative of the most dubious persuasion. Kuanpai soy sauce is just one example. It's "message" is conveyed in eardrum-stabbing copy that shrieks, "Kuanpai! Kuanpai! Kuanpai! A great respected soy sauce and leading Chinese trademark! Kuanpai!"

Such media wastage is colossal if one has the temerity to assume that advertising should, directly or indirectly, *persuade* people to buy a product. Awareness *is* a prerequisite to purchase; however, it is a necessary, but not sufficient, prerequisite. Effective copy must also communicate unique information, link "news" to the brand itself (rather than to a competitor), and persuade consumers that the proposition is relevant to their lives. Awareness in isolation does nothing. On the contrary, "unconverted awareness" can be, and often is, detrimental to equity. It cloys. It bombards. It alienates. Innocent victims, besieged with "overdelivery," look up to the sky and wail, "Free me!"

Frequency fixation often leads to a reverse dysfunction—chronic media avoidance and a parallel obsession with below-the-line tactical binges. Slek shampoo, for example, struck fear in the hearts of MNC manufacturers after its 1999 launch. The brand utilized extremely aggressive in-store sampling and oceans of point-of-sale material. Slek, however, invested practically nothing in television or print, and quickly achieved a near-miraculous 8 percent share. Unilever and P&G both feared that a terrifying new "model" had been unleashed, one mysteriously tailored to the "uniqueness of the China market." They were half correct. Indeed, local brands are an increasing menace and, as a cluster, now control almost 50 percent of shampoo market volume. But, due to their failure to forge coherent equity, none have any real staying power. Slek quickly peaked and faded into the background. Its story is not atypical. There are over 200 shampoo brands sold in the PRC. New ones are born every month. But they soon die, undernourished and unappreciated. The tide rushes in but no survivor is left on the shore. On the white goods front, every municipality, let alone province or region, seems to hawk its own air conditioner. (The market is flooded with over 150 brands.) To grab attention, appliance outlets morph into carnival grounds: promotional announcements blare over loudspeakers, barely clad girls offer sample sachets, and banners wave over the parking lot. And it is all a blur.

Celebrity usage is another common way of quickly establishing awareness (and often nothing else). Endorsements by the rich and famous can be powerful. Over the millennia, Chinese have been conditioned to respect status; they assume that people at the top are there by dint of ability, individual destiny, or heavenly mandate. Furthermore, celebrities signal perceptions of reliability, a valuable commodity. (PRC consumers are both apprehensive about the intimidating assortment of new choices and jaded from decades of poor quality, command-economy detritus.) However, celebrities should mean something. Usage should be optimized by linking a star's personality with that of the brand, lest viewers focus on what the star is wearing, not saying.

Unfortunately, celebrity usage is rarely optimized. For example, China Unicom invested $5 million in snaring Yao Ming, the most revered local sportsman of all time, as a spokesperson. (He is idolized for his successful "invasion" of the NBA and represents the victory of Chinese subtlety and understatement—*xuan*—over American brashness and bravado. Just as David slew Goliath, he brings down "the big guys." China Unicom, a new and scrappy competitor on the front line, is engaged in a similar battle with China Telecom, the telecommunication industry's 800-pound gorilla. The parallel between Yao's struggle and Unicom's ambition is striking.) Managed by engineers, the company has historically assembled pointless and visually egregious advertising. The television commercials, for example, depicted a child handing a basketball to Yao, who dunks it and grunts, "I love basketball. I love China Unicom." The print and outdoor material is even worse. Poorly laid out and cheaply reproduced, they show Yao standing there, idle, barely looking at the camera. (Hoping to improve its creative standards, Unicom appointed JWT as its advertising agency in 2005.)

It is perhaps instructive to compare the public resentment caused by Chinese manufacturers' "shock and awe" blitzkrieg with the goodwill generated by the timeless appeal of, say, a "Kodak moment" or "Absolut enjoyment."

Propaganda vs. Relevance

Since the 1949 revolution, freedom of expression has never existed in the Chinese mass media. The authorities meticulously delineate the contours of public discourse. Every sentence, quotation, and comma is laid down by edict. The regime—with impressive intellectual agility—mandates what the people hear and what they should think. The masses, adept at reading between the lines to uncover shards of insight, are in on the game. They know every news item and cartoon has been edited to put the CCP in the most "productive" light. The propaganda is immediately discounted.

The largest Chinese enterprises are and will remain state-owned enterprises, arms of one government ministry or another. Their leaders have been schooled to treat "customers" as controllable subjects, not persuadable targets. They continue to believe that the buying public gets its kicks by listening to corporate credentials. They remain tone deaf to messages crafted to meet consumers' needs. Their advertising, laden with statistics, bar-charted demo sequences, and hi-tech mumbo jumbo, emerges from the same department that dreams up the company's annual report. Haier, China's most respected brand, "announces" its G5 ("Five Goods") television set with the following ultrafunctional laundry list: ".62 precision display, 100 hertz line scanning, professional 5.1 Dolby surround sound, 'human' design, and global high-clarity with unlimited compatibility." One question, please: What are they talking about? Konka, a large television producer (and, as of late 2004, JWT client), spoke in industrial tongues when it promoted its 2003 "DSP" model: "All things in the world start with particles. Konka's special DSP digital super-fine matrix practically leaps analogue lines to digital particles, reaching a two million pixel display. (Super: Revolution from lines to particles!) The world has never been so clear."

On the other hand, the international brands more often push consumer desires to the fore. For example, Sony advertising shows the same person, from the time he's born until the moment he expires, sitting on the same couch watching the same television. Its message is both focused and relevant to the Chinese public, perhaps the most value-conscious lot on Earth. Philip's plasma display (PDP) TV leverages an empathetic proposition: "So vivid it feels like watching a movie in a theater."

Consistent Inconsistency

As we've discussed, a brand's vision and core creative concept (in JWT's lingo, the "branding idea") are long-term propositions. They should change only when there is a *fundamental* shift in the competitive landscape or *dramatic* evolution of consumer motivations. Most Chinese managers, intoxicated by the disorienting societal and commercial changes over the past years, don't agree. In 1990, they say the only means of calling your mother was the public (rotary) phone. Now there are 300+ brands of mobile handsets flooding the market. In 1995, few Chinese had a computer. Today, Lenovo, Dell, HP, IBM, Acer, and countless other players are struggling to capture a large slice of an ever-expanding pie. (There are probably over 100 million computer owners in the PRC.) In 2000, passenger cars were only owned by: (a) the Party's upper echelon, (b) SOE titans, and (c) corrupt businessmen. Today, they are a rite of passage for the new middle class, an indispensable status tool for the upwardly mobile. In 2002, the price of a lovely apartment in the center of Shanghai was $100,000. Today, the sky's the limit. Things change.

Indeed they do. The United States has been through a series of rapid changes as well—the birth of suburbia, the Red Scare, Freudian repression, poodle skirts, McCarthyism, Loving Lucy, Kennedy's Camelot and his assassination, the pill, the Beatles, women's liberation, the sexual revolution, "I Have a Dream," the assassination of Martin Luther King, Bobby Kennedy's murder, Vietnamese dominoes, baby booming anti-establishmentarianism, the Watergate scandal, the energy crisis, secularization of psychotherapy, Norman Lear sitcoms, hostage traumas, leisure suits, Jimmy Carter's malaise, punk, Punky Brewster, sunny Reagan conservatism, the fall of the Wall, the New World order, Gulf War I, sex in the White House, 9/11, Gulf War II, the Doctrine of Preemption, Katrina, and the final episode of *Friends*.

Of course, fundamental cultural values, while not absolute, evolve only imperceptibly and over long stretches of time. Today, self-reliance, individualism, and social mobility are still at the heart of America's psyche, just as they were when de Tocqueville did his walkabout. And one of the most successful trademarks in world history, Marlboro, has represented manly, rugged individualism since the early '50s. Five decades on, the cigarette's equity has remained remarkably consistent. How is this possible? When a brand taps into a core value or need (e.g., in the battery category, durability), it can pull an Energizer Bunny out of a hat and keep on going and going. P&G's Folgers has always represented the gold standard of coffee in the morning. Since its launch, the brand has been number one. Kraft's Maxwell House, on the other hand, has skipped from "Good to the last drop" to romance, to flag-waving jingoism ("America's coffee"). Its sales performance has been, to put it politely, checkered.

The beauty of a well-crafted brand proposition is that it is not static; it is alive. It has depth and dimensions. It has a left brain (function) and a right brain (emotion). It can grow, adapting itself to new situational factors, maturing as time passes. Like people, a great brand has an identity that remains consistent over time yet discovers new ways of self-expression. The best part of waking up has, for decades, been Folgers in a cup. But the drinker's worldview and ambitions have evolved. As long as there are teenagers, adolescent peer endorsement will always be Purgatory's currency. But what is "cool" evaporates or, at best, lingers for a year or two. Pepsi channels fairly fixed New Generation aspirations, but they are projected differently over time and across geography.

Like people, a great brand has an eternal, multifaceted, and dynamic soul, even more compelling than the sum of its parts.

Negative Leadership. Due to either a knowledge gap or structural inefficiency, the vast majority of Chinese companies never build a steady platform.

• Breaking sharply from textbook marketing, Lulu fruit juice, a well-known brand, has flirted with four benefits in three ads over two years. First, it embraced naturalness, the most common and nondifferentiating position in the category. Six months later, the brand aired another TVC that talked about the importance of Vitamin C for both: (a) a child's intellectual development and academic performance and (b) a mother's soft, wrinkle-resistant skin. Finally, consumers discovered that Lulu was also ideal for family bonding and cross-generational harmony. Lulu, needless to say, is not doing very well. Its sales are listless.

• TCL, regarded by financial analysts as one of the PRC's most sophisticated companies, is hobbled by fierce internal warfare. In four years, the television unit's marketing department has been purged three times, and it has fired as many advertising agencies, including JWT. Unsurprisingly, TCL's consumer position has leapt from "vivid excitement" to "digital window" (although JWT produced this copy, we still don't understand it) to "eye stimulation," and, finally, "the future of 3C communications." (Whatever 3C means.)

• Wanji, a privately owned, fading ginseng brand, can't decide whether: (a) it should target the young or old generation, (b) concentrate on seasonal "gifting" or daily consumption, or (c) maintain a "soothing" or "dynamic" personality. Fully aware that wobbling confuses consumers and the trade, the company's owners hired a "foreign expert" to treat Wanji's schizophrenia (an increasingly common, though futile, practice). The well-intentioned expert never made it past the family's highly regimented modus operandi.

Positive Leadership. P&G is king of the supermarket and prince of enlightened consistency. Two of its brands, Safeguard soap and Rejoice shampoo, dominate their respective categories by maintaining a focused image while growing with the times. As discussed previously, Safeguard, since an early '90s introduction, has been rooted in providing germ killing and family protection (i.e., mother love). But the balance has evolved. In the early days, it artlessly highlighted therapeutic efficacy with test tubes and "lab coats." Few were touched by "germs on the soap and under the microscope" demonstrations. As trust increased and sanitation improved, Safeguard inched away from an ultrafear approach into a friendlier, more lighthearted and part-of-the-family territory. Furthermore, while Safeguard's raison d'etre has remained consistent, the depth of its franchise has facilitated the launch of several variants (e.g., shower gel, kids' soap).

Rejoice's workman-like advertising—lots of computer-enhanced hair and smiling stewardesses—won't clean up at Cannes, but it's a strategic work of art and has achieved the trifecta of brand management: (a) ownership of the category benefit, (b) sales leadership and (c) a sustained price premium. For fifteen years, Rejoice has mercilessly hammered "soft and shiny hair" into the heads of China's twenty-something set. To boot, a breakthrough brand linkage device—the "no-hands comb drop" shot—has buttressed both awareness and the core proposition. The shampoo's single-mindedness has been relentless but Rejoice has never gone limp. First, it has gracefully segued from functional "hair performance" to "more confidence," a bull's-eye emotional motivation. (Functional and emotional benefits should never compete or "crowd each other out." Instead, they should mutually reinforce or, ideally, fuse as one unified idea.) Consequently, communications are increasingly connected to the lives of Rejoice's market—young Chinese women, an aggressively aspirational lot. Second, product and variant innovations are elegantly and regularly woven into the marketing mix. From "blacker and shinier" to "safe for color," Rejoice regularly pumps out "news" to bolster its primary benefit. (In 2004, during P&G's thrust to expand penetration into the "mass mass" market, the brand strayed from its foundations. It dropped price, kicked the men out, took mom out of the office, and plopped a four-year-old in her lap. In the process, Rejoice promptly hit the wall. At the time, the launch was limited to a couple of test cities so damage was contained but, for the first time, the brand's focus is an open question.)

The scale of Mars' Dove success is small but no less impressive. Any chocolate—from perky M&Ms to decadent hot fudge—is a comfort food. Any chocolate is a privately relished indulgence, savored alone after a hard day's work. When shared, usually with a boyfriend or girlfriend, it brings two people closer together. Milk chocolate, as you might guess from the name, is milk based. Therefore, the leading player will own "richness," "thickness," and "creamy texture." By consistently representing sensual pleasure with a proprietary brand icon (the "silk river"), Dove has grown to embody the category and epitomize the essence of chocolate. The property is integrated into all marketing activities, from advertising to sales force incentives to consumer promotions.

Beyond beating the pants off of Nestle and Cadbury, Dove's silky proposition has helped overcome a small marketing challenge: Chinese do not like chocolate. It is fine for special occasions but, as mentioned before, too "heaty" for regular consumption. In 2003, Mars transformed the brand from a foreign indulgence into more of a daily snack by introducing a variant with a light cookie inside, "the hidden treasure." Silk ribbons, representation of core chocolate values, remain a vital component of advertising. However, in the TVC, they were draped over lithe ballet dancers, perfect personifications of lightness and refinement. Sales have skyrocketed. In the end, a focused message, consistent over time, is liberating.

CHANGE IN THE WIND?

Rome was not built in a day. Or, as the Chinese say, a journey of 10,000 *li* begins with a single step (for those wondering, a li is about a third of a mile). China's liberation from the shackles of Communistic dogma is, by any historical standard, progressing at breakneck speed. Several industrial sectors—textiles, biotech, information technology, auto components—are clawing their way up the value chain. (Even *The Economist,* a mainstream publication cynical about the China "miracle," grants that the country has "progressed from the world's sweatshop to the world's tailor." China will rise and so will its brands. The former is an article of faith. The latter is a matter of economic common sense.)

Despite the previous section's intent to show where Chinese brands need real help, more than a few local brands have been making good progress. Gains are tentative and scattered, a grudging response to profit squeeze rather than some spiritual conversion to the glory of brands. In addition, few companies have fully implemented the structural reforms required to ensure continued momentum. But, nowadays, many firms *are* producing better ads. (A few are even maintaining stable relationships with international advertising agencies.) Specifically, they are: (a) using relevant brand logos and taglines, (b) incorporating insights into the core proposition, and (c) creating increasingly frequent product innovation.

The Basics: Logos and Taglines

A logo is a graphic representation of a brand's consumer proposition. A good logo is a relevant graphic representation. And a great logo is iconic, both relevant and visually distinctive. McDonald's arches ("happy land") are a meaningful icon. So is Nike's swoosh ("go!"), Pepsi's globe ("youthful energy"), the Pillsbury Doughboy ("sweet and warm"), and "Intel inside" ("magic ingredient"). Literally worth billions, they brilliantly project a product's essence. No Chinese company has designed anything with such impact. However, firms do recognize the value of a logo that looks good and says something meaningful about the brand. *Da Hong Ying,* a cigarette brand, incorporates a "V for Victory" in all mass media advertising and in-store material. Since more men than women smoke, the testosterone-injected symbol of masculine strength and pride makes perfect sense.

Jinzheng DVDs embodied "ripe" (i.e., reliable and user-friendly) technology with an apple that appeared in television, print, newspaper, in-store displays, promotions, posters, public relations, and interactive campaigns. Haier, China's mammoth appliance manufacturer, boasts scale-driven competitive advantages—reliability, superior after-sales service—but leverages them skillfully via its "two kids" logo that conveys "care."

In addition to evocative logos, there has also been progress on the tagline front. Historically, an integral part of the Communist Party machinery was mastery of slogan-based propaganda. From "China has stood up!" to "Let a Thousand Flowers Bloom," the Great Leap Forward ("Surpass Britain and France!"), and the economic reform period ("Cross the River by Feeling the Stones," "To Get Rich is Glorious," "Let Some Get Rich First!"), the CCP has always stressed—pounded home, really—the value of "taglines." As a result, most brands have traditionally hollered hollow corporate credentials ("China's leading yogurt!") or grandiose yet generic promises ("World-famous Chinese brand," "Making tomorrow better," "New technology, new life," "Our success is your success," "Health creates the future," etc.).

Now, however, several taglines spring from real consumer benefits.

- Da Hong Ying, the cigarette brand, is "Victory's Wings."
- Haier, purchased exclusively for the home, is "Sincerity Forever."
- Bird knows young Chinese men view mobile phones as more than communication devices or even productivity enhancers. They are macho status symbols, the ultimate competitive advantage of corporate warriors. Its tagline: "Mobile Phone Weaponry."
- Even Fujian province's Xue Jing (Sedrin) beer taps into the linkage between "networking" and "professional advancement" with "Buddies Forever." (Many Chinese friendships are the "wine and meat" variety, pragmatic acquaintances rather than deep bonds that have withstood the test of time. Beer "lubricates" trust, a precious commodity in a society devoid of institutions designed to protect individual rights. Western men, on the other hand, simply want to have fun.)

Of course most of the best local logos and taglines are still tepid affairs. In many cases, the connection between a unique product point of difference and insight is tenuous. That said, more local players now grasp the merit of rooting communications in fundamental consumer motivations.

Beautiful Insights

As discussed earlier, communications that leverage forceful insights hit the sweet spot of consumer desire. They base their communications in fundamental motivations for behavior and preference. They transcend corporate banality by transforming a hard sell into a soft kiss. More than a few local players have discovered that fertile insights make brands grow. Encouragingly, they have scored quick wins against deep-pocketed but ill-focused competitors. Six products, in particular, have made impressive leaps: Liushan shower gel, Yili dairy, Wandashan infant formula, Skyworth televisions, Diaopai laundry detergent, and Guibiewan health supplements. Some have even managed to sustain gains for more than a fiscal year.

Liushan has achieved and maintained a number four position in the hyper-competitive shower gel category, one dominated by multinational bigwigs, by tipping a hat to the value of green. In any country, "pure" is good and "polluted" is bad. However, Liushan astutely recognized, and leveraged, the fact that Chinese are fixated on all things natural. Daoism, the second most potent cultural influence after Confucianism, commands us to forge "harmony" with a universe composed, according to the *ba gua,* of eight elements: heaven, wind, water, mountain, earth, thunder, fire, and rivers. These natural forces, further clustered into four female (*yin*) and four male (*yang*) elements, must be meticulously "balanced" in every facet of daily life. Food, medicine, massages, art, exercise, architecture, interior design, and opera all reflect Daoist cosmological imperatives. Therefore, one can assume that any *unnatural* force—e.g., the corruptive power of money, or chemicals in soup—is bad, even evil.

(In pursuit of economic advancement, the PRC has raped the environment and is home to nine of the ten most polluted cities in the world. However, like a born-again evangelist weaning himself off the bottle, China's propaganda machine sanctimoniously preaches to the masses about the need to "love" Mother Earth. The central government now swears to the long-term importance of a "green GDP." China-based auto manufacturers claim to be on the cutting edge of hybrid-fuel innovation. Beijing's sky, however, is still yellow and Shanghai's Suzhou Creek is still dead.)

"Natural goodness" is an even more gripping proposition among Liushan's target, lower-income consumers suspicious of, or at least disoriented by, anything unfamiliar. Due to the prescriptive spirit of order-bound societies, traditional Chinese maintain a markedly prohibitive checklist of "good" (natural) and "bad" (artificial) things. Products composed of unfamiliar ingredients will be seen as particularly perilous by conventionally minded individuals. Liushan realized this, trumping competitors' laboratory-generated "performance" claims with a "natural" position in harmony with age-old edicts.

Yili milk brilliantly took "natural purity" one step further by maximizing its relevance among younger, upwardly mobile consumers. In doing so, the brand managed to kill two birds with one stone, reinforcing quality perceptions as well as modernizing a dusty, dated image. Changes ushered in by Modern Society, the ultimate man-made institution, are "corruptive" to all Chinese. New generation professionals lead particularly unhealthy lives, binging on (Western) fast food, residing in (Western) apartment complexes, and listening to new-fangled (Western) music. (Only Chinese instruments are said to produce sounds "pure" enough to unite Heaven and Earth, delivering us to the edge of Infinity.) In the past ten years, ever since skyscrapers rose and traffic jammed, "natural goodness" has become a very powerful motivator among nutritionally conscious yuppies. And there is no place more natural than Yili's home, the grasslands of Mongolia.

But the brand's appeal runs deeper than fear of biological contamination. On a loftier plane, many Chinese believe society corrupts. We are all born "good" but societal pressure spoils pure intention, hence Daoist and Buddhist emphasis on rejection of material (i.e., "illusory") temptation. Members of the new middle class, elite sharks who swim in contaminated water, have sold their souls to Louis Vitton and other twenty-first-century devils of enticement. The urban professional, more so than his parents or less "successful" peers, craves a return, albeit an abbreviated one, to a simple world, a time when moral transgression wasn't a daily fact of life. Yili, by tapping into the deepest reaches of the Chinese psyche, transformed Mongolian milk into a near-magical elixir for both body and spirit. (Unfortunately, two years after its strategic breakthrough, the company's senior management was purged, giving way to Paleolithic ads populated by cherubic moppets and dancing cows. The company was then embroiled in a huge embezzlement scandal. It is still trying to restore shattered credibility.)

Wandashan formula achieved an impressive number four share in a segment completely dominated by international competitors (Nestlé, et al.) until recently. The Chinese middle class has recently shed its malnutrition paranoia (in nightclubs, being heavy is no longer seen as a sign of wealth) and is as knowledgeable about "balanced" or "low-carb" diets as any Western health nut. However, the long-suffering masses, acutely fearful of illness and disease, are preoccupied with eating more, not eating right. (Mom will do anything to have her family gobble up what she cooks. The "empty plate" shot signals as much about nutritional intake as it does great taste.) Benefits are still relatively "lower order," mostly clustering in the "keep us healthy . . . deliciously" quadrant.

American and European companies tend to march into China armed with "transformational" models and benefit ladders. In the West, our kids should be taller, smarter, faster, happier, wittier, bouncier, prettier, more popular, more talented, and more intelligent. In China, a loving mother's most noble priority is to keep a child safe and alive. Mothers are angels; survival is sublime.

Of course, immunity is even more essential for infants, defenseless babes in the woods whose healthy development propels an entire clan's social and economic advancement. While Western players promised benefits such as "quicker mental development," or "faster growth," *Wangdashan* seized the high ground of the *Chinese* category with an immunity proposition. The brand further capitalized on local beliefs with a great support point: "immunity ingredients from the milk of a pregnant cow." In doing so, it achieved an impressive 7 percent share in a market flooded with both MNC and local competitors. To boot, *Wangdashan* pulled off this coup with a price *higher* than market average. (In the PRC, a market chronically afflicted with commoditization and deflation, there are only two price-inelastic product clusters: status- and fear-based brands. Baby food, perhaps the only *terror*-driven FMCG category, can actually wield price as a competitive advantage. When a baby comes into the scene, the sky's the limit.)

Skyworth television—yes, *television!*—has also carved a nice niche by respecting Chinese protective values. (TVs, by the way, are exceptionally price sensitive. Unless a set guarantees its viewer the key to paradise, a premium means death. International brands, burdened with high cost of goods, simply can't compete; they are usually forced to rely on inequitable "strategic partnerships" with local players to achieve even a modest foothold in the market.) Most manufacturers communicate generic benefits such as "vividness," "clarity," or "stylish design." A few have moved onto a flimsy "innovative technology" platform with propaganda about "the future of home entertainment" or "our glorious future, your glorious home." Skyworth, a private (albeit "local-style") enterprise, shattered a few eggshells with its "healthy TV" benefit. In a Confucian society where a parent's most sacred obligation is to shield children from harm, anything and everything is dangerous. Soap can be germ-ridden. Paint can be toxic. Milk can be contaminated. Food can be poisoned. Skyworth, in a series of ads filled with sparkling eyes and clapping hands, uncovered a new threat: the radioactive TV set. Each of its variants boasted a distinct "health benefit," from "microwave-free," to "shock resistant" and "comfortable for children to watch." For a few years, until early 2004, Skyworth's "healthy TV" was quite successful, achieving a number four market share. (Unfortunately, the narrowness of its position made long-term consistency all but impossible, forcing the brand to abandon a promising emotional territory. Had it broadened the position to, say, "caring technology," Skyworth would have been in a better position to capitalize on early gains. Insights are necessary, but not sufficient, ingredients of a lasting brand vision and sustained consumer loyalty.)

Diaopai laundry detergent is the most successful local brand in China. It paradoxically manages to charge a premium while focusing on affordability. And Diaopai is no niche brand; it wields a market share in excess of 20 percent and is, by far, the largest player in an ultracompetitive category. It has established a bond with the lower strata of society, safety seekers whose boats have not yet been lifted by a rising economic tide. Beautiful advertising articulates both the other half's fear of "losing it all" and anger at having fallen through a shredded safety net. Their copy, however, is more than sentimental pap. By cleverly framing value as "more washes for less" rather than absolute price, Diaopai has established itself as a friend in times of need. (In a typical TVC, a young girl tells her family's story: "Recently mom was laid off. No one would help her. She didn't see me, but I heard her crying. I wanted to give her a little surprise by doing the laundry. Mom told me that with just a little bit of Diaopai, we could wash lots and lots of clothes. Oh! It cleans so beautifully. Mom, I'll help you help the family get by.") Furthermore, by avoiding words like "cheap" or "discount," Diaopai has transformed bargain-hunting, demeaning behavior in Confucian societies, into face-saving smart shopping. Diaopai's empathy will ensure market leadership for years to come, assuming it finds a way to integrate more tangible claims of performance superiority into the emotional platform. (In 2005, Diaopai lost a significant share to P & G's Tide.)

Guibiewan health supplements' gifting strategy gets to the ambivalence at the heart of China's generation gap, a yawning chasm present ever since the launch of economic reforms. Instead of positioning the product for individual consumption, Guibiewan is sold as a present for parents, the "easy" way to express appreciation for (or alleviate guilt elicited by) their sacrifices.

To proud Chinese intent on demonstrating why the West is selfish, accusations of "parental abandonment" come quick and often. "I couldn't live with myself if I stuck my parents in a home," they say with reproach. (Despite the universality of loving parents, most Asians do not recognize that the desire for self-sufficiency—no matter at what age—is one manifestation of Western individualism.) "Filial piety" epitomizes Chinese culture. The anti-individualistic father-son rapport is a sacred covenant, the crux of a Confucian worldview. Life is a cycle. Young children are protected by young parents; elderly parents are protected by adult children. To boot, every good son surrenders a chunk of his salary, no matter how modest, to his parents.

Despite near-absolute loyalty to parents, the new generation does bridle against smothering love and judgmental looks. This increasing disenchantment is driven by three unstoppable forces:

First, Western individualism is romanticized everywhere. Pandora's Box has swung open. There are glossy fashion magazines, overseas study programs, ecstasy-flooded nightclubs, illegal DVDs, imported commercial holidays (Christmas and Valentine's Day are now practically de rigueur), aggressively managed Western companies, and an American car culture. Individualism, often confused with egoism, has emerged as a highly aspirational value. In the new era, categorical obedience to the older generation is not easily swallowed. (On the other hand, the ingredients of true individualism have never existed in China. Admiration for people who forsake societal approval to achieve a dream or appreciation for legal systems that safeguard rights to life and liberty are elusive.)

Second, the centrally mandated single child policy, still the (weakening) law of the land, has had a huge impact on the new generation's collective sense of self. All parents unconditionally love their kids. However, in Confucian societies, the young are also investments with the potential to yield both material comfort and elevated social status. The singleton is the key to an entire family's success and, therefore, the king of the world. He or she develops an exaggerated sense of self. "I" comes to the fore. (However, once adolescence hits, the shock of regimentation—six-to-a-room university dorms, militant bosses, and more militant mothers-in-law—precludes self-awareness from ripening into full-blown individualism.)

Third, lifestyle options have exploded. Worldviews have broadened. Compared to their parents, young professionals earn a fortune. They can afford to go places—Paris, Rome, Las Vegas—*ma* and *ba* never dared to dream about. An appetite for the "excitement of a new era" has been whetted. Anything standing in the way of grabbing the gold ring is, at the very least, resisted. (On the other hand, wings are clipped by fear of familial ostracism. Most Chinese yuppies can afford to buy their own apartment. But most young adults lack the courage to announce a move out of the house unless preceded by an engagement proposal. Not surprisingly, hotels charging hourly rates are everywhere.)

Guibiewan knows modern values have loosened the traditional ties that bind father to son, mother to daughter. Today's youth are, by historical standards, estranged from parents, both physically and emotionally. However, present-day freedoms conflict with a timeless respect for familial obligation. Every "independent" Chinese under the age of forty flip-flops between selfishness and selflessness. The brand's insightfulness helps address a basic conflict—i.e., the desire to reciprocate parental sacrifice while forging a self-actualized lifestyle. In Guibiewan's most famous TVC, an adult man narrates, "When I was young, every day was like my birthday. It seems like *baba* never had a special day. Every father knows his son's birthday. But how many sons know their father's? Dad, I'll always remember your birthday."

The discovery of insight propels sales. As long as Chinese business leaders, supremely practical people, continue to leverage consumer-driven marketing strategies, they will constitute a formidable threat to complacent MNC players.

Innovative Sparks

In addition to creating relevant icons/taglines and leveraging real consumer insights, a few indigenous brands are becoming more nimble on the innovation front.

(Editorial comment: The PRC's shortage of any country's greatest natural resource—the creativity of its people—cannot be explained away by low per capita income figures, material dialecticism, or Maslow's hierarchy of needs. China has never rewarded challenges to conventional wisdom; threats to established order are viewed as heretical. For 5,000 years, China's greatest technological breakthroughs—from gun powder to the printing press—have taken root only in the rarefied climes of the ruling class. Independence of thought, or lack thereof, may well affect growth, particularly when, years down the road, China evolves from a production- to a service-based economy. Hopefully, post-WTO *institutionalized* ties with the world (the first in China's history) will give the country enough confidence to overcome the yoke of the past. Taiwan's metamorphosis from police state to resourceful democracy suggests that "creative Confucian" is not necessarily oxymoronic. That said, this is a challenge for Generation Next. For the next twenty years, China must maintain a clear focus on productivity and efficient allocation of resources.)

Sanyuan's three-in-one breakfast milk addresses a powerful, albeit functional, insight—the conflict between contemporary professionals' morning time shortage and an ancient belief in breakfast as the most important meal of the day. (A Chinese breakfast should be warm, comfortingly familiar, and starchy—e.g., buns, congee, or dumplings.) Sanyuan's breakthrough product—a mixture of milk, egg, and cereal—has been very intelligently positioned as "morning nutrition made easy." On an emotional level, its advertising pulls off a quintessentially Chinese trick, lightheartedly linking the functionality of a basic product with aspirational career advancement. We see a split-screen image of two sleeping men, both of whom wake up in a rush. The Sanyuan drinker glides through his morning rituals and, at the end of the commercial, is seated confidently at his office desk. The other guy, depicted as a four-eyed dunderhead (he sleeps with his glasses on), spills his milk, drops the toast, and never gets out of his pajamas.

Suyixian's MSG-free soup base gives the universal taste-nutrition trade-off a distinctive local twist. MSG, as everyone knows, is essentially Chinese salt, sprinkled onto or mixed into lots of food. It helps mom bring out the *xian*—a straight-from-the-slaughterhouse freshness unique to meats and hearty vegetables but not applicable to, say, apples. She knows, however, that MSG has negative effects on her family's health. Suyixian resolved this conflict by launching "The xian of bullion without the MSG," quickly establishing itself as a viable competitor of MNC titans such as Unilever's Knorr.

(Like everything else in life, Chinese "balance" food to maintain harmony with the universe. Some categories such as chocolate and black tea are masculine and "heaty"; others such as fruits and green tea are feminine and "cooling." By incorrectly calibrating a meal's *yin/yang* ratio, the flow of the body's *qi* will be interrupted. This is no small matter. In the minds of more than a few, an improper diet will lead to illness and then a concatenation of crises—time away from the office, job insecurity, financial risk, tension between husband and wife, imbalance within the family, divorce, social disgrace, loss of face in life, and ignominy in the afterlife. Smarter multinationals are catching on quickly to "harmony of opposites" and, in the process, are building healthy consumer franchises. For example, Nabisco's PRC Ritz range is dominated by the sandwich format; many variants have sweet filling inside that takes the salty/heaty factor down a degree or two. PepsiCo's Lays introduced a lemon potato chip, a smart, go-native "flavor balance." Häagen Dazs hit it out of the ballpark with green tea ice cream. (Granted, this brainstorm was imported from Japan; the Japanese are also picky about how, when, where, why, and with whom they eat. Kellogg's, much more successful in Japan than China, tested three nutritional platforms for a late '90s adult cereal launch: "balanced," "light," and "more." "Balanced" won, hands down.)

Even *Haier,* an unwieldy Shandong-based white goods conglomerate admired for its scale and not for its brand-building capabilities, has developed a razor-sharp understanding of how Chinese use appliances. Despite a rather stingy R&D budget, the company pumps out a stream of innovative products, often facilitated by "strategic alliances" with foreign enterprises (e.g., Sanyo). Within any given segment, Haier's product range, down to microniche level, is impressive. It offers everything from mini–washing machines designed for "sensitive," close-to-the-skin clothes (e.g., underwear, bras, and other germ-ridden unmentionables) and portable remote-control washing "systems" with LED displays to table-top wine coolers and mobile refrigerators. It sniffs out opportunity gaps and fills them. Haier's deep insight into consumer preferences (and not its frustratingly shallow brand equity) has even created an opening in the American market. The brand now controls a 45 percent share of compact refrigerators sold in the United States, products targeted primarily to college dorm residents. (It is not surprising that two out of these three examples are food brands, products that directly spring from Chinese cultural beliefs and worldview about which Westerners remain dangerously ignorant. Across all MNC categories, food and beverage competitors most frequently fail to strike gold and then quickly pull up stakes. Why? They kill themselves with self-inflicted wounds—specifically, a failure to: (a) adjust cost of goods in these ultra-price-sensitive categories and (b) mine insights for driving preference and beliefs about things that go into the body.)

In innovation, Sanyuan, Suyixian, and Haier are still exceptions, not the rule. However, even the most cynical China hands avoid downplaying the resourcefulness of a new generation of aggressive, ambitious Chinese. This space should be watched.

Relevant taglines and icons, insight-driven advertising, and a spurt in new product innovations are three areas in which local brands have made impressive strides over the past few years. Despite structural inefficiency, domestic companies' ravenous hunger for success probably means ultimate acceptance of international practices. Recent gains will only accelerate. But fasten your seatbelts, it is going to be a bumpy ride.

MNC COUNTERATTACK

Leading foreign companies are not sitting still. They are fighting back and often winning. (After initial surges, local mobile phone brands suffered a setback, falling into the vicious cycle of overproduction, commoditization, falling prices, and razor-thin margins. One marketing director admitted off the record that his company shipped 200,000 handsets per month in 2005 versus close to a million in 2003. As Barbara Bush once said, "We keep seeing the same movie.") Specifically, they have belatedly begun to adopt the following strategies:

1. Localizing product appeal;
2. Grabbing the perceptual high ground while broadening the consumer franchise;
3. Arbitraging on structural shifts taking place within the economy, particularly rising incomes;
4. Leveraging deep pockets and a research and development advantage;
5. Communicating a core proposition visually.

Localize!

A memo to all foreigners, but particularly our French friends who are only slightly less emotionally invested in their cultural heritage than the Han: please do not assume the Chinese will—*et viola!*—like your product. If you do, your company isn't ready for the Mainland.

The reliability of international brands is, indeed, a selling point but not enough to seal the deal.

• Starbucks knows this. It also knows Chinese don't like to drink coffee (again, too "heaty"), so it: (a) introduced tea, (b) broadened the sandwich menu, (c) identified prime site-to-be-seen real estate, and (d) expanded average store size. Starbucks in China is not only a comfortable environment to drink a cup of coffee. Starbucks, from Day One, successfully established itself as a public place in which professional adults go to snack, linger, and, most importantly, proclaim their affiliation with the New Generation Elite. The brand, now on every Beijing and Shanghai corner, has been integrated into the fabric of their daily lives.

• Most auto companies manufacture no two-door models, offering a wide range of choices between large and extra-large sizes. Image-driven Chinese men must project status with every step—hence Ford's decision to christen its Lincoln Navigator as "The President," targeted to those who aspire to stride down the corridors of power with confidence and grace. (SUVs will be huge here, both in size and popularity.)

• Ketchup just is not sexy in China, so Heinz shrewdly introduced nutritious but quick to prepare *Babao* ("eight treasures") congee, a dish that is normally labor-intensive. The product helps mom resolve a dilemma of wanting to give the best food for her family but not having time to prepare it.

• Unilever's Hazeline shampoo (Sunsilk in other markets) localized its range with a black sesame variant, a food believed to make hair blacker and shinier. Other locally relevant ingredients (ginseng for weak hair, green tea for oily hair) have also been well-received. (Since its 1998 launch, Hazeline has shifted positions fast and furiously. It has gone from "naturally safe" to "confidence" to "cements boy-girl relationships," "rescues you from social disaster" and now back to "naturally safe." In addition, media spending has been anemic, particularly when compared to the P&G Rejoice juggernaut. The brand, lucky to still be around, has survived only because the product itself has been brilliantly tailored to conform to Chinese beliefs.)

Leveraging the Lab

Global companies are, by and large, bigger investors in research and development than local enterprises. This competitive strength springs from three key factors, only one of which will remain in place as China becomes a more mature economy. First, state owned enterprises (SOEs) and other Chinese entities have relatively short histories and, therefore, have not aggressively reinvested capital. Second, the growth of per capita income has been largely driven by productivity gains that occur as underemployed "rural fringe" workers are integrated into China's thriving urban economy. Gains do not spring from the technological innovation that occurs in developed economies. (China's urbanization rate has no historical parallel. During and after the American industrial revolution, it took fifty years for the percentage of the people living in cities to double from 20 percent to 40 percent. China accomplished the same increase during the past *twenty* years and, as a result, has rescued hundreds of millions from abject poverty.) Third, as already repeatedly mentioned, China is a Confucian culture. Supremely "practical," it is not and never will be a "land of detail." Virtually all knowledge—from scientific to observational—is "applied" to concrete (i.e., immediate) problems. In such a hard-driving utilitarian environment, the long-term payoffs of primary research will rarely be fully embraced. Japan, a land of nuanced detail, is just the opposite; it is obsessed with style, sometimes even at the expense of substance. (Its toilets are so multifunctional, they do everything but the dishes.) Innovation springs from intellectual curiosity, a trait suppressed in cultures where questioning conventional wisdom is verboten.

In a country where technological leapfrogging is often the only route to market penetration, examples of innovation-led gains abound. P&G's Olay, recently the Mainland's most heavily advertised brand, is a titanic force, powered to number one by full-throttled R&D. Its Olay Total Effects 7X Visible Anti-Aging Vitamin Complex hits the high C, shattering perceptions of what a mass market cosmetic line can affordably deliver. Unrivalled hi-tech credibility also enables Olay to sell a huge range of lower-rent items (including soap) without debasing its image. Japan's Unicharm, maker of sanitary napkins, diapers, and incontinence products, is "reinventing mopping." Equipped with an expertise in state-of-the-art polyurethane technology, the company could introduce Wave, already on the market in Japan, at any time. Its microfiber dusters, ultra-lightness ("Sweep with one hand!"), and flexibility ("No crevice is too narrow!") would make a big splash on the Mainland. In the early '90s, another P&G brand, the oft-mentioned Rejoice, profited from deep R&D pockets when it introduced two-in-one shampoo (cleanser plus conditioner), a format that now dominates the value-conscious, "more is better" Mainland.

Leading the Masses

As discussed at the opening of this chapter, until very recently MNC brands were, for the most part, relegated to niche status, targeting only the coastal cities' crème de la crème. Meanwhile, local players flooded the "white space" to meet the needs of a price-sensitive mass market. A few MNCs are now wising up to the importance of scale—i.e., a broad-based consumer franchise—in establishing a deep foothold in China. As usual, Procter & Gamble is leading the charge. Its strategy has three pillars: first, dramatically slashing retail prices, particularly in low-involvement categories with limited product differentiation (e.g., shampoo and soap); second, heavy media and R&D investment within high value-added categories (e.g., cosmetics, sanitary napkins); third, ruthless domination of distribution channels. P&G is graceful on the insight front, but its real strength remains unleashing massive scale to conquer the hinterland. Smaller players, however, must adopt more elegant means of expanding their consumer base.

Most local companies are sales-driven. Flitting at the fringes of commoditization, they offer me-too products at a me-too price. Most MNCs offer superior products but are inaccessibly priced. Recently, however, more international brands have adopted a two-pronged strategy. They wield cutting-edge products to drive image and "vanilla" ones to generate sales. General Motors, for example, has been a huge success from Day One. By entering China with an upscale brand (Buick), GM generated a halo strong enough to add luster to recently introduced cheaper cars. Volkswagen, on the other end, was born as a low-end taxi. Its shoddy door handles, late '70s design, and tin-can chassis were not optional. Now Passat and newer, more expensive "subbrands" are swimming upstream, struggling valiantly against a tide of a faded image and declining market share. It competes as much with local brands like Cherry as it does with the Detroit and Tokyo big boys. Ford, on the other hand, was a slow starter. It was rescued by Mondeo, *Motor*

Trend's 2004 China Car of the Year. The upscale sedan's $30 million launch was many times larger than earlier support for the unsuccessful mass market Fiesta; as a result, Ford erased a dowdy first impression. The company has just accelerated momentum with the launch of the cheaper ("B Class") Focus, targeted to younger "individualists."

The strength of international mobile phone imagery is largely the fruit of Nokia, Sony Ericsson, and Motorola's disciplined use of above-the-line (mass) media to promote premium phones and below-the-line (in-store) blitzes to push price-competitive models. After falling from a strong number three to a laggard among the also-rans, Sony Ericsson was a dead man walking. It then bet everything on camera phones, a "killer ap" that took China by storm, and ended up winning big. Nokia's stylish image makes it young China's preferred brand (although Samsung is making a run for the money). It has remained popular by satisfying the New Generation's thirst for sexy *and* cheap phones, a one-two punch landed by (a) advertising trendy devices to generate a powerful across-the-line image and (b) "signature design elements" to give mass phones cachet. By skillfully leveraging high-end badge value, the MNC players, after touch-and-go flirtation with quick-fix discount strategies, have beaten back the tide of local competitors, now relegated to the "lower mass" market. (Siemens' PRC failure is instructive. After slashing its media budget, abandoning a winning "Be Inspired" campaign, and failing to rein in distributors, its share plummeted from 12 percent in 2002 to less than 4 percent in 2004. The company was forced to partner with Bird, an eager-but-spastic local manufacturer and finally purchased by Taiwanese electronics manufacturer BenQ. The German brand's demise highlights the limitations of technocratic management in China, an industrial landscape already sullied by its own disciplined army of robotic engineers.)

It is not only "high involvement" items that have begun to use "vanilla" to satisfy mass market tastes. Fast-moving consumer goods (FMCGs) have caught on. Colgate has been wildly successful in balancing three variants on three price tiers with three different functional benefits. Colgate "Total Oral Care," premium toothpaste composed largely of imported ingredients, costs approximately 200 percent more than local brands and maintains a 3 percent share. Colgate "Herbal" and Colgate "Strong," however, use local ingredients, have a lower cost of goods and are priced slightly higher than or at parity with local brands. The combined Colgate franchise controls a phenomenal 25 percent+ of the toothpaste market, one with hundreds of regional and national competitors. Colgate has been triumphant in extending its reach downward by simultaneously enhancing a gold standard image with advertising and stealthily downgrading the quality of cheaper variants. (See figure 15.1.) This sleight-of-hand would not have been possible had consumers been able to "notice" the degraded quality of mass variants. Pulling it off within something like sanitary napkins, a category in which the perceived gap between cotton local brands and polyurethane MNC products is wide, has been trickier. P&G's Whisper "Cotton" launch was uncharacteristically clumsy and seems to have degraded quality perceptions of the mother brand. Low-end "Cotton" was introduced with much fanfare, practically screaming, "We're going native!" (Whisper's key competitor, Unicharm, took a more enlightened route when it introduced its own cheaper product. First, it avoided "corrupting" its premium Sofy brand by creating a new name, Charm; the company was leveraged as a "seal of reassurance." Second, it forged a positioning of "not sacrificing softness for dryness" that, unlike Whisper, didn't call attention to the product's less expensive cost of goods.) (See figure 15.2.) Neither Colgate "Strong" nor Colgate "Herbal,"

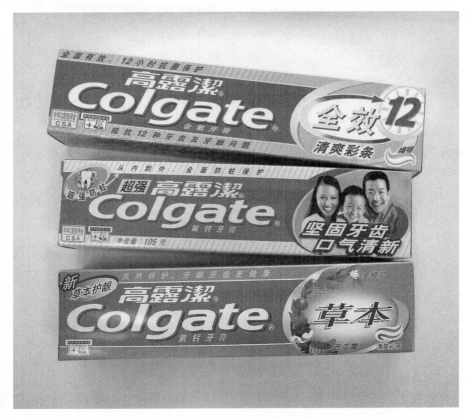

Fig. 15.1. Colgate Total vs. Colgate Strong and Colgate Herbal is probably the best example of downward brand extension. It works particularly well because the consumer can't really notice a lower cost of goods.

Fig. 15.2. The Sofy-branded items—top—are premium quality. Charm is made with a cheaper cost of goods and leverages the Sofy brand only as a basic quality guarantee. An example of downward brand extension to increase sales volume without degrading the mother brand's equity.

on the other hand, ever had significant media support, not even during launch periods. Both quietly appeared on supermarket shelves armed only with a familiar logo and a friendly price.

Reading the Tea Leaves

Multinational companies can divine the future. Taiwan's Kangshifu, for example, knows noodles. More to the point, it knows how instant noodle preferences evolve when income rises and a middle class emerges. Specifically, growing wealth comes hand in hand with increased time pressure, triggering a demand for instant noodles. Kangshifu got in there early, dominated instant noodles when they were only indulgent novelties and, today, owns a massive market. To boot, they are also well poised to dominate the next big thing, cup noodles. (Noodles, by the way, are Chinese comfort food and come in every shape, size, and flavor. Satisfyingly nonnutritious, they are donuts, ice cream, and potato chips rolled into one. Businessmen slurp them after a tough night of wheeling, carousing, and karaoke. Teenagers eat them after cram school. Working professionals take a break from the ego-challenging regimentation of corporate life with noodles.) In facial foam, currently a niche market, Boire is now investing the same "get them when they're young" strategy. Based on its experience with rising incomes in North America and Europe, it can map the shift from soap to body gel to facial foam with mathematical precision. Sharp is also an early bird; it currently has a tiny share of the TV market. But it hopes to dominate liquid crystal display (LCD) sets, the segment of the future.

Eye Candy

Finally, MNCs—without mincing words—still are better advertisers. For the reasons limned in this and the previous chapter, they grasp the value of bull's-eye consumer insights, consistent messages, and the economic efficiency of both robust brand equity and a strategic media plan. Despite the skepticism with which marketing consulting gurus regard the advertising profession, Western companies acknowledge the supreme importance of a well-crafted benefit statement. Furthermore, the best of them are masters at developing visual brand properties. In a market where "Keep It Simple" carries the same weight as Biblical commandments, the ability to vividly communicate a proposition can be a do-or-die imperative (see figure 15.3). Rejoice's comb-drop shot (hands-free, it falls through soft, shiny hair) is perhaps the most effective

Fig. 15.3. This 999 itch cream's advertising is extremely simple. The product works better than a back scratcher.

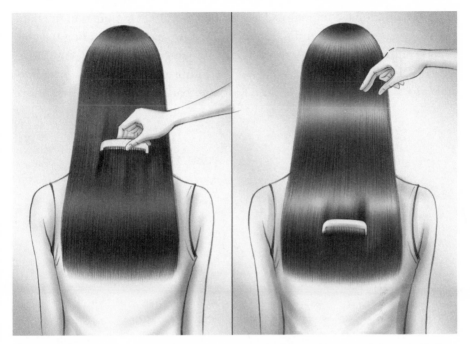

Fig. 15.4. Like P&G's Safeguard visual, its Rejoice "comb drop" shot is one of the most effective visual devices in PRC advertising history and instantly communicates the brand's soft and smooth proposition.

demo sequence in advertising history (see figure 15.4). Cadbury's two-glasses-of-milk shot is integrated in every scrap of communication from television and in-store displays to packaging. With no copy at all, it reassures moms that chocolate can be delicious and nutritious—well, at least not total junk food. Dove, a chocolate targeting a more youthful segment, has consistently used a lovely silk ribbon device to reinforce its "sensual and indulgently creamy" proposition.

Wrapping it Up

Local brands are still hobbled by key weaknesses including: (a) inconsistent messages, (b) failure to distinguish between consumer-relevant copy and corporate propaganda, and (c) confusion between brand awareness and brand equity. That said, Chinese companies have made significant progress. More and more, they weave insight into communication. Furthermore, Mainland enterprises are now more skillful in leveraging aspirational taglines and mnemonic devices. And they are taking baby steps on the product innovation front. Multinational competitors have spotted the threat looming on the horizon. They have finally begun to brandish "MNC weaponry" including the ability to localize products, grab the perceptual high-ground via high-end SKUs, dig deep into R&D pockets, arbitrage on future trends, and design memorable visual properties. The Middle Kingdom battleground grows ever more interesting.

CHAPTER 16

CHINESE CULTURAL RELATIVISM AND GLOBAL BRANDING

It is strange. Despite the satisfaction some marketers take in dismissing the contributions of advertising agencies, there is no topic more political and angst-ridden than the freedom of local managers to decide copy. Why is this? Articulating and addressing consumer needs is intellectually stimulating. It is a sexy—albeit touchy-feely—conceptual challenge that contrasts starkly with the humdrum monotony of daily operational duties (sales force motivation, distribution management, pricing optimization). When jurisdiction over advertising—the tangible manifestation of consumer insight—is taken away, "higher order" cachet evaporates. Some executives do not consider themselves "legitimate" unless they manage their brand's advertising. (In its recent mammoth restructuring, Unilever created a two tier marketing culture, with regional hot shots heading "Brand Development" and local staff handling tactical "Brand Building.") Copy decisions made by Chicago-based bosses without passports do not go down smoothly in China. Although Chinese are generally anti-individualistic, they are ego-driven and nationalistic. They know the PRC is a blossoming superpower. To them, enforced mandates from afar smack of cultural arrogance, even hegemony. Failure to acknowledge China's greatness practically guarantees resentful, passive-aggressive local staff. (Chinese and Americans share an important trait; both believe their country sits at civilization's epicenter. Chinese think China is the world's most cultured country. Americans think America, one nation under God, is its most moral.)

Despite the messiness of Global vs. Local food fights, the proud instincts of Chinese are spot on. MNC brands must speak to the Mainland's special characteristics. The media's coverage of China's economic "miracle" has been sensationalistic, sometimes breathlessly over the top. Nevertheless, the PRC, vast and untamed, *is* the New Frontier. And "close enough" is fatal if your competitors, many of them local, gun for perfection. Furthermore, China's economic and cultural conditions are unique, requiring a tailored marketing mix. However, the need for optimization is not an excuse for local rebellion or stone-faced passive aggression. Happily, executing locally relevant copy isn't inconsistent with the concept of global brands. Smart multinational companies have implemented marketing structures that both ensure cross-market consistency and sanction local "interpretation." (FMCG companies such as P&G and Unilever, albeit far from perfect, are pretty good at maintaining this precarious balance. But they have learned the hard way; bloodied walls are still drying. High-end cosmetic and fashion brands are still all thumbs. There are still blond ice goddesses, all frowns, on Chinese billboards.)

What is a global brand anyhow? The term usually conjures up the so-called icon brands, products that are beloved because they embody a universal aspiration. Kodak, from Brazil to Bali, owns nostalgia. McDonald's has a lock on family fun. Nike embodies irreverent, youthful individualism. Icon brands often leverage global creative to reinforce both emotional relevance and stature. Coke, for example, taught "the world to sing" decades ago. And, today, Apple's iPod and Absolut vodka often run the same print everywhere. (Even the most global brands, however, must balance foreign copy with local executions. Pepsi, the personification of New Generation Cool, knows that Chinese youth idolize Beckham and Ricky Martin but relate to jazzy soccer star Li Tie and Aaron Kwok, Canto pop's pretty-boy king. Nike rotates global "Olympic spirit" TVCs with celebrations of Chinese athletic breakthroughs.)

How can we assess whether a brand is global?

LOOK

On the most rudimentary level, the same logo must be used everywhere. Packaging is usually the same, too, give or take a few modifications mandated by local regulatory authorities. MNC brands are transnational symbols of clarity ("There's shampoo in the green bottle" or "The tilted blue and white heart means this is a wireless computer") and reassurance ("I can get a pretty good hamburger when I see yellow arches"), so getting consumers to recognize physical markers is a critical—a necessary but not sufficient—first step.

Helpful hint: logos and brand names should be in Chinese *and* English. The masses don't speak English but the language signals quality. Furthermore, a brand name should be translated in Chinese with characters that: (a) sound similar to the English name and (b) reflect the product's benefit or personality (i.e., have meaning). Coke, to cite a famous example, is "Ke-kou-ke-le"; interpreted roughly, it means "makes mouth happy." Pepsi is "bai shi ke le" or "a hundred joys." Some other examples appear in table 16.1:

Table 16.1

Brand	Chinese Pinyin	Meaning
BMW	bao ma	treasure horse
Apple	ping guo *	apple
Mercedes Benz	ben chi	racing gallop
B&Q	bai an ju	"hundred safety" home
Nike	nai ke	stamina-overcome**
Rejoice (shampoo)	piao rou	floating softness
Head & Shoulders	hai fei si	flying silk of the sea
Sprite	xue bi	emerald snow
7-Up	qi xi	seven happiness
KFC	ken de ji	certain-moral-base **
Nokia	nuo ji ya	promise-base-Asia**
McDonald's	mai dang lao	wheat-when-labor**

* No phonetic similarity
** No semantic relevance and, hence, a lost opportunity

PERSONALITY

A multinational brand must also avoid a schizophrenic character. Nokia should not be warmly accessible in emerging markets and coldly hi-tech in developed ones. Tony should be the type of cat that "brings out the tiger in you" no matter where a twelve-year-old eats Frosted Flakes. Marlboro personifies the essence of masculinity in every corner of the globe. Consistency of tone and manner matters for two reasons. First, failure to project more or less the same image will confuse consumers, especially high-end ones who travel. (Again, a brand is an organizing concept, a mental framework.) As the world becomes more interconnected, we instinctively look for familiar "signposts" that alleviate the anxiety of disorientation. A consistent brand personality is one such tool. Second, a steady image is operationally efficient. Brand "equity" both defines a product's consumer relationship and guides resource allocation within the corporation. For example, if Nokia mobile phones are premium in some places and mass in others, new product development could never be headquartered in Frankfurt. Asia would require its own new product development (NPD) center. If Rolex epitomizes "achievement" in New York and "trendiness" in Tokyo, it must implement two of everything: two product lines (one stately, the other flashy), two ad campaigns, two sponsorship series, and two retail strategies.

MESSAGE

The need to maintain a consistent look and style is accepted by all but the most high-maintenance local manager. However, to maximize efficiency and optimize capital investment, global brands must also deliver the same benefit—i.e., the role played in consumers' lives—across markets. BMW means "driving excitement." Everywhere. Mercedes means glitzy status grounded in German technology. Everywhere. Apple encourages people to "think different." Everywhere. IBM has shifted from selling PCs to providing IT solutions. Everywhere. Does this mean the advertising always has to be the same? No, and this is where people get confused. Driven by cultural imperatives, the *expression* of an identical consumer benefit will vary from place to place. Chinese project "status" differently than do Americans. "Creativity" might not have the same relevance in Confucian, rule-bound markets as it does in individualistic Protestant ones. (Only high-end, *functional* brands can successfully adopt a one-size-fits-all creative strategy. For example, the needs of all globe-trotting businessmen are pretty much the same; Cathay Pacific and United Airlines, therefore, produce the bulk of creative centrally. IBM—"Solutions for a Small Planet"—does develop local advertising in priority markets but often employs its agency network as distribution outlets, "fast adapting" global creative for air in local markets.)

That said, the need for tailored creative is not an excuse for organizational anarchy. Happily, countries "cluster" according to key cultural and economic dimensions. (China's importance often results in it being a cluster of one.) Protestant Northern Europe and the United States are less "rule-bound" than Catholic Southern Europe and Latin America. The Chinese, Koreans, and Vietnamese are Confucian, conflicted by a desire to simultaneously stand out and be socially accepted. Thailand and Japan, different in so many ways, are both Buddhist, enamored by nuance and detail. Emerging markets—countries with limited disposal income—are unified by a wide range of factors including price sensitivity and fear of disease. The best MNC corporations optimize a balance between efficiency ("one size fits all") and relevance ("my market is different") with firm yet flexible "brand architectures." These "templates" both fix a brand's iron-clad underpinnings (visual identity, personality, and core benefits) and liberate a manager to fine-tune communications based on traditions and values. (The frame of a house mandates whether it will end up ranch-, Tudor-, or colonial-style. But the owner can decorate a den as he or she pleases.) Pfizer's Listerine, for example, is universally known for "germ elimination"; the "payoff," however, varies according to disposable income. In developing economies, germ kill is often linked to fresh breath. European and North American advertising, on the other hand, is much more therapeutic, connecting germ elimination with oral care ("Kills the germs that cause bad breath, plaque and gingivitis"). Cadbury Adams' Halls is a mint candy that delivers a "hit of refreshment" to Asians but soothes throat and nasal discomfort in Northern, cold-and-flu-prone countries. All advertising, however, highlights "mentholated vapor action."

WHERE'S THE BEEF?

Enough theory. It is all well and good to say that China is different. But, what precisely *are* those differences and how do they translate into a need for Mainland-specific communications? No matter what your category is and to whom you advertise, PRC copy should:

1. Remember the predominance of the single-child household;
2. Avoid overemphasis on regional differences;
3. Dramatize a practical win or "step forward" in life;
4. Reflect the conservative nature of Chinese society;
5. Reflect the hopeful (i.e., not cynical) nature of Chinese society;
6. Adhere to censorship standards;
7. Enhance the social (i.e., public) context of a product proposition;
8. Use Chinese talent except in special circumstances;
9. Convey messages simply;
10. Focus on the big picture (i.e., long term) and own the category benefit.

SINGLE CHILDREN

This is the litmus test of complete ignorance. Do not put two kids in the back seat of the SUV. A model family in the PRC consists of one mother, one father, and one child, preferably a boy. Chinese soccer moms do not exist. And the kid, the manifestation of a clan's future potential, should radiate perfection.

ONE CHINA?

Very often, those unfamiliar with the Mainland use China's diversity to justify localized copy. They fret: "How can we use one TVC around the whole country when we know the PRC is, in fact, made up of several regions? Beijing and Shanghai are so different. The people are different. Their preferences are different." Well, this argument does not wash. Score one for the centralists. China's cultural roots are deep and consistent across different provinces. Everyone is Confucian. Family relationships assume the same shape everywhere ("revere the old, mold the young . . ."). Cosmological, societal, and legal views are identical practically everywhere. Since the Middle Kingdom rose, there have never been civil institutions to: (a) protect the rights and economic interests of individuals and (b) avert the chaos of dynastic disintegration. "Culture" was the "dark matter" providing the gravitational pull to keep the Chinese universe in order. Absolute, unwavering belief in the supremacy of Chinese thought was a de facto national religion.

However, geography is actually a confounding variable, masking two dimensions that do, in fact, militate against a one-size-fits-all approach to inter-province copy development: income and age. (Of course, this is true anywhere. But, in China, the differences between rich and poor and young and old are stunning.) First, individuals not belonging to the middle class exhibit much more conservative buying behavior than do their wealthier comrades. They are unfamiliar with brands and are extremely price-conscious. They are deeply fear-based and, in general, not optimistic about their ability to "move forward" in life. Second, the New Generation (i.e., people who have come of age during a period of relative openness and economic reform) digest communications differently than their parents. The former are more involved in the message and appreciate creativity for its own sake. They treat brands as identity surrogates. The older generation—and, again, anyone over forty is "old," immune to seduction—simply wants information. Madison Avenue's razzle-dazzle simply doesn't work. They are more socially conservative, twice as easy to shock.

Regional factors play a role only for products with "physical" benefits—for example, soy sauce (taste), soup (nutrition), and soap (hygiene). In the past, Chinese were not allowed to move from province to province. Furthermore, the Mainland's topographic and agricultural conditions vary greatly. As a result, local cuisines are distinct. (East is sweet and oily. North is grainy and mushy. Southerners are *dimsum*-crazy. Westerners like it hot.) Soy sauce is used for dipping in Guangzhou and braising in Tianjin. People south of the Yangtze eat rice. Chillier climes prefer wheat. Traditional Chinese medicine is dominated by beliefs about do-good ingredients, many of which have been incorporated into local recipes. Finally, climatic factors—cold and dry in the North, hot and wet in the South—impact everything from shampoo usage (anti-grease versus anti-dry) to skin care needs ("moisturizing" versus "refreshing"). Overall, however, it is easy to pay too much attention to regional particularities and not enough to national similarities.

MOVING FORWARD

When the opportunity presents itself, Chinese are stupendously skillful ladder climbers. Products, therefore, require practical "payoffs." Lipton tea should enable the professional man to gather himself before the big meeting. Even beer must deliver *something*. In Western countries, "Letting the good times roll," or "Making weekends great" is enough. Fun is fun. In China, beer must: (1) bring people together, (2) reinforce trust, and (3) optimize opportunity for mutual (financial) gain. Diamonds shouldn't just sparkle; they should dazzle and enhance social status. Knorr soup base should help mom *achieve* by enhancing domestic authority, fulfilling her Confucian obligation to "protect," maintaining harmony, demonstrating culinary skill, whatever. The payoff from big-ticket items—cars, jewelry, university tuition, insurance policies, etc.—must be even more obvious. A Ford Mondeo is an *investment*. It must project status and "open doors."

In a country of limited disposable income, "intrinsic" benefits aren't big. "Feelings" or "enjoyment" evaporates. "Experience," however, lingers. This is particularly true for expensive luxury products; "self-indulgence" will always lose to self-advancement. Silk scarves—publicly displayed apparel—will sell better than satin sheets. Expensive (i.e., "branded") wine will go down easier than expensive (i.e., generic) caviar. In Japan, self-pampering is its own reward. A wonderful bath is enjoyed as a beautiful private moment. Toto spray-wash toilets, the ultimate private indulgence, are ridiculous to Shanghainese, a pointless extravagance. "Pampering" must recharge batteries for another round of shopping or aerobics.

DO NOT OFFEND

The Middle Kingdom cracked open its doors in 1978. They were blown off in 1992, following Deng Xiao Ping's epoch-shaping Southern Tour. China, therefore, has been part of the "modern world" for fifteen years. "Western thought" is titillating, even aspirational, but it's dangerous, synonymous with moral decay and social chaos. "Spiritual pollution" offends everyone, not just bureaucratic stiffs and tea ladies. Anything racier than a boy-attracts-girl plot shocks. (In a 2000 Halls' Orange Vita C commercial, a shirtless man danced through "Fruitopia." While awareness reached 60 percent within four weeks, consumers didn't stop writing complaint letters until 2002.) (See figure 16.1.) Despite the presence of sex shops every other block (in big cities) and a booming commercialized sin industry (everywhere), Chinese are prudish. They still discuss matters of the flesh with cute metaphors (e.g., menstruation is "that time"; in the south, erectile difficulty is "six o'clock"). Only a (sizable) minority of college students have had intercourse by the time they graduate. Sex education is rare. AIDS education has only recently begun to filter into secondary and tertiary cities. Prostitutes offer services by asking, "Massage?" Homosexuality is beyond taboo because, outside decadent primary cities, it is not even a concept. To the vast majority of the population, it simply doesn't compute. So avoid explicit sexuality in this vast G-rated kingdom. For that matter, avoid wicked ads with: kids sassing parents, parents sassing kids, husbands nagging wives (wives *can* henpeck husbands), ugly people, anything remotely "anti-China," product comparisons, failed marriages, and impolite teenagers. Every spot must glow with the wholesomeness of a Norman Rockwell painting. Contemporary China likes to think of itself as *Father Knows Best* in color.

SPARKLING SHEEN

The Chinese are the world's least cynical people. The middle class believes, as Scarlet O'Hara might say, "Tomorrow is another day" (to make money). The masses, ferociously focused on maintaining calm, also have a gift for transcending grittiness and finding beauty in the most modest corner. Antiauthoritarianism barely exists in China; it is tantamount to suicide. Physical survival and social advancement are inextricably bound to absolute acceptance of the conventional wisdom. Rebellion, on every level, has no payoff. (Failure to pay homage to the government is dangerous, even for expatriates.) Gritty, countercultural films bomb. "Fifth generation" director Zhang Yimou, known in the West for sumptuously shot historical work (e.g., "Raise the Red Lantern," "Ju Dou"), flatlined when he went contemporary with movies such as "Keep Cool." (He fared much better with martial arts flicks including "Hero" and "House of Flying Daggers.") Practically all "sixth generation" directors (young Turks fixated on gritty urban reality) remain frustratingly anonymous, spurned by both censors and the public. Defiant modern artists who capture repressed angst are cutting edge but not cool.

Advertising, therefore, should—fully and passionately—embrace optimistic consumerism. A trip to Carrefour is not a slog through traffic; it is a journey to a wonderland of discovery. Nike's "Just Do It" can be challenging but should never be brash. The rebellious U.S. "Agassi vs. Sampras" spot featuring an impromptu tennis match, clogged traffic, and befuddled cops would never fly.

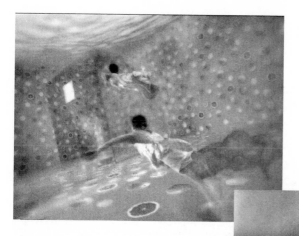

Fig. 16.1. This Vita C TVC achieved a 60%+ awareness after only four weeks on the air. Its sexuality, however, was provocative and still represents the outer limits of acceptability. (One censorship rule: the length between throat and neckline must not exceed 13cm.)

Kitchens should glisten. Offices should be ultramodern. Every stitch of clothing should shimmer. Chinese consumers are not the least bit cynical about brands; indeed, they are the most advertising-friendly folks on earth. Consumerism should never become an object of postmodern ridicule. In a repressed, regimented society, material acquisition is the most potent form of individual expression. Similarly, advertising, despite being directed by the invisible hand of some corporation, is the most open "public forum." (Journalism is only slightly less controlled now than it was fifteen years ago.) Western-style "I know you know I know" winking cynicism does not endear. San Miguel's "Take a Fresh Look" campaign poked fun at empty advertising. It was a hit in Hong Kong but not in adjacent Guangdong. Even the famous Energizer Bunny campaign ("It keeps going and going and going. . . !") wouldn't be appropriate here. Big or small, subtly or blatantly, the urge to splurge must not be ridiculed.

AVOID THE CENSOR'S KNIFE

Foreign newcomers fear the censor more than the Grim Reaper. Yes, one must develop a sixth sense of what does and does not work; but social conservatism puts more of a lid on creative expression than even the government does. (Note: Beijing TV's standards are the strictest, so if you get a script through them, you're pretty much in the clear.) Here is a handy list of what to avoid:

- *Sex.* No eroticism. No cleavage. No "bad men." No mornings after. No premarital titillation. (Come to think of it, we don't even see married couples in bed together.) No homosexuality. No condoms. No AIDS. No massage parlors. No sensual skin stroking. Belly buttons are vulgar.
- *"Unsafe" or "uncivilized" behavior.* Good fathers and governments defend the welfare (i.e., safety) of sons and workers. So, no driving without a seatbelt. No jaywalking. No running on busy sidewalks. No blocking traffic. No playing on the roof. No rolling around the grass of a public park. No spitting. No burping. (Yawning is allowed but not advised.) No dogs on the run. No food-contaminating civet cats.
- *Disrespecting the political hierarchy*—i.e., groups being "led" by anything other than the military or the CCP. (Pizza Hut was forced to delete a kid standing on a desk extolling the taste of the "Edge" pizza. The ten-year-old, unwittingly, was an "alternative center of authority.") Well-behaved crowds, on the other hand, are fine. They reinforce national unity. Having fun with any political figure—Mao, Deng, Jiang, Hu (Jin Tao), Wen (Jai Bao), the local Party secretary, "good" emperors, and any Party member—is, of course, strictly forbidden.

- *Disrespecting the social hierarchy.* Father is always smarter than son. Teacher is always smarter than student. Elder brother is always smarter than younger brother. Senior citizens are always the wisest of all, save the emperor (or Party leader). Round-faced children are obedient disciples of all things Chinese.
- *Affronts to China.* As described previously, Mainlanders are nationalistic. Any slight, perceived or real, elicits howls of righteous indignation. National symbols—dragons, phoenixes, the Great Wall, the Temple of Heaven, Tiananmen, Ne Zha, Kung Fu masters (Nike got burned here), and Sinopec—are sacrosanct. Furthermore, when relevant, failure to explicitly recognize China's greatness is risky.
- *Affronts to competitive products.* Comparison advertising—e.g., "The Pepsi Challenge"—is unambiguously illegal, so do not even try. You cannot even have Sprite's *colors* (yellow and green) next to a 7-Up cart.
- *Affronts to neighborhood pharmacists.* Over-the-counter drugs are highly regulated due to concerns for: (a) public welfare (older, less advertising-savvy consumers are the primary market target) as well as (b) the industry's fossilized state-owned enterprises and distribution arms. You cannot show doctors. You cannot show patients. You cannot show symptoms. You cannot show cures. You *can* use abstract, difficult-to-understand metaphors and dancing stomachs. (See figure 16.2.)

A SOCIAL CONTEXT

In China, individualism is a clever interpretation of convention. It does not carry the slightest hint of rebellion. Confucian to the core, banishment to the Land of Outcasts is the deepest fear of the Chinese. People can't survive without occupying a rung on the social ladder. Therefore, every commercial should be fueled by the electrifying buzz of peer endorsement. Aesthetic grace, in and of itself, is pointless. It must be twisted into "style," or "cool," or "trendiness." Even Nike, history's most powerful proponent of "Me!," never raises eyebrows. (In a masterfully edited 1999 soccer spot, a boy fails to score a goal and a superimposed phrase appears: "Heroism doesn't depend on winning or losing." Then an invisible audience bursts into applause.) A mother's child-rearing skill must be societally sanctioned. The darling is public property, a future contributor to the nation. Unilever's Knorr bouillon, slow to take off but now chugging forward, uses a chef—i.e., a widely recognized "expert"—to speak on behalf of the brand's "real chicken taste." Ford's Lincoln Navigator SUV was not launched as a symbol of rugged individualism. Instead, it is a projection of power (see figure 16.3). In advertising, the vehicle is called *zong tong* or "The President," a majestic leader, albeit one who wins elections.

Fig. 16.2. In OTC ads, censorship restriction is severe. No patients, no doctors, no illness, and no cure can be depicted. The results? Lots of happy stomachs, as in this early JWT 999 Wei Tai print work.

Fig. 16.3. Even for the most expensive products—i.e., those targeted to the most "self-actualized" and successful men—it's important to reinforce one's social position. Lincoln's Navigator has been branded the "President," the same noun used to describe the U.S.A.'s Commander-in-Chief. Advertising should never be "internal."

True individualism—i.e., the "right" to make decisions based on personal satisfaction irrespective of collective opinion—is extremely aspirational. (Remember, Chinese are ambitious; egos are huge.) But individualism is like Eve's apple, an enticing but forbidden fruit. Savvy marketers know how to concoct oxymoronic "safe self-expression." For example, Ford's Mondeo, a show-off car, celebrates the man whose "status springs from substance." A successful guy never broadcasts his own achievements, lest he be tagged an egomaniac. Cosmetic brands such as Olay and Avon promise blemish-free skin that gets noticed, not glowing white skin that attracts a crowd. They do not nail a woman to the pedestal. (Women never shine. They sparkle. And so do their diamonds.) Yao Ming is worshipped because he is understated, not a trash-talking, fan-punching NBA boor.

Executionally, social endorsements should not be wrapped in cliché. Nodding heads in unison, "boyfriend admiration" sequences, a "thumbs up" shot, and bosses patting shoulders are all turn-offs here, too. In a land of stealth social climbers, understatement is a prized asset. To capture someone's attention, whisper.

GO LOCAL

The Chinese are matchless ethnocentrics. Fiercely nationalistic, they are willing to die defending their civilization. (But, contrary to conventional wisdom, they don't believe *the country itself* sits at the center of the universe. *Zhong guo* or "Middle King*doms*"—Mandarin does not have a plural form—is a Zhou-era reference to the *series* of small states that existed along the Yellow River. It constituted the geographic core of China's "cultural footprint.") People don't want "acceptance" by the world community. They demand acknowledgement of their nation's inevitable rise as a superpower. Therefore, actors, except in rare circumstances, should be Chinese. Many cheap local brands employ off-the-street white talent and the result is not pretty. Caucasians with bad haircuts speaking bad Mandarin do not enhance brand equity. Unless they are superstars, Western celebrities are best avoided. Over the past few years, the Chinese entertainment scene, while still not a cornucopia of creativity, has become a bit more fertile. Young talent is manufactured efficiently. Some stars (Maggie Cheung, Stephen Chou, Chow Yun Fat, Tony Leung, Andy Lau, and Jacky Cheung) and directors (Zhang Yimou, Wong Kar Wai) are now icons.

Detour: In Japan, there is a curious "recessive nationalism." It's a land of detail, nuance, and conformity. Unlike the Chinese, Japanese derive satisfaction from kowtowing to tradition. One whispers, even in the street. Public brawls are evil. Even today, a relatively cynical time, streets are filled with soothing Musak and baby-talking sales ladies. In this self-effacing context, using white actors works. Even B-list celebrities carry cachet.

MAKE IT SIMPLE

Unaffordable pricing is the most frequent in-market mistake. Complicated messages are the most frequent on-air blunders. Chinese consumers are inundated with choice. They are confused. Making matters worse, the media scene has exploded. The number of TV stations skyrocketed from 9 to 545 over the past 10 years. Between 1996 and 2004, television spending increased from $1 billion to approximately $15 billion. In the consumer world, cars of all shapes and sizes are seen on Shanghai roads. As late as 2003, this was not the case. And in grocery stores, practically every category boasts hundreds of brands. The shopper's mind, therefore, boggles. Young and old, coastal and inland, North and South, middle-class and mass . . . simple sells.

How can you tell whether you are triggering information overload?

• First, can the question "What is the one thing I want my audience to remember?" be answered in a few words? Every execution should have a clean, direct center of gravity. Do not burden advertising with more than one "key response." Trust us. Consumers do not want to know everything there is to know about a product. They are asking, "What's in it for me?" They have no time for philosophy or encyclopedia entries. Messages with "both . . . and" clauses are confusing.

• Second, does every execution—TV, print, newspaper, or web—have a "key visual?" And does it dramatize what you want to communicate? Chinese do not digest wordy copy. Subtitles, text blocks, and quick cuts are dangerous. Some companies are learning to embrace the "magic frame." The aforementioned Knorr chicken bouillon TVC had a chicken being "pulled" from the farm into a restaurant kitchen. Halls mint candy dramatizes "refreshing cool" with a "flash" of surreal pleasure—a roller coaster flying to the moon, a girl floating in the air, an escalator turning into a water slide (see figures 16.4 and 16.5).

• Third, does your media plan rely too much on television? Advertisers who believe only in TV (e.g., an otherwise brilliant Unicharm) have no choice but to stuff thirty- or fifteen-second commercials full of "supporting" information. Different media are consumed differently. Television and outdoor billboards are not "elective"; people passively receive an ad whether they want to or not. Print and newspaper advertising, on the other hand, is more actively digested. Magazines can convey relatively complicated information, as long as it supports a core proposition. Both television and print *must* be used for "high-involvement" products—i.e., important to self-esteem/identity (cars, mobile phones, diamonds), progress in life (cars, education, investments) or health (hospitals, insurance).

THE HIGH GROUND

Given the tremendous opportunity fueled by China's reemergence, it is fitting that this book's final point is more a call for boldness than an appeal for caution. The PRC is actually beyond the Wild West. It is uncharted, virgin territory. Take Buick's resurrection, for instance. In the United States, Buick was last hot around the time of Nixon's "Checkers" speech. But Detroit's embarrassing aunt is the Mainland's life of the party. GM did practically everything right: focused, insightful advertising; global standards implementation; productive joint venture partnerships; and, finally, a product designed with Chinese in mind (a roomy back seat, aggression-releasing "road hug," and a large, impressive chassis). Buick is now a gold standard (see figure 16.6). How was this possible? How

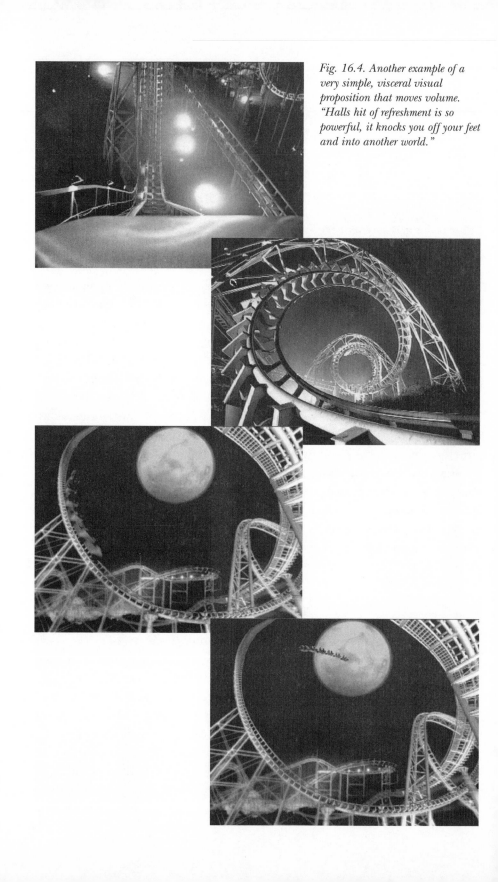

Fig. 16.4. Another example of a very simple, visceral visual proposition that moves volume. "Halls hit of refreshment is so powerful, it knocks you off your feet and into another world."

Fig. 16.5. Halls "Waterslide" ad.
Make it simple.

Fig. 16.6. A beautiful example of the art of the possible. Buick, a dead brand in the United States, has risen from the grave in the PRC to assume the form of Category Leader.

did Detroit's dancing elephant blow Volkswagen out of the water? (VW's recent sales have been, inevitably, a disaster. The brand started as a taxi and then tried to go "premium." In hindsight, it was never going to work.)

In China, GM started over. They learned from mistakes made in the United States and did not repeat them. (Let's hope the inspiration continues. The company's gifted China CEO, Phil Murtaugh, resigned in March 2005.) The PRC, gloriously, is the ultimate high-risk/high-return investment. Missing the mark will create woe. But a bull's-eye means a foothold at the base of a new global economic pillar. Success, even for late entrants, is still possible. The competitive environment, while fierce, is amorphous. Nothing is set in stone (yet). Product differentiation, the most primitive dimension of brand equity, has barely begun. The luxury market, for example, is a shining clump of tangled jewelry. Louis Vitton, Gucci, and Hugo Boss are "prestigious" but boast no distinctiveness. High-involvement goods such as cars and computers have not established loyal franchises. Even mobile phones—China's most differentiated, image-driven category—continue to experience volatile share movement. Pharmaceutical products are clumped into "safe Chinese" or "effective but risky Western" piles. Tylenol, for example, has been around for years, and, what is more, is manufactured by J&J, a well-regarded MNC. But it is still just a pill. It is not too late for a new international competitor to steal volume by forging a long-term brand vision. The consumer landscape is fertile but not yet harvested. In wet shaving, Gillette dominates, but: (a) penetration is low and (b) its advertising is middling, largely imported American copy. The creative fails to address a Chinese man's internal conflict between aggression and anxiety. There is no "conquering." There is no "edge." If it had the verve, Energizer's Schick could take the high ground and become the category leader.

So, there we are. We have been given an incredibly rare and special gift. Every year, approximately ten million Chinese enter the hallowed ranks of the middle class. The growth has only just begun. A flattening slope is decades away. In large ways and small, the Chinese market battleground is chaotic. It is muddy and unformed. There are a few power brands—Pepsi, Nike, Rejoice, Safeguard, Olay, and McDonald's—but not many. The opportunity for both local and international marketers to define and own consumer desires is wide open. With courage, investment, and respect for China's culture and worldview, the gold ring—ownership of the category benefit—is still within reach. We hope more focused, savvy corporate heroes stand up and grab it.

INDEX